American Historians and the Atlantic Alliance

AMERICAN DIPLOMATIC HISTORY
Lawrence S. Kaplan, Editor

Aftermath of War
Americans and the Remaking of Japan, 1945–1952
Howard B. Schonberger

The Twilight of Amateur Diplomacy
The American Foreign Service and Its Senior Officers in the 1890s
Henry E. Mattox

American Historians and the Atlantic Alliance
Edited by Lawrence S. Kaplan

American Historians and the Atlantic Alliance

edited by Lawrence S. Kaplan

The Kent State University Press
Kent, Ohio, and London, England

© 1991 by The Kent State University Press, Kent, Ohio 44242
All rights reserved
Library of Congress Catalog Card Number 90-47720
ISBN 0-87338-431-8 (cloth)
ISBN 0-87338-438-5 (pbk.)
Manufactured in the United States of America

Three of the essays—those by Ernest May, Walter LaFeber, and Joan Hoff-Wilson—have appeared as part of a special commemorative issue on "NATO Over Forty Years" in the Fall 1989 issue of *Diplomatic History,* and are printed with permission.

Library of Congress Cataloging-in-Publication Data

American historians and the Atlantic Alliance / edited by Lawrence S. Kaplan.
    p.   cm.
    Includes bibliographical references and index.
    ISBN 0-87338-431-8 (alk.) ∞ — ISBN 0-87338-438-5 (pbk. : alk. paper) ∞
    1. North Atlantic Treaty Organization. I. Kaplan, Lawrence S. II. Series
D845.A66 1991
355'.031'091821—dc20   90-47720

British Library Cataloging-in-Publication data are available.

Contents

Acknowledgments	VII
Introduction	
LAWRENCE S. KAPLAN	1
The Formation of the Alliance, 1948–1949	
ROBERT H. FERRELL	11
NATO and the Korean War: A Context	
WALTER LAFEBER	33
The American Commitment to Germany, 1949–1955	
ERNEST R. MAY	52
Charles de Gaulle and the French Withdrawal from NATO's Integrated Command	
SAMUEL F. WELLS, JR.	81
"Nixingerism," NATO, and Détente	
JOAN HOFF-WILSON	95
The SS-20 Challenge and Opportunity: The Dual-Track Decision and Its Consequences, 1977–1983	
GADDIS SMITH	116
The INF Treaty and the Future of NATO: Lessons from the 1960s	
LAWRENCE S. KAPLAN	135
Notes	155
Bibliography	179
Index	183
Contributors	192

Acknowledgments

The idea of gathering American diplomatic historians for a symposium on the role of NATO in the history of United States foreign relations originated with Dr. Barry Fulton, Public Affairs Adviser of the U.S. Mission to NATO. That he was successful in mobilizing the resources of the NATO headquarters was demonstrated by the high level of support he received from leading members of the organization. U.S. Ambassador Alton G. Keel, Jr., not only welcomed the Americans to Brussels on 14 May 1989, but delivered an introduction on the following day in which he looked ahead to what the next decade might bring. Jan G. Reifenberg of the *Frankfurter Allgemeine Zeitung* shared his views on the state of the alliance at a dinner address. Moderators of the panels included Morris Honick, SHAPE Historian; General Barry McCaffrey, Deputy U.S. Military Representative to NATO; John Kornblum, Deputy U.S. Permanent Representative; Jean Claude Renaud, Director, Economics Directorate; Dr. Lawrence Legere, Defense Adviser, U.S. Mission to NATO; Dr. Henning Wegener, Assistant Secretary-General, Political Affairs; Michael Legge, Assistant Secretary-General, Defense Planning and Policy; and Dr. Jamie P. Shea, Special Projects Assistant to the Secretary-General.

The participants were served by the comments of European scholars from six member nations of NATO. They included Professors D. Cameron Watt of the London School of Economics, Helge Pharo of the University of Oslo, Denise Artaud of the CNRS, Theodore Coloumbis of the University of Thessaloníki, and Omer de Raeymaeker of the University of Leuven. The foregoing served as commentators for the papers of Robert Ferrell, Walter LaFeber, Samuel Wells, Gaddis Smith, and Lawrence Kaplan, respectively. Professor Ennio Di Nolfo of the University of Florence prepared a commentary on Joan Hoff-Wilson's paper, which was read by his colleague, Dr. Leopoldo Nuti. Dr. Sherri Wells of the U.S. Department of State Historical Office provided comments for Ernest May's paper.

This volume, like the symposium itself, owes a debt to its NATO sponsors and to those who attended the sessions officially and unofficially. The revised papers that appear as chapters have benefited from the observations and criticism of the commentators. They have also benefited from the attention given to the book's production by the Kent State University Press. I am appreciative of the contributions of the senior editor, Julia J. Morton, assistant editor Linda Cuckovich, and of the director of the Press, John T. Hubbell. Not least among the contributors of this book have been Ellen Denning, secretary of the History Department, and, as always, Ruth Young of the Lemnitzer Center. Mark R. Rubin, administrative coordinator of the Center, coordinated with his customary skill. A special word of thanks to Sean Kay, NATO Center Fellow, for his efforts. I am grateful to all who have given their time and talents to this project.

> Lawrence S. Kaplan
> Lyman L. Lemnitzer Center
>   for NATO Studies
> Kent State University

Introduction

Fifteen years ago I published a note in the *AHA Newsletter* inquiring why American diplomatic historians have neglected or downplayed the importance of the North Atlantic Treaty in the history of American foreign relations. My comments were made on the occasion of the twenty-fifth anniversary of NATO, a reasonable time to make some evaluation of the significance or insignificance of the organization in this nation's history. The North Atlantic Treaty marked the first entangling alliance with any European country since the termination of the Franco-American treaty in 1800.

If this description of the formation of the alliance is accurate NATO should have been a magnet for American historians. But this was not the case in 1974. The contribution of historians to the enormous body of NATO literature had been minimal. A student seeking information on the alliance's history in its first generation had to look to political scientists such as Robert E. Osgood or to essayists such as Robert Kleiman or Ronald Steel. Insightful and useful as their works were, their discussions of NATO were either illustrative or polemical.

The reasons for the silence of historians fifteen years ago may be explained partly, I suspect, because NATO was an ongoing alliance, an open-ended issue historically, with no end in sight. Had NATO been a failed alliance, with a beginning, middle, and end, it might have attracted the attention of such distinguished historians as Thomas A. Bailey and Robert H. Ferrell, who dealt respectively with the Treaty of Versailles and the Kellogg-Briand Pact. Incidentally, they published their books just twenty-five years after their subjects came into being.

There are other explanations for the silence. Conceivably, the absence of records inhibited scholars awaiting the publication of the State Department's relevant *Foreign Relations* volumes.

While this is an understandable reaction, the alliance by the 1970s had undergone sufficient change in its development for issues to be susceptible to scholarly analysis. If archives remained closed, many of the major actors on the scene had published a profusion of primary materials.

The most serious reason for neglect went beyond the scarcity of primary materials or the need for more temporal distance from the subject. It was a matter of priorities. For most students of the Cold War at the time, whether identified as "court historian" or "new left," the framing of the North Atlantic Treaty was a minor matter, subsumed in the major break from isolationism. Their eyes were on the Truman Doctrine as the symbol of the Cold War and the policy of containment. The treaty, if it had any meaning at all, was a logical consequence of the containment policy. It may be worth observing that in 1974, the twenty-fifth anniversary of the North Atlantic Treaty, the Harry S. Truman Library in Independence, Missouri, held no ceremony and sponsored no conference, although in 1975 it was the setting for a major conference on the Korean War, where the principal political and military leaders of 1950 shared their reflections with historians.

Much has changed since that time. The alliance has survived as a troubled but viable institution that after forty years may claim considerable credit for both the normalization of relations with the Soviet Union and the establishment of a united Europe, the two major objectives of the treaty in 1949. But since those accomplishments were not fully realized in 1989—and may not be even in the 1990s—the need for the alliance to provide stability in transatlantic affairs may keep NATO alive another generation.

But if NATO should survive, will it be meaningful? The idea of NATO being in a terminal state has been a topic for pundits since 1950. If it remains troubled, its troubles are on the front pages of newspapers, not in the back pages of the *New York Times,* where SEATO and CENTO had their obituaries in the late 1970s. Unlike those alliances, NATO is relevant today.

The durability of the alliance may or may not be a factor in the attention it has received in recent years. The opening of archives has attracted doctoral students to the field. Their interest has centered on the 1950s rather than the 1940s, now considered excessively worked over. In the early 1970s the list of current research projects assembled by SHAFR or of dissertations in Warren Kuehl's *Dissertations in History* and the *Comprehensive Dissertation Index* revealed how little interest there was in NATO. A hasty review of bibliographies today shows a different story. It should be added that European scholars, in recent years, have made special contributions to the formative period of NATO's history.

Yet as historians deal with the problems of Germany's accession to the alliance or the impact of the Suez crisis on NATO, they frequently operate on an assumption that the passage of the treaty was a foregone conclusion. The vote of 82 to 13 in the Senate seems to have been a triumph of bipartisanship, with Senators Arthur H. Vandenberg and Tom Connally vying for credit. In a sense too many of us still accept the judgment of historians who have filed NATO under the Truman Doctrine. If the nation had accepted containment in 1947, obviously it followed that the Truman Doctrine had eased the way for the treaty two years later. This is a mistaken assumption, whatever the vote may suggest or whatever textbooks tell the student.

To deal with these and other historiographical problems the United States Mission to NATO, in collaboration with the Lyman L. Lemnitzer Center of Kent State University, organized a symposium on the occasion of the fortieth anniversary of the signing of the treaty. The organizers invited several American diplomatic historians to meet in Brussels on 15–16 May 1989 to examine the role of the alliance in the history of American foreign relations. They presented seven papers, each centering on a major issue in the past forty years, beginning with the framing of the treaty itself in 1949. Subsequent crises became milestones in the evolution of the organization: the Korean War; the accession of the Federal Republic of Germany in 1955; French withdrawal from NATO but not the alliance in 1966; the effect of the Harmel initiative and détente on NATO in the late 1960s and early 1970s, the dual-track initiative of 1979 involving concurrent movement toward defense buildup and negotiations for arms limitation; and finally, the projected effect of the Intermediate Range Nuclear Forces Agreement of 1987.

In this book the historians present a history of the past forty years from an American perspective, placing the alliance within the larger frame of America's foreign policy as a superpower. Their interpretations benefit from their intimacy with cognate issues on which each historian has written over the years. While their evaluations cover most of the issues facing NATO, there is nothing homogenous about their findings. Their personal perspectives differ, and the availability of materials presents its own problems. NATO students of the 1970s and 1980s come to more speculative conclusions than those of their counterparts with access to archives of the 1940s and 1950s. But whatever their individual interpretations each reveals the important role NATO has played in fashioning the "American Century."

Robert Ferrell recalls vividly what the passage of time understandably has obscured: the sense of disarray in which the postwar world found itself in 1947 and 1948. World War II had destroyed most of Europe, and the survivors were fearful of the future. The Soviet Union, though badly damaged by the war, had become the major power of the continent, ready, it seemed, to impose its communist system upon the Western democracies. It is not surprising that it was European initiative, particularly the work of British Foreign Secretary Ernest Bevin, which induced Americans to consider an entangling alliance.

Ferrell develops a theme that the late Armin Rappaport touched upon a generation ago when he identified the alliance as "the American Revolution of 1949." The duty of responding to the Bevin initiative was left to leading members of the Truman administration who shrewdly wooed the many constituents that were needed to support a treaty. The result was a departure from an old and honored tradition.

What is often overlooked in examination of America's entry into the alliance is the risks that were involved. Ferrell notes the fragile nature of the deterrent the U.S. was offering Europe. Although recognizing America's potential as a military giant, it was more potential than reality in 1949. The allies relied on a Strategic Air Command providing very little credible retaliatory or deterrent force until it was reorganized by General Curtis LeMay a year after the treaty was signed.

Walter LaFeber examines the first major crisis in the history of the alliance: the Korean War. That conflict might have awakened isolationist passions in the United States, leading to an abandonment of the relatively recent priority it had given to Europe. Instead, the war focused attention on a divided Germany replicating a divided Korea. The lesson of the Korean War in this instance resulted in the reorganization of the alliance into a military organization that could cope with Soviet aggression, direct or indirect, in

Europe. It meant too that German resources had to be brought into the enterprise. Consequently, much of American statecraft from 1950 until the Federal Republic joined NATO was directed toward winning Germany's acceptance by the allies.

LaFeber's principal judgment is that the Korean War was no watershed. Rather, it was the occasion to solve systemic problems that had disturbed the alliance before June 1950. Problems included the shortcomings of the Marshall Plan, the inadequacy of European conventional forces, and an uncomfortable recognition of the global implications of the Atlantic alliance in such areas as Southeast Asia. But the most critical problem, he writes, was the German question. Rather than seeing West German rearmament as a consequence of the Korean crisis, he finds that conflict in East Asia opened an opportunity for the United States to press for a Franco-German rapprochement, which Secretary of State Dean Acheson and his colleagues believed was a prerequisite to NATO's acquisition of West German troops. The war in Asia seemed to offer solutions to problems that had eluded American leadership in the first year of the alliance's history.

West Germany is a focal point also in Ernest May's examination of the Federal Republic's accession to NATO in 1955 and its significance in the 1950s. But his is a different perspective. What attracts his attention is less the service that Franco-German collaboration might give the alliance or the manpower West Germany could provide its allies; he looks instead at an anomaly of history in which a superpower allows its troops to serve as hostage to its smaller allies. Powers in the past have made their allies pay far more than did the Atlantic allies for the service of a powerful nation. Why Europe received the American commitment without providing service of equal value may be explained, May suggests, by the special geopolitical circumstances of the time and by the special tradition of America's domestic politics.

If the 1950s was the apogee of NATO, with American military power protecting Western Europe and permitting it to develop national economic miracles and even to take steps toward an economic community, the 1960s was a difficult decade, arguably the most critical in the alliance's history to the present time. It was in the 1960s that crises over Berlin and Cuba led the world to the brink of catastrophe. It was the decade in which the Soviets claimed equality with the United States as a superpower, and General Charles de Gaulle led France virtually out of the organization. NATO might have collapsed under the weight of these challenges. The Gaullist challenge was especially divisive. France had been a difficult ally from the beginning, concerned on the one side with an Anglo-Saxon domination and on the other with a revived German threat. Under de Gaulle it seemed determined to go its own way. But as Samuel Wells points out, it was a carefully calibrated way.

France did not leave the alliance. De Gaulle assumed that the dangers from the East had abated, and that a connection on his own terms would permit France a freedom it could not have alone or inside the organization. It was possible, as Wells speculates, that greater sensitivity to French amour propre, as President Dwight D. Eisenhower recognized and John F. Kennedy and Lyndon B. Johnson did not, might have kept France inside. He concedes that it was an unlikely possibility.

There is a connection between France's withdrawal from the organization in 1966 and the positive reception of the North Atlantic Council to the Harmel Report a year later. While de Gaulle had been less fearful of Soviet power than his colleagues in the alliance, he had also been less willing to both enter into negotiations with the Soviets and grant more authority to the smaller allies in the alliance. With respect to the former, he believed the West would gain no advantages in negotiations; Soviet intentions centered on neutralization of Europe or removal of nuclear arms, both issues the French opposed. As for the smaller allies, France had no more interest in granting a greater voice to the smaller nations than did the United States. After 1966 the smaller nations did find a voice in the Nuclear Planning Group and a revitalized Defense Planning Group. They had seats in committees with greater influence on military planning. The Harmel Report, under the leadership of representatives of smaller nations, called for an effective détente with the East bloc, for disarmament and balanced force reductions by both sides. This did not mean that defense plans were irrelevant; it meant that détente was as essential a function of NATO as military preparations.

The United States from 1967 to the mid-1970s appeared to share the drive toward détente, as it approved Germany's Ostpolitik, the anti-ballistic missiles (ABM) and Strategic Arms Limitations Talks (SALT) treaties. But, as Joan Hoff-Wilson observes, the term "détente" was so loose as to be almost indefinable. It was translated into the Nixon Doctrine in which the United States, driven by the imperatives of war in Vietnam, sought retreat from the burden of responsibilities it had assumed under the Truman Doctrine. Among the new relationships was a linkage with the Soviet Union in which the United States attempted to pull the Soviets into a more normal relationship. Such intention, initiated by President Richard M. Nixon, nurtured by national security adviser Henry Kissinger, and amalgamated under the sobriquet "Nixingerism," had some elements in common with Europe's conception of détente. But the differences made for conflict and misunderstanding in the early 1970s, as the United States pursued a global policy while the Europeans concentrated on regional issues. So even though Nixingerism paid lip service to the primacy of Europe in the Nixon Doctrine, and to collaboration with NATO partners, it was an uneasy partnership, marked by America's resentment over Europe's behavior in the Yom Kippur War of 1973 and by Europe's anger over such unilateral policies as devaluation of the dollar in 1971. Although détente was a by-product of the Nixon Doctrine, it was central to Europe's hopes. It had a pragmatic value for Nixon and Kissinger, and when that value seemed to fail it was abandoned—and abandoned without consultation with NATO allies.

In the mid-1970s the hopes that had been invested in the Mutual Balanced and Force Reduction (MBFR) talks in Vienna, in the SALT talks between the superpowers, and in the Helsinki Agreement of 1975 were not realized. Although there was little progress in arms reduction talks, the condition of NATO was better than in the 1960s when flashpoints in Berlin or Cuba might have precipitated full-scale war. By the late 1970s it was obvious that Berlin and Cuba had receded as problems, that the danger of unilateral U.S. withdrawal had declined with the end of the war in Vietnam and with the ongoing MBFR negotiations.

Yet there was a malaise that was damaging the alliance. It emerged from the mutual suspicions of Europeans and Americans over their loyalty to NATO. As Gaddis Smith observes, on one level the crisis developed from the rapid modernization of Soviet arms, particularly missiles, and the deployment of increasing numbers of SS-20 missiles targeted on Western European cities. NATO's response was to counter Soviet moves with cruise and Pershing II missiles. At the same time, it sought to preserve the principles of détente by coupling this action with negotiations to limit theater nuclear weapons on both sides. But this is too simplistic a description of the action, as Smith notes. Neither SS-20 nor cruise missiles did more than add marginally to the weapons alignment in Europe and could be identified simply as part of the modernization process on both sides.

The missile crisis of the 1970s masked internal conflict within NATO, much of it deriving from the personalities of President Jimmy Carter and Chancellor Helmut Schmidt. Carter disconcerted the allies by the priorities he would give extra-European issues, such as the Third World or morality in government. Although his character may have been respected, his sense of direction was not. He appeared erratic in his relations with the Soviets and was identified as an unreliable partner by Schmidt, the leading European statesman of the day. In this context the council's decision to link deployment of cruise missiles with negotiations for reduction of arms was a means of reviving the credibility of the U.S. commitment. Despite the continuing presence of American troops in Europe, Carter's decision to shelve the neutron bomb and his apparent insensitivity to European concerns in SALT II talks required a new effort.

The virtue of the dual-track decision of the North Atlantic Council in 1979 was the linkage of defense preparations with arms control, in the spirit of the Harmel initiative of 1967. Its drawback was the length of time between the decision and deployment in 1983, which gave opportunity for opponents on the Left and Right to mobilize. The Reagan administration seemed interested only in the military aspect of the decision, with an indifference to the second track. Smith observes that the dual-track decision encouraged the revival of powerful antinuclear movements in both the United States and Europe, which also slighted the second track by its concentration on the deployment issue.

The year 1983 was arguably the year of decision in the second generation of NATO's history. The menacing walkout of the Soviets from negotiations and their efforts to intimidate West German and British electorates in that year backfired; public opinion in the NATO countries remained loyal to the alliance. NATO passed the test as European legislatures accepted deployment.

But toward the end of the 1980s, the Soviets offered an even greater challenge to the alliance as a new leader, Mikhail Gorbachev, reversed Soviet positions on all kinds of international issues, and not only engaged in constructive dialogue with Western leaders but seemed to promise a genuine end to the Cold War. The return of the Soviets to the negotiating table in Geneva led to summit meetings in Reykjavík in 1986 and Washington in 1987, where an arms reduction treaty was finally signed. President Ronald Reagan responded by embracing, to the consternation of his allies, a Soviet proposal to remove all nuclear weapons from Europe, and then, with the widespread approval of his allies, by agreeing to a treaty removing intermediate nuclear ballistic missiles from Europe.

The INF treaty could have signaled the termination of the alliance. Its goals were either realized or well on the way to realization. European integration was becoming a reality. Europe had not only recovered but was potentially as strong or stronger than the two superpowers. The Communist challenge had dissolved, partly because of failure to serve as an ideological guide to the world, partly because of failure to provide acceptable economies for people living within the system. If Gorbachev's Soviet Union had changed so drastically, what functions would NATO serve?

My own view looks to the past as well as to the future. NATO in the 1960s was considered to have met its goals, as Western Europe recovered and the Soviet Union accepted "peaceful competition." The alliance survived, and the reasons for survival a generation ago may be applicable over the remaining years of the present century. The rapidly changing events of 1990, notably the apparent breakdown of the Soviet empire and the uniting of the two Germanies, could not have been predicted a year before. The Gorbachev initiatives in the Soviet Union may have opened the way for a permanent end to conflict in Europe, to a new order for Europe. It also may have set in motion civil war and chaos in the East and a German-dominated community in the West. Whatever the course of history in the next few years, it is likely that NATO will have important functions to perform. Not least among them would be the association of the United States with Europe as a stabilizing factor, ensuring a sense of security against a powerful Germany in the West and potential chaos in the East.

The alliance has always been more than a military organization, and West-West relations more often than not have figured more prominently than East-West confrontations. Removal of most of the American troops from Europe could follow reduction in arms and in tension without necessarily terminating the treaty of alliance. Even if the machinery of SHAPE and SACLANT were dismantled, wholly or partially, the transatlantic ties could keep the treaty intact, not as a empty shell but as a bond of reassurance to Europeans (East and West) as well as to Americans. Until new institutions have come into being or until a full sense of security has been achieved in the West, there is justification for the maintenance, and even the deepening, of the transatlantic relationships that have been established over the past forty years.

ROBERT H. FERRELL

The Formation of the Alliance, 1948–1949

In retrospect of forty years, and after pondering the frailty of judgments about contemporary history, it does seem that the North Atlantic Treaty has changed the foreign policy of the United States beyond recall, thereby ensuring the future—military, economic, political—of Western Europe. So one concludes from looking back over the years of NATO's existence, overlooking the confusions, irritabilities, and even failures, the ups and downs that mark international affairs as surely as they beset individuals. Anyone old enough to remember the state of international affairs in the late 1940s can behold enormous change, indeed so much as to constitute a veritable revolution. One hesitates to use the word "revolution," hackneyed as it has become. Historians are fond of it. Still, it seems the appropriate word to describe the present, as against the now remote—and riddance to it—past after World War II, the opening years of the Cold War.

Consider this revolution for what it has meant to aging students of contemporary history who remember the climactic last year of World War II in Europe, the dull thud of buzz bombs and V-2 rockets upon defenseless, broken-windowed London, and across the Channel, the sirens on the tanks moving up the country roads of Normandy. After such experiences they wanted some sort of assurance that their nations would not make the same errors as after World War I. As it turned out, they were much surprised that upon defeating one foe in Europe it was necessary to confront another. They were not keen on a permanent American presence in Europe, but if such was necessary, they were for it. Fortunately, they thought, President Harry S. Truman, Congress, and the American people took the essential measures. Almost 150 years before the revolutionary beginning in 1949, the American nation in the now-forgotten Treaty of Morfontaine had escaped from its first—and for a century and a half, only—alliance. With the North Atlantic Treaty there was again involvement, an enormous change, if one chose to think about it. As for Western Europeans, the treaty of 1949 gave hope to, and then substantial defense against, what was a dangerous situation; beginning with the Korean War the treaty led to a respectable, if never convincing, military balance with the forces of the Soviet Union. This allowed Western Europe's economic revival, initially through the Marshall Plan, in course by 4 April 1949 and commencing in the summer of 1950 the huge offshore American purchases during the Korean War. The result, economically speaking, was revolutionary; in the words of Walt W. Rostow, Western Europe's economies "took off." The European Community nations now are admiring the prospect of another takeoff at the end of 1992. And Western Europe's economic miracle has helped reduce the Continent's political nationalism. It has played some part in bringing to power the regime in Russia that is breaking with the communist and tsarist past, with all such a regime can mean for European and world peace.

It is possible that history may make another turn, of 180 degrees, and go the wrong way, a veritable revolution in reverse. In international and personal affairs such revolutions have occurred. Hugh R. Trevor-Roper has pointed out the melancholy result of the Pacification of Ghent in 1576, as forgotten a moment as Morfontaine in 1800.[1] In the sixteenth century a great prince had seemed to triumph by uniting the Low Countries in favor of enlightened religion and, so far as concerned the burghers, even more enlightened commerce and manufacturing. According to the scheme of William of Orange, all Europe would look to Ghent as a beacon for its progress. Not for a moment would it be possible for the sovereign of Spain, Philip II, to challenge light with his regal darkness. But as Trevor-Roper told so well, history met defiance in the person of the Spanish monarch, whose advisers told him that by eliminating William of Orange, through assassination, much good would follow. All the monarchs and princes did it, the advisers said; a small sin could result in far greater good. William therefore passed to his heavenly reward, the Low Countries became a charnel house of war, and in the next century the Thirty Years War raised nationalism as the end-all of Europe, with war as its handmaiden, and doomed the Western world to three hundred years of darkness. Even our own century, as John Lukacs has shown in a brilliant but, alas, unpublished essay, has been a theater of nationalism, the curse of Philip II. It is rival nationalism, not capitalism versus communism, that has marked the international calamities of our time.

We nonetheless must take courage. Trevor-Roper's exposition is entrancing; this master essayist can set up his purposes and by analogy take his readers the way he wishes them to go. The year 1576, he makes us believe, was a point of change, a great moment, and history went the wrong way. But facing another moment in 1949, history surely went the right way, and may well continue to do so.

A few years ago the author of a book on the United States Strategic Air Command during its initial years, including the period of the foundation of NATO in 1948–49, wrote plaintively that before drawing the meaning of great international policies historians ought to look at the military hardware and the military technicians that were to take those policies into the realm of fact. Part of the problem, as Harry R. Borowski drew it, was that information on the Soviets was not forthcoming, and crucial American military records were not available until 1974.[2] Also part of the problem, perhaps, was the tendency of all of us to equate the ideal with the real, especially if it involved—as in Borowski's book—an organization led by a man who boasted about taking people back to the Stone Age. Similarly, it was tempting not to look at SAC because it dealt in hardware that all of us essentially disliked.

The truth is that the military position of the Western nations in 1945–50 was appalling, and only at the very end of the half decade was there the beginning of change—because of Lieutenant General Curtis E. LeMay's reforms in SAC and the opening of the Korean War, which led to large increases in conventional armament.

Beyond question the war plans of the Western European nations and of the United States were ambitious to a fault, and on the American side if carried out would have placed an immediate foundation under what Melvyn P. Leffler has described as "the American conception of national security."[3] On both sides of the Atlantic, however, the staff statements of the time started resolutely and ended in doubletalk. They were English compositions and, in a sense, unworthy of the intelligent officers and their assistants who sat around tables forty and more years ago. In reading the plans of the staffs, not merely those of the Brussels powers of 1948–49 but of the Joint Chiefs of Staff in Washington, one has the impression of generals and admirals, some of them principal figures in the recent war, sitting around highly varnished tables and talking of dreams—the troops, and the bombs and planes, were not in existence.

Perhaps the less said about Western European plans for defense, the better, for those plans were crude in the extreme. Indeed, there were none until the time of the Brussels Pact. That is, there were none save for plans of evacuation of the occupation troops from the Channel and the Pyrenees, if the occupation troops were able to get to them after the Russian hordes started to move west.

But Brussels demanded plans, and the question became how far east the pact's forces could make a stand. At the beginning, and in the end, the decision was swathed in meaningless words, such as the plan communicated to Ambassador Lewis W. Douglas on 14 May 1948: "The five powers are now assessing their resources and fully recognise that an attack in the near future would find them militarily weak."[4] The plans did not move much beyond that point, although there was considerable discussion, with suitable expression of national interests, of who would command the nearly nonexistent troops. Here the French, who were supposed to contribute the largest forces to the Western European army (but possessed no equipment and already were harried by the requirements of Indochina), were terribly concerned that they might be under command of the British, who undoubtedly would then produce a scheme to bring in West German troops of some sort. The five powers agreed to have a French army general, French admiral, and British air marshal placed in command. By this time discussions were proceeding for some sort of wider pact in which the United States would participate, and the Brussels powers suggested an American supreme commander. General Lucius D. Clay in Berlin thought of resigning if American troops went under command of a Brussels general. Washington advised him that it did "not want an American commander too closely associated with the overall initial debacle."[5]

In September 1948, the Western Union defense organization made Field Marshal Sir Bernard Montgomery chairman of the commanders-in-chief committee, with headquarters eventually at Fontainebleau. Montgomery, military-political schemer that he was, then got to work. According to an equally irrepressible American State Department official, Theodore Achilles, one of "Monty's" earliest secret telegrams to the War Office in London was, "My present instructions are to hold the line at the Rhine. Presently available allied forces might enable me to hold the tip of the Brittany peninsula for three days. Please instruct further." Montgomery also began to annoy the French by proposing a command setup modeled on that of the British and Americans during the Normandy invasion, namely, two army groups above the army corps organizations. The French knew that one group would be under American command and the other under British, with General Jean de Lattre de Tassigny becoming an errand boy to the corps commanders.[6]

While the Brussels nations in 1948 were playing with command problems and stating their essential problem in as many words as possible, the Americans in Washington were not doing much better. For the first three years after World War II the United States had no joint strategic plan, as a commission chaired by Thomas K. Finletter discovered late in 1947. The five members of the commission inquired as to whether a plan was available. Finletter went to Truman, who promised to obtain it. Shortly afterward Admirals William D. Leahy and Chester W. Nimitz and Generals Dwight D. Eisenhower and Hoyt S. Vandenberg met with the Finletter group and presented the plan, "pages thick, pages and pages," accompanied by an oral exposition. The group found the briefing very confusing, and after several questions General Eisenhower apologized.

"I'm sorry, I guess my mind is worse than I thought it was," he said. "I can't understand what the war plan is."

After more discussion he continued, "Gentlemen, these five civilian gentlemen who are here are just patriotic American citizens trying to do something they've been asked to do by the President. I think we owe it to them to tell them that there is no war plan."[7]

In these years the services made do with such ad hoc plans as the air force–generated "Makefast," which hypothecated six B-29 groups operating from Cairo and England within four months of the opening of hostilities, and believed that such a force could destroy three-fourths of Russia's petroleum-producing capacity in nine months and destroy the mobility of Soviet ground and air forces in one year. The plan left open whether planes would carry nuclear or conventional bombs.[8] Two-thirds of the Soviet petroleum industry was in seventeen cities, and by July 1948 the joint chiefs came up with a "short-range emergency war plan," "Halfmoon," which called for dropping fifty atomic bombs on twenty cities important for petroleum and other items, in order to cause "paralysis of at least 50 percent of Soviet industry." Upon being briefed on May 5, President Truman ordered an alternate plan based on conventional bombing. The president thought the bomb might be outlawed by the time war came, through the Baruch Plan or some such arrangement. As the

Berlin crisis deepened and turned into a blockade, with the Western airlift at first a chancy proposition, Truman reluctantly assured Secretary of Defense James V. Forrestal that "if it became necessary" he might use nuclear weapons, and he endorsed NSC-30, a National Security Council document that looked in that direction. Halfmoon, incidentally, called for forces in Germany to withdraw to the Rhine ("but it is probable that U.S. forces will withdraw through France either to French coastal ports or to the Pyrenees") and envisioned SAC planes deploying to bases in England, Khartoum-Cairo-Suez, and Okinawa.[9]

But was it not true that behind the inability of the military staffs, foreign and domestic, to guarantee the safety of Western Europe by conventional means, there was a merciful if not providential reliance on what the political scientist Bernard Brodie in a widely read book of the time described as "the ultimate weapon"? Certainly people in Western Europe and the United States believed that Western Europe's security rested ultimately with the atomic bombs carried by the U.S. Air Force's Strategic Air Command. So did officials, including even President Truman on occasion (he could wobble, as in his analyses of Halfmoon). On 9 February 1949 the president was talking with the chairman of the Atomic Energy Commission, David E. Lilienthal, who unknown to friends and acquaintances was keeping a massive diary. Truman told Lilienthal that "the atomic bomb was the mainstay and all he had; that the Russians would have probably taken over Europe a long time ago if it were not for that."[10]

The arresting fact of the West's reliance on the American SAC in the early postwar years was that it was entirely misplaced. Here the merciful or perhaps providential part was probably that the Russians did not know this. Forcing the American armed services into ever smaller budgets prior to outbreak of the Korean War had so reduced conventional forces that only nuclear bombs could have saved the West. And yet, even with the ultimate weapon—partly because of budget constraints, mainly because of very poor leadership—SAC was no reliance at all.

The budget question was only in lesser part the problem of SAC. When things changed for the better the necessity in terms of personnel was only an increase of about 20,000 men, from 52,000 to 71,000, no large matter within a total armed forces strength of about 1.5 million. The budget, to be sure, was tight, and for fiscal year 1950 (1 July 1949 to 30 June 1950) the administration asked for $14.4 billion and received $13.9 billion. But this was not too far from an acceptable budget, according to a man who should have known. General Eisenhower wrote in his diary for 19 February 1949 that "I personally and very earnestly believe that $15 billion to $16 billion per year is all that this country need spend for security forces, if it is done every year (with some additional amounts to cover past deficits)."[11]

Most of the problem lay elsewhere, in leadership. And here the lesser part of the difficulty was in supervising production of fissionable material and fabrication of bombs. The stockpile, of course, was quite insufficient for the hopes placed upon it by the president and the State Department and Department of Defense, not to mention the European allies. David Alan Rosenberg first published the figures for 1945–48, and Steven L. Rearden in his official history of the Defense Department has corroborated them, showing two weapons ready by late 1945, nine by 30 June 1946, thirteen by mid-1947, and fifty by mid-1948.[12] As Rosenberg also related, Forrestal and Nimitz provided recommendations on production rates of bombs; neither knew the size of the stockpile or the current rate of production, but each assumed the other did. Rosenberg has stressed, too, the necessary slowness in assembling bombs, the short time that a bomb could remain within an aircraft, and the manner in which the life of workable bombs was limited by the polonium initiators: bombs in the stockpile seem to have been unassembled until some crisis or other, and it took twenty-four men nearly two days to prepare each weapon; a bomb could remain in a plane only forty-eight hours before having to be partly disassembled to recharge batteries powering the bomb's fusing and monitoring systems; and the initiators, needed to increase the neutron background in the cores to ensure fission of the critical mass at the proper moment, had a half-life of 138 days.

But SAC's worst problem was its bumbling leadership, until LeMay took over in October 1948. Such is the conclusion of Borowski, who has made an exhaustive study of SAC's difficulties. The command's extraordinary ineptitude may have derived from the air force's straining to become independent, which took so much of the energy of its leaders. SAC's first commander was General George C. Kenney, a subordinate of General Douglas MacArthur during World War II, who was a good speaker and spent a great deal of time giving air force speeches around the country. The air force's first chief of staff, General Carl Spaatz, may have been doing much the same thing. Whatever the reason, this meant that SAC's deputy commander, Major General Clements McMullen, a name that has not gone down in history, was the architect of many of the problems that plagued the command until LeMay took over.

To recite—in an essay dedicated to the origins of NATO—the problems of General McMullen is to go into too much detail. Suffice it to say that the foundation of Western military retaliation rested with this virtually unknown general, who through a device of organization known as cross-training nearly reduced the Western world's defenses to a shambles. McMullen believed that air crews were the best people to do all the jobs in the air force. He also thought that to cut staffs would make the boys more efficient. His motto was "Give them half of what they asked for, work them twice as hard, and they will get twice as much done." The result was a series of inefficiencies, and putting them all together they nearly spelled disaster. Morale plummeted as the air crews worked ever harder and General McMullen sent the non-fly-boys to various air force Siberias. The theoretical became the possible until proved otherwise, and in the case of cross-training it did not stop until LeMay, replacing Kenney and McMullen, stopped it.

Meanwhile the air force realized that the quickest route to the Soviet Union lay over the North Pole, and thus the best course was to put bomb groups on Ladd Field near Fairbanks, Alaska. But there the men soon found what it was like to fly in appallingly cold weather, when even to start the engines was an excruciating experience of several hours, and then to get the planes to stay up, when lines were freezing, was worse. Moreover, they were scared out of their wits at becoming lost. As Borowski has written, "If one were to remove that portion of the globe north of the Arctic Circle and position it over the geographical center of the United States, it would cover the entire nation, Mexico, most of Cuba, large portions of the Pacific and Atlantic Oceans, and nearly all of the Canadian provinces."[13] If a flier bailed out he would not last long, and if he went down on the polar ice cap or in the area of continual winter darkness he would have only time enough to say his prayers.

Other problems arose, such as "silverplating" B-29s. This involved much more than strengthening their frames and opening up wide hatches for the five-ton "fat boy" bombs of the time, the plutonium bombs of Alamogordo and Nagasaki. By the end of 1946 only about half of the forty-six so-modified planes remained from the recent war. To silverplate each new plane required six thousand hours.

Then there was the business of getting a bomb on target, which LeMay discovered that his predecessors in command had virtually ignored. He set up an exercise that was not like the sitting-duck arrangements that SAC had known during the time of McMullen, in that it simulated what would be known about cities in the Soviet Union. He gave crew members a 1938 photograph of Dayton, Ohio, and told his bombardiers to go to it. In January 1949, the command made a simulated wartime assault on Dayton, flying at thirty thousand feet, and the mission was a complete failure. SAC had been flying at low altitudes, but this time flew at high altitudes and the equipment failed. Radar operators could not read the targets. Thunderstorms made the weather uncooperative. "You might call that just about the darkest night in American aviation history," the general said years later. "Not one airplane finished that mission as briefed. *Not one.*"[14]

The weakness of Western forces at this time was drawn in the starkest terms at a meeting of the NATO foreign ministers with the highest American officials—President Truman, Secretary of State Dean Acheson, Secretary of Defense Louis Johnson (who had replaced Forrestal)—on the evening before the treaty was signed, 3 April 1949. A stenographic account of the meeting, incidentally, has recently come to light in the Truman Library in Independence, Missouri, and only Lawrence S. Kaplan, the indefatigable NATO researcher, had seen this document before its reincarnation.[15] During that outspoken session, with no outsiders present, Secretary Johnson said that "neither the signing of the Atlantic pact nor any initial U.S. military aid program is going to enable us to hold the Rhine line. It will be some years, assuming continued U.S. aid and probably increasing rearmament by Western Europe itself, before we can feel confident of our ability to do this." The president himself was no more comforting, and in one respect less. "We must not close our eyes to the fact that, despite the huge U.S. war potential," he said, "the Western nations are practically disarmed and have no power sufficient to prevent the five hundred Soviet divisions from overrunning Western Europe and most of Asia. To be sure, we have the atomic bomb; but we must recognize the present limitations of our strategic methods for delivering it . . ."[16]

In the American system of government the president of the United States sits in his office in the west wing of the White House and presides, as his title indicates, over the work of his subordinates.

But that is what the Constitution of the eighteenth century prescribed, and from the outset there were great practical differences from the written document. One might have thought that Secretary of Defense Forrestal was at least presiding over his sprawling cabinet office, but of course that was not true. One day President Truman's naval aide, Rear Admiral Robert L. Dennison, was in the Oval Office and Truman looked at him owlishly through his thick glasses and said,

"Do you know who the secretary of defense is?"

Bob Dennison played along with the president and said, "Yes, sir, Jim Forrestal."

"You're wrong," was the response. "*I'm* the Secretary of Defense. Jim calls me up several times a day asking me to make a decision on matters that are completely within his competence, but he passes them on to me."[17]

One can only be thankful that Truman, who had an acute sense of how to run the government of the United States and possessed an essentially civilian point of view, presided over civil-military relations in the early postwar years. In 1948 Forrestal wanted the military to have possession of the atomic bombs, and Truman would have none of it. Perhaps it made no difference, for the military could not have dropped them effectively if they had had them.

In the generally commonsense way that the government worked during the Truman administration, the president was vastly assisted by two excellent secretaries of state, whose qualities were epitomized in a remark by Acheson to the historian Gaddis Smith. General Marshall once told Acheson there were two kinds of men: those who dealt with action and those who dealt with description. Acheson was no man to hide his light, and added: "He [Marshall] was entirely the former. I have been both."[18]

Truman, Marshall, and Acheson had plenty to be levelheaded about, whether active, descriptive, or both, during the years 1948–49 when the North Atlantic Treaty took shape. In the developing historiography of the Cold War, Melvyn Leffler has written that there were no real fears of Russian conquest, that year after year the intelligence agencies predicted no Russian attack, but that the American military, aided and abetted by the president and his State Department assistants, listened carefully to the accounts of Russian capability, decided to counter them with economic and military programs of their own, and created the strained relations with the Soviet Union that they said they hoped to avoid.[19] Still, there were real scares, real war scares. Regarding General Clay's cable of 5 March 1948, Leffler has written that for the first time he, Clay, thought war was really possible. He relates that Clay was only trying for increased defense expenditures. But a State Department memorandum of the same date showed, on an attached note in Truman's hand, that the president was highly uneasy. Truman listed trouble spots beginning with Turkey and Greece and asked, "Shall we state the case to the Congress, name names and call the turn? Will Russia move first? Who pulls the trigger?" There followed, to be sure, other surprisingly worried moments for a man as unflappable as Harry S. Truman. On 13 September 1948, he was scared: "Have a terrific day. Forrestal, Bradley, Vandenberg (the general, not the senator), Symington brief me on the bases, bombs, Moscow, Leningrad, etc. I have a terrible feeling afterward that we are very close to war. I hope not. Discuss situation with Marshall at lunch." Nearly a year later, on 31 August 1949, after the North Atlantic Treaty had been signed and the organization itself was under way, there was another scare; during the president's staff meeting he told the group that the country was nearer war than it had been at any time—this over the Russians' contention with the Yugoslav government of Marshal Tito. On this occasion Truman added that the United States had very little arms should it be plunged into war.[20]

The North Atlantic Treaty was drawn up in 1948, at a time of crisis, especially at the outset of the year—the Czech coup of February, followed by the death of Foreign Minister Jan Masaryk, and then the rapid worsening of relations with the Soviets that resulted in the Berlin blockade beginning in June. In the autumn matters seemed to straighten out, what with a virtual Soviet peace offensive (less pressure through Communist parties in France and Italy and failure to place heavy demands on Finland and Norway, as expected). The statesmen of the West could hardly take comfort, however, in what they assumed to be only a lull. It is instructive that the second secretary of the British Embassy in Washington, Donald Maclean, attended the early meetings of the Western nations looking to the formation of NATO; Maclean was spying for Moscow. He fled to the Soviet Union in 1951 and must have sent word in 1948 that the Washington deliberations were altogether pacific and defensive. The Westerners had no mole in the Kremlin to inform them of Russian intentions.

The man who got the treaty negotiations going, beyond doubt, was the foreign secretary of Britain, Ernest Bevin, who spoke with

Secretary Marshall just after the failure of the first London Conference in December 1947—the conference that was supposed to settle the German problem but instead succumbed to a series of intransigences perpetrated by Vyacheslav M. Molotov. Bevin acted, even though the omens for his being an agent of change were hardly good. At the conference's end Marshall had worked out an arrangement whereby he and Bevin would cooperate in breaking up the meetings, but Bevin, through sheer fumbling Dean Acheson later thought, failed on his part of the bargain and Marshall had to do the job himself. As for Truman, he confidentially believed Bevin to be a boor and, more to the point, a son of a bitch, perhaps because Bevin had testified openly about Truman's Palestine policy. But Bevin acted anyway, and when Marshall came to dinner for what he thought was a social chat, Bevin began to talk unintelligibly (to Marshall) about two circles. As soon as Marshall got back to his hotel he told his assistant, John D. Hickerson, "I wasn't prepared for it. If I had known he was going to talk about this I would have taken you down. You've got to go down and see what the guy has in mind." Bevin was talking about negotiations for the Brussels Pact, which was one circle, a tight one, and he wanted another circle including the United States and Canada, not as tightly drawn.[21]

What happened thereafter is well known. The foreign secretary made a speech in the House of Commons in January, and the British ambassador in Washington asked for talks, which began soon after in Washington.

In all this Bevin was helped somewhat by former Prime Minister Winston Churchill, whose favorite line of verse was "Westward look the land is bright."[22] Churchill was championing what became the Council of Europe, an idealistic organization with no powers to which nations sent representatives. Bevin thought that organization useless, and also dangerous, and in his cockney accent made one of his best remarks about the danger: "If you open that Pandora's Box you never know what Trojan 'orses will jump out." Churchill, meanwhile, was muddying the international waters by advising his American cousins to tell off the Russians ("tell the Soviets that if they do not retire from Berlin and abandon Eastern Germany, withdrawing to the Polish frontier, we will raze their cities").[23] Nonetheless, the former prime minister's more sensible agitations helped Bevin's more sensible proposal.

Once conversations began in Washington between the ambassadors, the details were pretty much up to the Americans, for the

Brussels Pact powers needed American power and the price would have to be paid mostly by the giver, despite the brave talk on both sides about mutuality. Bevin did not care what form the association of the United States with Western Europe took, so long as there was a presence.

As it turned out, some American officials were helpful and some were not. Hickerson and his associate in the State Department, Achilles, were the ringleaders in pushing through a form of agreement that would work. After Marshall had sent him over to talk to Foreign Office officials about the two circles, Hickerson had jumped at the possibility of extending the Brussels Pact. He took a ship back to the United States with the Republican delegate to the London conference, John Foster Dulles, and converted Dulles to the project. Fortifying himself with fish house punch on New Year's Eve 1947, he told Achilles, "I don't care whether entangling alliances have been considered worse than original sin ever since George Washington's time. We've got to negotiate a military alliance with Western Europe in peacetime and we've got to do it quickly." There followed committee meetings and "ulcer lunches of stale sandwiches or gummy beans from the scruffy newsstand snackbar across the hall" and the working group essentially came up with a draft treaty, ready by the beginning of September 1948.[24]

In the arrangement of the treaty's terms, Hickerson may well have been the principal designer, and he was so designated by his friend Achilles. At the outset Hickerson wanted the Brussels Pact, which was being negotiated in February, directed generally, at an unspecified enemy, not at Germany as was the Dunkirk Treaty of 1947. He suggested the Rio Treaty formula: an attack against one would be an attack against all, with each nation choosing weapons according to its own constitutional processes. Undersecretary of State Robert A. Lovett—for weeks at a time Secretary Marshall was out of the country attending international conferences—did not want to do that and said, "I don't think we had ought to do this. Let's just give it our blessing." Hickerson said he felt very strongly. Marshall, a good staff man, gave Lovett's draft his blessing, but said, "Now, give this back to Hickerson. He feels strongly. Tell him to call in the British ambassador and give him all this [Hickerson's suggestion] orally, but on the record this [the blessing] is all we've done." Hickerson sent for Lord Inverchapel and gave him the signed note and said, "Now here is the note *I* wanted to send, and I'm authorized by the secretary to let you see this." He added a sly explanation: "If your memory were perfect you could memorize that, so I'll just give you a copy of it. It has no status except to refresh your memory. I read it to you, and in your memorandum of conversation you may quote this."[25]

Curiously, the two senior department people who one might have thought would have taken the lead with ideas and action—and they were at least talented with the former—did little to advance a North Atlantic Treaty. The counselor of the department, Charles E. Bohlen, believed military aid would suffice and a treaty would only get in trouble with the Senate. The head of the Policy Planning Staff, George F. Kennan, talked about a dumbbell arrangement, the U.S. and Canada and perhaps Britain on one end, the Europeans on the other. Sometimes he looked in the direction of Europe as a third force, what later was known as disengagement. John Lewis Gaddis has drawn their disillusion in terms of a paradox: in 1945 Bohlen favored a third force, Kennan a sphere of influence, and by the time of negotiation of NATO they had changed positions. Bohlen, Gaddis contends, reflected the mainstream of official thinking in Washington; Kennan, as so often, was the outsider. But the truth may be that both of these well-known department idea men simply found NATO uninteresting, perhaps because it fuzzed up the U.S.-Soviet conflict.[26]

In the negotiations in Washington and Europe in 1948 the positions taken regarding non–Brussels Pact nations were sometimes piquant and always interesting. In the former category was a conversation that the doughty Marshall had with Foreign Minister Bo Östen Undén of Sweden, who took advantage of the secretary's presence in Paris in October to explain Sweden's traditional neutrality, which by that time, Undén said, had lasted some 135 years. Even during the late Soviet-Finnish war the Swedes were virtuously neutral, and the Russians had appreciated that, as well they might have. Relations with the Soviets at the moment were good. He feared that any move by Sweden to ally with the West might affect Finland, which the Russians were leaving alone. Marshall in return said that there had been a feeling of neutrality in the United States, and he inquired what the effect might have been if Presidents Woodrow Wilson and Franklin D. Roosevelt had maintained such a policy. Undén admitted it would have been tragic but said that the United States was a great power. Marshall retorted that the U.S. among almost all the other countries of the world could best afford from its own selfish security point of view to be neutral. Undén said that

Sweden was like Switzerland. Marshall said there was a considerable difference geographically. Toward the end Undén made the comment that the problem of Swedish neutrality, 135 years of it, was his problem. Marshall agreed but said that as Undén had spoken frankly, so he, Marshall, had sought to speak.[27]

Italy desired an invitation to join the Atlantic treaty, and the Americans refused until the Italians—whose military contribution might be less than nothing—asked for an invitation. Involved in their inquiry was their need (since they would be inquiring) not to mention their territorial ambitions in Africa. The Portuguese government, an embarrassment under the conservative guidance of Antonio de Oliveira Salazar, at first sniffed and talked about the exclusion of Franco Spain, but then asked for a ticket.

Canada contributed Article 2 of the treaty, the Canadian article, what Acheson described as the "pie in the sky" article. Because the Canadians in Quebec would not desire external commitments that were exclusively military, the Canadians wanted an article that would look toward a real Atlantic community. Achilles later discussed with Escott Reid, by that time out of the Canadian foreign service, the obstacles to Article 2 that Reid espied and Achilles did not see, obstacles that the persistent Canadians overcame. But both Reid and the then undersecretary (later secretary) for foreign affairs, Lester B. Pearson, took a feeling of considerable accomplishment from Article 2.[28]

It remained to take special care with the Senate, which in 1948 was a part of the famous or (according to President Truman on the electoral circuit) infamous Eightieth Congress. There was not even a Democratic majority in the Senate. Moreover, it was necessary to take care with the American people who, like the Republican senators, were much concerned about any possible interference of the proposed treaty with the American Constitution and with the United Nations. The constitutional problem required preserving the right of Congress to consent to a declaration of war. The UN problem required attention to Articles 51, 53, and 54 of the charter. The former difficulty was resolved by fuzzing the terms of decision over how to repel an attack, which for Europeans lost the pointedness of the Brussels Pact article that set out the mechanics of decision. But here the opinion of Bevin, that the form was unimportant so long as the engagement was made, proved wise. As for the decision to establish an organization in accord with Article 51 of the charter, a regional organization, that was impossible to reconcile with Articles 53 and 54, which required authorization of (53) and information to (54) the UN Security Council. As Lawrence Kaplan has written, "The North Atlantic Treaty could meet neither requirement."[29] Russia was a permanent member of the Security Council. This, however, was no more quixotic an arrangement (to stress one article of the charter that conflicted with two others) than the fact that the North Atlantic Treaty had arisen directly because the United Nations had proved almost a failure as a result of the veto power—the constant Soviet vetoes. Americans had forgotten that at the San Francisco Conference in 1945, Senator Tom Connally had dramatically demanded that the charter give each permanent member of the Security Council a veto. Before the members of one of the conference's committees he had said, "If you want a charter, you can have a charter with the veto or no charter at all," whereupon he tore up a copy of the charter.[30]

For the Truman administration one of the most difficult tasks might have been getting the nearly revolutionary treaty (with its confusion over membership and yet independent constitutional process) and over three articles of the UN Charter through the Senate, where unfriendly senators and their constituents might have had a field day. For this purpose the president and Secretary Marshall delegated Undersecretary Lovett, a man of infinite patience and subtlety, which he needed for the task. Lovett had to deal with Senator Arthur H. Vandenberg, he whom Acheson later credited with the intellectual necessity of opposing any suggestion from a Democratic administration or even a rival politico of his own party, then undergoing a conversion and thereafter arranging a resurrection of the once-perverse suggestion in the form of a Vandenberg Resolution.[31] Lovett spent hours in what were known as "500 G" meetings—500 G being Vandenberg's suite at the Wardman Park Hotel. The essence of the negotiation appeared one day when Lovett ventured the possibility of a presidential declaration of willingness to negotiate a North Atlantic treaty. He met with a resounding "No!" "Why," asked Vandenberg, "should Truman get all the credit?"[32] The senator introduced his own wordy resolution, which the Senate perhaps in boredom adopted on 11 June 1948, in a vote of 64 to 4.

When the North Atlantic Treaty was signed on 4 April 1949, relations of the signatories with the Union of Soviet Socialist Republics had settled down markedly from the fears and, apparently, confusions of the year before. It is fair to describe April 1949 as a sort of poised moment, much like the era of the Geneva summit meeting in 1955. Everything appeared to be going the way of the West. Fighting renewed in Greece between government and Communist forces, but this time the government quickly gained the upper hand, and for all practical purposes, mainly because of Tito's defection from the Soviet orbit, the trouble in Greece was over. By this time the Berlin blockade was about to end, saved by the airlift. In the United States the new secretary of state, Acheson, was known to be pro-British. Truman had been elected and no longer was subject to the slighting remarks and the almost automatic conclusion of his political enemies that he was an accidental president. In the Attlee cabinet Bevin held an unassailable position, as in pushing for the treaty he had triumphed over the perhaps indifference, and certainly the Commonwealth preferences, of his chief, Prime Minister Attlee.[33]

The strategic picture in the North Atlantic area was still clouded, but there was hope. The assumption of "Offtackle," the plan approved by the American joint chiefs in December 1949, was that the Soviets would overrun West Germany. "While the countries which have signed the Atlantic Pact will have improved economically and militarily, they will be unable, with the exception of the United Kingdom, to effectively resist being overrun and occupied by Soviet forces." The plan envisaged holding a substantial bridgehead in Western Europe, or if this was infeasible, the earliest practical return of troops, in order, as the expectedly turgid document explained, "to prevent the exploitation and Communization of that area with long-term disastrous effects on U.S. national interests."[34]

The hope in the strategic picture was not Offtackle, which was only one more high school essay by the joint chiefs, but another essay that promised something for Europe, the medium-term defense plan to be completed in phases by 1954. It did not merely promise a stand at the Rhine, as Montgomery had hoped for in 1948, but anticipated shifting supply lines and national responsibilities. It projected ninety ready and reserve divisions, and a tactical air force of eight thousand planes. "Charade though the medium-term defense plan may have been," Kaplan has written, "it checked the deterioration of morale which had greeted the short-term program"[35] of cut and run.

The medium-term plan became the basis for American military aid, to which Congress gave consent after some notable hesitation. The day after the treaty was signed, on 5 April, the Western Union countries announced their arms requests, and the United States responded the next day. The administration request was for $1.45 billion, and more than two-thirds of the money was to go to NATO countries. By this time, however, the political complexion of Congress had changed; the Eighty-first Congress was Democratic, and Senator Vandenberg's role as leading man in the Senate's foreign relations had come to an end, with his replacement being the equally histrionic Connally. Not about to be taken from the stage, Vandenberg led a revolt against arms grants, against "the warlord bill which would have made the President the top military dictator of all time." The United Nations was resurrected, against the proposed Mutual Defense Assistance Program. On 29 August the Soviet Union detonated a nuclear device, Vandenberg underwent his usual conversion, and on 6 October Truman signed the act for $1.3 billion, with $1 billion for Europe. Its effect was slow and undoubtedly not too sure, for the European allies needed far more arms than the act allowed. But it was a start. By 30 June 1950 Truman had obligated most of the 1949–50 military-aid funds, although only $49.3 million had been expended. Moreover, and unlike the Marshall Plan, MDAP assistance promised to go on indefinitely.[36]

Soviet detonation of a nuclear device confirmed what already had become American strategic policy, and thereby the policy of the Atlantic treaty—that the foundation of resistance to the Soviet Union would be nuclear retaliation. The Soviet explosion of course persuaded the Truman administration to go for the H-bomb. Truman confronted a three-man advisory committee, of Secretaries Johnson and Acheson and Chairman Lilienthal of the Atomic Energy Commission, on 31 January 1950. When Lilienthal attempted to hold out against development of the "super," Truman cut off the chairman in the middle of his exposition, saying that he, the president, had no alternative. He announced his decision, which was released to the press that evening.[37] Already, though, the pinched budgets of the armed services had dictated nuclear reliance.

Truman did not like such an affirmation of strategy but had to tolerate it. He never was the ardent supporter of nuclear weapons that his critics beheld, a sort of antediluvian character who sat behind the desk in the Oval Office and grinned as he signed appropriations to the AEC, or himself went up in a B-29 and sat behind the cross hairs as he "dropped the bomb" on his international adversaries. Shortly before he went out of office in 1953 he responded to a letter from a member of the AEC, Thomas E. Murray, who wrote that it was an error to make nuclear issues stand apart from other issues of warfare. "I rather think you have put a wrong construction on my approach to the use of the Atomic bomb," was the response. "It is far worse than gas and biological warfare because it affects the civilian population and murders them by the wholesale." The H-bomb avowedly was a weapon of mass destruction, for it could not be aimed. Truman knew this, and accepted such weapons with intense reluctance.[38]

Fortunately, with the confirmation of a nuclear strategy the United States and its allies were able to rely on a revived SAC, under the efficient management of General LeMay. By 1950 the command was becoming efficient at aerial refueling, exchanging a difficult hose-and-reel system for a relatively easy flying boom. It was operating 225 nuclear-bomb-carrying aircraft, including silverplated B-29s; B-50s, which were B-29s built for longer range and for carrying nuclear bombs; and thirty-four of the new and huge B-36s. The latter were outmoded before they came in, as the original design had been drawn in 1941 when it appeared that Britain might go under, unable to resist the Luftwaffe, and America needed a plane that could bomb Germany from North American bases. The B-36s were to last only a few years, until the B-52s—those venerables of the air that are still flying—came in in 1953–54. Possessing eight huge propeller-driven engines, the B-36s towered over their predecessors and successors—in the air force museum at Wright-Patterson Field near Dayton, the prize exhibit at the present time is the B-36, which spreads its wings across the entire football field–sized hangar, almost covering the motley collection of other planes. But with this plane and its smaller cousins LeMay readied 263 combat crews by 1950 and was training forty-nine more. He had eighteen bomb-assembly teams and was adding four. He was trying to forget the bombing of Dayton, the air force's darkest night, and was flying his bomb groups over Baltimore, a city that resembled Soviet targets, with far more success.[39] Cross-training, and General McMullen, no longer represented SAC.

Always ready for theoretical organization, the North Atlantic Treaty nations quickly placed the "O" in their arrangements, and NATO came into existence. The transition was both diplomatic and military. Diplomatically speaking, the arrangements included a council, a defense committee that set up a military committee (with a standing group representing the United States, Britain, and France), and other groups. The council in May 1950 established a council of deputies "to meet in continuous session in London," a full-time body of "highly qualified persons."[40] Militarily the new organization, to the disgust of the French, succumbed to American giganticism. The appearance of the Americans was not unwelcome to the French, for the Americans balanced off the British, who had wanted to dominate the Brussels group but contribute no troops (not until March 1950 did the British cabinet consent to reinforce its continental occupation force upon outbreak of war). Still, the Americans brought their overorganization. When de Lattre de Tassigny gave up and went to Indochina as high commissioner in December 1950, this meant the appointment of General Eisenhower as supreme commander. Eisenhower, of course, believed in the American way. To the irritation of de Lattre de Tassigny's assistant, André Beaufre, it meant "submitting to the cumbersome American administrative machinery, which perceives organization only in the form of highly complex diagrams." The "period of painstaking craftsmanship," as Beaufre described the perception of his chief, had ended, and "though the armed forces could be built up only slowly and in a limited way, a torrent of staffs and departments suddenly appeared which in themselves equaled the effective force of a good army."[41]

Meanwhile, the Korean War had opened and would change many things in NATO. It always seemed that when the West was having the most difficulties, the Soviets extended a helping hand. This was one of the niceties of Stalinist diplomacy that the analysts of Kremlin shrewdness often chose to forget. In February 1948 it had been the takeover of Czechoslovakia, which gave the Soviets assured access to the large Czech arms industry, to the only European source of uranium, and to a convenient invasion route into Western Europe. It inspired the Western nations to plan for the North Atlantic Treaty. The Soviets then reinforced this result with the Berlin blockade. Then when MDAP was faltering in the American Congress, the Russians thoughtfully detonated their nuclear device, and shortly afterward MDAP sailed through the House and Senate. The fulfilling of some of the military requirements for NATO would then come after the opening of the Korean War, for which the Soviets had given a green light in conversations with the North Koreans and Chinese.

NATO, one may conclude, represented a great change in American foreign policy, "the American Revolution of 1949," in the words of the late Armin Rappaport. It also represented a sea change in the fortunes of Western Europe. On the American side there was the obvious conversion of the great body of Americans to the belief that the country could not remain apart from the world, that alliances were essential, and that alliance with Western Europe was the most essential (as Senator Vandenberg, with his unerring instinct for linguistic insecurity, would have said). Asked on the evening of 3 April 1949, during the remarkable session of the foreign ministers with the highest American officials, whether Western Europe was the center of American attention, Secretary Johnson responded "Absolutely."[42] On the European side, NATO militarily would create enough of a balance to deter the Soviet foe. Politically it established a lasting regional organization.

The Rio Pact, NATO's prototype, never placed the "O" in its acronym, and indeed never had an acronym. SEATO and CENTO disappeared, in 1977 and 1979, respectively. NATO has functioned much better than the two principal supranational organizations of our century. Compared to the United Nations, which has shown continual signs of near failure, NATO looks good. Compared to the Wilsonian League of Nations it looks equally good, for Wilson's ideas about Europe were vague and insubstantial and very probably never could have worked, even with American presence, German good will, and Soviet cooperation rather than idealistic hectoring. And as mentioned at the outset of this essay, it is easily possible to testify for NATO in terms of economics—by giving a respite from fears of a Soviet invasion and occupation, it helped create Western Europe's economic plenty of the moment, and may well follow with another economic miracle after 1992. This later prospect, if realized, would mean fulfillment of the Canadian article, the "pie in the sky" proviso, Article 2.

The detractors of NATO, one need hardly add, will always be with us, and it often is difficult to confute their testimonies. The British historian Peter Foot has written that NATO was a scheme for European integration, for "security on the cheap," so Americans could take their dollars elsewhere.[43] This is a plausible explanation, if the historian himself offers few proofs other than what he styles "perceptions" of the American mood, including what many Americans might describe as humbuggery, such as congressional resolutions and other such effusions. David P. Calleo, a trenchant writer about the Atlantic economy, has recently described NATO as providing "hegemony on the cheap" and says that this era of need has ended, the Europeans can take up the burden. His view, widely shared in a time of American budget deficits, sounds like neo-isolationism, although Calleo is too sophisticated a student to subscribe to that word.

Agreeable change is not really what critics like. They never desire the moment ("jam tomorrow, and jam yesterday"). One should also inquire how they would have felt about a United States that had turned in upon itself, or at best sought to draw a Monroe Doctrine line around the Western Hemisphere, with Europe succumbing to the military, political, and economic ways of the Soviet Union.

All in all it is difficult to think of a single international instrument that has accomplished as much as NATO in such a short time, for so little American money, for so many of America's friends.

WALTER LAFEBER

NATO and the Korean War: A Context

The Korean War "was a turning point in the history of the [North Atlantic Treaty Organization (NATO)] alliance," according to the leading United States historian of that alliance, because the conflict led to a "massive increase" in U.S. military assistance (including the commitment of American troops in 1951), the restructuring of NATO's organization, and the expansion of the alliance's "geographic shape" with the inclusion of Greece, Turkey, and the Federal Republic of Germany. Moreover, because of the war "the German question was revived and acquired an urgency that had been lacking before June 25, 1950."[1] All that is of course true, although it may be suggested that these turning points had roots that reached back months before the beginning of the Korean War. Moreover, the U.S. policies that transformed NATO were reacting less to that war than to a deeper, systemic crisis that, in the view of Washington officials, had been developing and threatening the whole of their foreign policies for nearly a year.

The conflict in Korea was a watershed in the history of American postwar foreign policy, but like all watersheds, it had indispensable tributaries. The war did not mark an abrupt break, or turn, in President Harry S. Truman's foreign policies, but formed part of a continuum that had its more important origins ten months before when the Soviets exploded their first atomic device and it became clear, with the writing of the State Department white paper, that the United States had to accept the conquest of China by the Communists. So too, important changes in the NATO alliance did not suddenly become real after June 1950[2] but had begun in the fall and winter of 1949, when despite the absence of Soviet military threats against Western interests—an absence acknowledged by top State Department experts—the United States began the institutional

33

restructuring of its foreign policy that produced many characteristics of the Cold War as we have since known it.

This essay also advances a secondary argument: One of the key changes in the perception of NATO by American and West European officials was a new, evolving relationship between the alliance in Europe and Western interests elsewhere on the globe. The history of how Washington policymakers and, at times, European leaders tried to use NATO to resolve problems beyond the geographical bounds of the alliance itself is instructive, if intermittent, and that theme too made a significant appearance in the months before the Korean War broke out.

NATO's primary importance has not been as a military alliance to stop a probable Soviet invasion, but as a means to deal with more immediate problems—integrating the Federal Republic of Germany into the West, easing of Franco-German hatreds, anchoring a Great Britain tossed between continental and Atlantic-Commonwealth interests, and solving a systemic economic crisis that preoccupied officials in both Western capitals and Moscow in 1949. Early in that year, however, Secretary of State Dean Acheson expressed great optimism about the alliance. Praising the changing French attitude toward the Germans, Acheson told an executive session of the Senate Foreign Relations Committee in May that France accepted West Germany's integration into the rest of Europe "solely and only on account of the North Atlantic treaty." When asked whether NATO had given Europe confidence against a resurgent Germany, he responded, "Yes. It works in all directions." From the United States perspective, moreover, it worked cheaply. Americans, led by President Truman himself, believed that major U.S. contributions to NATO consisted of financial aid and a number of atomic bombs controlled by the U.S. Air Force. As a British Foreign Office minute warned in June 1949, such a belief was "to some extent ... an extension of an isolationist feeling in that the idea of strategy based on inter-continental bombers with the U.S.A. having a monopoly of such bombers & of the atom bomb, will prevent Americans having to fight another land war in Europe."[3]

By late August 1949, both Acheson's optimism and the "old isolationist feeling" were badly shaken. The imminent conquest of China by the Communists posed problems for NATO nations' interests in Asia, problems that Washington had largely ignored just months earlier. The Soviet atomic explosion produced an earlier-than-expected end to the U.S. monopoly. And the Marshall Plan, which was to restore the economic health of the NATO and neighboring nations, was not working rapidly enough. "We are faced with a terribly serious world situation, a world financial situation," Truman told his top staff. Britain "is practically 'busted' and unless a solution to the problem is found our world recovery program is going to smash up and all our post-war efforts will go to pieces."[4]

Western experts working inside the Soviet Union meanwhile noted that the Kremlin seemed to be changing tactics: from trying to "carry Western Europe by direct assault" (as through the Berlin blockade of 1948–49), to exploiting "the break in prices and the growing unemployment figures in the United States [and aggravating] the situation by undermining confidence and spreading alarm, especially in the Western European countries," as a British diplomat phrased it. In December, British and American analysts in Moscow agreed that Stalin's foreign policy would grow tougher and more obstinate, yet less confrontational and dramatic, as he waited for the climax of "an economic crisis [that] is already under way in the West," a crisis that the Soviets expected "to be more severe than the crisis of 1929." A Central Intelligence Agency warning in September reinforced such fears. The CIA advised that while the Soviets cracked down in Eastern Europe, in Western Europe they would try to undercut NATO by comparing the Communist peace congresses with the U.S. military buildup. Moscow would also contrast the "real difficulties" of the Marshall Plan "with the mutual benefits to be derived from increased East-West trade."[5] In western eyes, the grave dangers obviously did not suddenly appear with the invasion of Korea.

Acheson privately doubted that unilateral U.S. private investments could solve the intractable economic problems. Investors were too skittish about the safety of their funds. The old days were over: "In China when things got rough we'd just send in a gunboat and shell hell out of them to protect our holdings." But now, Acheson added, "We must realize that the U.S. is in a helluva fix today. The United States needs allies." Those allies, furthermore, as he told Congress in August 1949, were discovering that "economic measures alone are not enough." Economic recovery requires "a sense of security," and such security in turn demands "a firm belief in the ability of the free nations to defend themselves against armed aggression. Such a belief is notably lacking in Western Europe today." The Europeans' self-defense forces "must be increased, largely by their own effort," so "economic recovery" could proceed. But

Acheson's insight clashed with Truman's determination to maintain a $13 to $14 billion defense budget. The president informed his budget aides and key cabinet members in July 1949 that he wanted a "balanced program," and added that "it was never his intention to embark on a constantly rising program of National Defense and International aid." At least one public opinion poll showed more support for his policies than might have been supposed. When asked whether the United States should send arms and money to nations who wanted to build up military defenses against a possible Soviet attack, 46 percent approved and 40 percent disapproved. Only 50 percent of Democrats and 42 percent of Republicans surveyed approved.[6]

Deeply worried officials in London understood that Acheson believed the economic crisis required more military security, but they also understood Truman's sentiments and the public opinion figures. As the British Chancery told the Foreign Office, the U.S. budget deficit for fiscal 1950 was $5.5 billion, or a little more than Marshall Plan and Mutual Defense Assistance authorizations for the year. " 'The folks back home,' " Chancery concluded, "are clearly not in a mood to forego domestic benefits" for the sake of Europeans. Chancery noted a Seattle woman's statement that her parent-teacher group " 'can't understand why Washington is financing socialism in England while asking everybody to fight it here.' " Meanwhile, the British minister of defense, A. V. Alexander, told U.S. Secretary of Defense Louis Johnson that the recent radical devaluation of the pound in September, plus the sliding British economy, "made it impossible" to keep up both overseas commitments and "provide adequately for the re-equipment of the Armed Forces."[7]

The growing economic squeeze directly affected NATO planning by late November 1949. After examining the probable military and political effects of the Soviet atomic bomb, the U.S. chiefs of staff wanted the North Atlantic Regional Planning Groups to "accept as a basic premise that war will be forced on us on 1st July 1954." The British strenuously objected and counterproposed 1957 as the basis for such NATO planning. London officials, indeed, wanted to avoid mentioning any date at all because only then could they also avoid "demands for equipment to be delivered to a fixed programme which could not be met without affecting our economic recovery." The British chiefs of staff backed up this proposal with an assessment that Stalin wanted to avoid major war. Sounding much like

George Kennan and Charles Bohlen, the two top U.S. experts on Soviet affairs, the British military concluded that Stalin's first priority was consolidating power in the satellite bloc and then restoring the Russian economy.[8] If this assessment was correct, it would be difficult to convince Congress and the American people to increase U.S. defense and foreign aid budgets by warning that the Soviets were threatening to move militarily.

U.S. officials, and especially those in the Pentagon, assumed that they could not wait until 1954 or until the overt threat of Soviet troop movements before they began solving the fundamental problems that now afflicted the West's policies. These officials were especially becoming haunted by the German problem in the aftermath of the Soviet A-bomb blast. In the spring of 1949 Acheson had assured Congress that "the disarmament and demilitarization of Germany must be complete and absolute." As late as 30 November 1949 (or some three months after the Soviet explosion), he denied that the State Department had under consideration any plans for a West German role in West European defenses. At the same time, however, the U.S. Embassy in Moscow warned Acheson and Truman that "in view of favorable developments on the atomic energy and China fronts, the Embassy believes that Moscow may consider this an opportune time to regain the initiative on the German question"—although the embassy was not certain how Stalin would try to regain it. In the meantime, U.S. military officials told British counterparts that in case of a Soviet attack, American forces would probably not be able to reach the Rhine in time to be helpful. The Pentagon, led by its Joint War Plans branch, began to develop an all-out program for German militarization at the moment Acheson denied the State Department was considering any such program. British military planners, inspired by remarks of Field Marshal Bernard Montgomery, decided in December 1949 that a new German army could be formed "within the North Atlantic Treaty, whilst the other [NATO] Powers would be responsible for the navy and air force. A German arms industry would, however, be required for the equipment of the German army." The West Germans were not slow in picking up on these developments. Significantly, about three weeks after Acheson visited West German chancellor Konrad Adenauer in November 1949 (a visit in which the American hinted that a West German defense contribution might well be expected), Adenauer began mapping the political strategy for rebuilding his nation's military units and placing them within an integrated European army. As

Adenauer later recalled his thoughts, "Rearmament might be the way of gaining full sovereignty for the Federal Republic. This made it the essential question of our political future."[9]

Given the important evidence on Acheson's views at this time, and given the Pentagon and British military planners' willingness to move rapidly on plans for West German rearmament, the question is why Acheson did not fully and more publicly support that rearming. Why did he wait for nearly a year, or until three months after Korea erupted? The answer seems to be that Acheson understood there was an absolute prerequisite to bringing West Germany within a European defense force. That prerequisite was an economic arrangement between Bonn and Paris that would both integrate West Germany more fully within the Western system and at least diminish French fears of a revived, remilitarized, and increasingly uncontrolled Germany. As Acheson told French ambassador Henri Bonnet in early December 1949, he was disturbed about rearmament rumors because they were "interfering with the main task before all of us which was the integration of Germany into the European scene. The rearmament of Germany was not part of this integration and the talk was disturbing and upsetting." Or as Acheson told his close friend, British ambassador Oliver Franks, in November, "the boys" in the State Department had given much thought to "a real French-German rapprochement, economic and political," so Germany could remain with the West and have "an economic outlet in Western Europe. She had to have one somewhere." Acheson "did not reject the suggestion," as Franks reported the conversation, "that he wanted the work of Charlemagne redone after 1000 years."[10]

Acheson's analysis was echoed at private study sessions of the New York Council on Foreign Relations, sessions in which Paul Nitze (Kennan's replacement as director of the State Department's Policy Planning Staff) and Frank Altschul (a council leader and chair of General American Investors Corporation on Wall Street) took the initiative. The two men agreed that, in Altschul's words, "the Marshall Plan will not achieve what was expected of it by 1952." A new plan was required. Harvard economist John Kenneth Galbraith added that unless something was done soon to solve the need for dollars in Western Europe, "the logical course for each European government is to work toward some degree of autarky by 1952. And that is what is actually happening.... This is very bad from the point of view of the European economy as a whole, and for the prospects of American exports."[11]

The economic and political costs of immediately trying to rearm West Germany would greatly worsen, not help remedy, this growing crisis. The first concrete steps of economic integration, with French cooperation if not leadership, had to be taken before rearmament began. The fear of 1948–49, that without the shield of NATO the Marshall Plan could be ineffective, now somehow became neatly reversed. The argument was developing that the Marshall Plan faced such danger that truly building up NATO conventional forces as an offset to the Soviet possession of the atomic secret could smash the West's recovery plans. The deep systemic problem had to be resolved, in part through French-German economic cooperation if possible, and only then could the military problems be addressed. An effective NATO had to be the result, not a cause, of more efective political and economic cooperation. And so it proved. As Kennan wrote in a kind of farewell note to Acheson on 17 February 1950: a "period of gradual economic adjustment" was required. "The end of this period of adjustment should be a complete absence of tariffs and subsidies, except where genuine security considerations intervene; and even in these cases we should treat other members of the Atlantic Pact group as allies rather than potential enemies, and try to spare them from being the victims of security considerations."[12]

In an earlier letter to Acheson, Kennan had urged a fundamental reevaluation of U.S. foreign policy, in the wake of the Soviet atomic explosion, before the administration embarked on a disastrous nuclear arms race. During an October discussion with India's leader, Jawaharlal Nehru, Kennan and Acheson agreed that a new approach was indeed required. Despite the Truman Doctrine, Marshall Plan, and NATO, the two Americans believed that "our actions since World War II had not been based on any broad global plan, but that, to the contrary, a great deal of improvisation had been necessary." Or as Acheson recalled the crisis some five years later, the Soviet bomb "changed everything . . . and within a month [Truman] had put the machinery of government into operation to work things out." The result, Acheson observed, was NSC-68, or National Security Council paper number 68: "This is the fundamental paper that still governs the thing; it's the basic thing." Drawn up under Nitze's supervision during the first four months of 1950, NSC-68 approached NATO and the West European problems by noting how threats to Western Europe, because of the buildup of Soviet war reserves and arsenal capabilities, could be neutralized (at least in part) by the implementation of the Marshall Plan and the 1949 Mutual Defense Assistance Act. But "unless the military strength of the Western European nations is increased on a much larger scale than under current programs and at an accelerated rate, it is more than likely that those nations will not be able to oppose even by 1960 the Soviet armed forces in war with any degree of effectiveness." An "essential element in a program to frustrate the Kremlin design" had to be economic aid and military assistance to NATO allies.[13]

Economic integration, however, remained a prerequisite. As the Marshall Plan neared its end, there was no "possibility of achieving ... a satisfactory equilibrium with the dollar area. [Western Europe] has also made very little progress toward 'economic integration,' which would in the long run tend to improve its productivity and to provide an economic environment conducive to political stability." Then came a pivotal point: "In particular, the movement towards economic integration does not appear to be rapid enough to provide Western Germany with adequate economic oppportunities in the West." The economic and military buildups had to occur rapidly or otherwise "our allies and potential allies" could, "as a result of frustration or of Soviet intimidation drift into a course of neutrality eventually leading to Soviet domination. If this were to happen in Germany the effect upon Western Europe and eventually upon us might be catastrophic." Avoiding such a crisis required both a military budget that would quadruple from its current $13 to $14 billion level and an alliance that rested securely on economic integration and a carefully planned military buildup.[14]

As Nitze began drafting NSC-68, Acheson explained the basics during a closed-door session with the Senate Foreign Relations Committee. The Soviets' "aggressive imperialistic attitude" had of course, to be discussed, but "even if there were no Russia, if there were no communism, we would have very grave problems in trying to exist and strengthen those parts of the free world which have been so badly shaken by the ... two wars and the consequences of both of them." The subtlety of that problem, and the threat of its long-term costs, posed grave political dangers for Acheson and, as well, for NATO's prospects. Those dangers increased as the Soviets, in the words of a British analyst, had apparently decided in early 1950 "in favour of creating a détente in the hope of relaxing American hostility." Another Foreign Office expert (this one an expert on North American affairs) added that "the United States Administration were always worried lest an apparent change of front by the Russians should lead Congress to weaken its support for the Administration's foreign policy."[15] It seemed that Truman and Acheson could not, as they had so successfully during the Greek-Turkish dilemma of 1947, point to imminent Soviet expansion as a means of prying more military and economic aid out of Congress.

The administration indeed ran into strong domestic opposition to its budding plans in early 1950. In a widely noted speech of January, Walter Lippmann declared that Tito's defection from Stalin's bloc and the appearance of India, Pakistan, and Indonesia as independent nations meant that the "two coalitions" were breaking up. The United States, he implied, had to stop thinking in terms of a simple bipolar world. Moreover, the Soviet A-bomb explosion "has changed the balance of military power" and reinforced in "the exposed and vulnerable countries around the periphery of the Soviet Union . . . their natural impulse to disassociate themselves from the two coalitions." Consequently, "Western Germany cannot become a military ally of the West, as Field Marshal Montgomery so fondly hopes, because Britain and America cannot with certainty and effectiveness promise to defend Western Germany against Russian aerial attack." The Germans would develop a "middle position" between the two superpowers. Japan would assume a similar position for similar reasons. Lippmann warned that the United States must not "resist this process and . . . attempt to reverse it."[16] In other words, he struck at the fundamental assumptions on which NSC-68's argument was to rest.

Acheson's and Nitze's hope that NSC-68's grand plan would lead to a reinvigorated and strengthened NATO also ran into problems within the administration. Secretary of Defense Louis Johnson took Truman's affection for balanced budgets seriously and refused to listen to plans that could mean a major increase, let alone a possible quadrupling, of military expenditures. Acheson's assistant secretary of public affairs, Edward W. Barrett, read the secret NSC-68 draft and then warned the secretary of state that "we are going to run into vast opposition among informed people to a huge arms race." Even if Acheson succeeded in getting such a race started, "I fear that the U.S. public would rapidly tire of such an effort. In the absence of real and continuing crises, a dictatorship can unquestionably out-last a democracy in a conventional armament race." In the Senate, Robert Taft of Ohio took the initiative on foreign policy lost in early 1950 by the terminally ill Arthur Vandenberg of Michigan.

The Republican leader had earlier fought ratification of the North Atlantic Treaty. Months afterward, Taft told a friend that the "Atlantic Pact and the military assistance program" was "more likely to lead to war than to peace, although I hope I am wrong." He wanted to contain communism, especially in Asia, but believed *"there is no threat"* to Western Europe "at this time." Taft argued that NATO could only "proceed on [the] basis that Russia will not go to war."[17] He implied that this was a highly dangerous basis on which to rest any foreign policy, and it could be unacceptably costly if NATO were to be built on more than a bluff.

By the winter of 1949–50, U.S. officials were determined to make NATO more than a bluff. They pushed ahead on two different but parallel paths. On one they and some West European partners worked for an "integrationist strategy," as Michael J. Hogan has called it, a strategy that revolved around a common strategic concept and balanced collective (rather than balanced national) forces. The strategy for NATO formed part of a larger overall policy of creating an integrated, open, market-oriented Western Europe. Acheson also drove U.S. policies down a second path: he linked his policies toward pivotal NATO members with U.S. policy objectives elsewhere in the world. A North Atlantic alliance began to have global implications. The paramount example became the U.S. commitment to helping the French hold their Southeast Asian colonial empire so Paris officials would be more cooperative on NATO policies.[18]

The United States' commitment to Indochina occurred before, not after, the Korean War began. The commitment was driven by multiple causes, the most important of which were the restoration of Japan's economic complex by giving it resources and outlets in Southeast Asia and the need to keep the French as a major NATO partner. As the economic cost of France's effort reached $600 million in 1950, and as losses of troops climbed (one estimate concluded that the yearly rate of officer casualties had already reached a figure comparable to the size of the annual class graduating from Saint-Cyr), Acheson decided to swallow his objections to French colonial policy. In March 1950 he and Truman committed U.S. economic aid to Indochina. By May, U.S. aid missions were established in the region.[19]

Acheson went into Vietnam with his eyes open. By the end of March 1950 he was telling the Foreign Relations Committee, behind closed doors, that the situation required the United States to pressure the French to act more intelligently, but "the thing that we have to be careful about is that we do not press the French to the point where they say, 'All right, take over the damned country. We don't want it,' and put their soldiers on ships and send them back to Europe." The alliance was making claims on U.S. policy that had not been evident before August 1949. In May 1950 Acheson flew to London and pleaded with the British government for more help in building up defenses. In a pessimistic analysis of the situation, the secretary of state worried that unless something was done "there was a danger that some of the weaker and more exposed countries now in the western camp might, when a crisis arose, change sides." Without mentioning NSC-68, Acheson declared that the United States was preparing to do much more, but it needed help from its friends.[20]

Prime Minister Clement Attlee and Foreign Secretary Ernest Bevin responded that when the time arrived that Great Britain could get along without aid, it might be possible to consider giving more aid to others. The British, indeed, were entertaining quite other ideas than using the NATO alliance as a cockpit from which to guide policies in other parts of the world. Foreign Office officials had drawn up a paper, which they hoped Acheson and Bevin would initial, that constituted a U.S. agreement to treat Great Britain as a partner. The British believed they could then look increasingly westward, rather than eastward, for help. This plan was quite moderate when contrasted with an alternative program that other Foreign Office officials had devised. Their outline suggested that NATO might well be only "a temporary phase, and that the real object should be to organize Western Europe into a 'Middle Power,' co-equal with, and independent of, the United States and the Soviet Union alike." This new Europe could then cooperate with "the bulk of the African continent" and be in "loose association with other members of the Commonwealth, to run an independent policy in world affairs which would not necessarily coincide with either Soviet or American wishes." Supporters of this plan in Great Britain, the paper noted, included "those who find American capitalism little more attractive than Soviet communism, and those who feel a natural dislike of seeing this country in a dependent position." This alternative program was discarded and the British presented Acheson with their partnership proposal. He dismissed it with the remark that "it was quite impossible to allow it to be known that any such paper had been drawn up or that it had been agreed to." The focus,

Acheson stressed, had to be on the NATO nations. Back in Washington, Senator Millard Tydings (Dem.-Md.) observed: "The nut of it all is that our great hope for the future of ourselves and those associated with us lies primarily in Europe. If that is swept away, Malaya and all those other things are infinitesimal." Acheson agreed: "Yes, sir, I think that is entirely right."[21]

The emphases in the buildup outlined by NSC-68 during the spring of 1950 were, therefore, on Western Europe and on the use of American power that had the widest possible freedom of action. The new and, as it turned out, historically significant commitments made before 25 June 1950 in Indochina and the Middle East (for example the tripartite agreement between the United States, Great Britain, and France to try to control military outbreaks, especially around Israel) moved out of the changing U.S. view toward what Tydings had called "the nut of it all," and—especially in the case of Indochina—toward Japan in the crucial months between September 1949 and June 1950.

As these policies intensified in the spring of 1950, the West German rearmament question moved to the center of discussion. At a New York Council on Foreign Relations study group, Henry Byroade, head of the State Department's German desk, agreed with the observation of New York City lawyer Goldthwaite H. Dorr that "the problem seemed to be that if Germany was not integrated into western Europe it would be integrated with the Soviet Union. . . . Mr. Dorr went on to point out that this had been the basis of two world wars." Byroade emphasized that German rearmament had to wait: "To place military integration before any other kind of integration would be disastrous on the continent. Moreover the Germans do not want to rearm. . . . We cannot say the Germans will be disarmed forever," but economic integration came first. When Byroade was asked who would defend West Germany if the United States and the Soviet Union withdrew from Central Europe (much as Lippmann and Kennan had been suggesting), he replied it would be "somewhat comparable" to Korea, with a Soviet-supported army in one part and a U.S.-supported force in the other. He stressed, however, this was mere speculation because there were no plans to remove U.S. troops from West Germany.[22]

Two months later, Byroade's key precondition began to be met. In May 1950, the French proposed the Schuman Plan for integrating the French and West German iron and steel complexes. Oddly, however, the initial reaction in Washington and London was less than joyous. Bevin and Acheson, in the British official's words, were in "general agreement that the French Government had behaved extremely badly in springing this proposal on the world at this juncture without any attempt at consultation with H.M. Government or the U.S. Government." Neither the Americans nor the British intended to make any quick commitment to the plan. Five top British cabinet members "agreed that it showed a regrettable tendency to move away from the conception of the Atlantic community and in the direction of European federation."[23] It seemed that U.S. and British leaders wanted West Germany integrated into Europe, but the process had to include close non-French supervision. Integration-before-rearming required certain qualities.

The Pentagon, however, was less particular. U.S. Army planners pushed forward their blueprint for rearming West Germany, and on 30 April 1950 the Joint Chiefs of Staff approved it. The chiefs then wisely decided to delay their request for approval from Truman, who strongly opposed such a plan. In public statements during May and June, the JCS chairman, General Omar Bradley, pointedly observed that in the wake of the Soviet atomic bomb blast, conventional forces were urgently needed. The NATO Council meeting in May supported Bradley. Winston Churchill had already stated in the House of Commons that Germany should be rearmed within a European force. (Churchill's comment provoked from Bevin a strong public response that included the phrase: "The Hitler revolution did not change the German character very much. It expressed it.") When the joint chiefs tried to play on this growing public debate by proposing to raise the issue at the NATO conference, the State Department split. Acheson finally decided the issue had to be delayed. On 5 and 6 June 1950, however, even Acheson and Secretary of Defense Johnson admitted to a congressional committee that European conventional forces were "totally inadequate." Bradley further testifed that "I think we must all admit that the security of Western Europe would be strengthened if they [the West Germans] were included in it." He quickly added that he understood the political considerations of the problem that had to be resolved "with all the angles considered."[24]

Three weeks later, on 25 June, those political considerations rapidly changed, but it should be emphasized that some of the politics, not the planning, needed to be changed after the Korean War began. The essentials of the strategy were in place: a rapidly growing consensus that NATO required West German conventional forces, the meeting of the prerequisite of at least initial German-French economic integration, the realization that the disappointing progress of the Marshall Plan meant that other kinds of fixes were required if Western Europe was to be made secure, and finally, the existence of a Pentagon plan for creating a West German force. The Korean War accelerated the progress of this strategy and made the politics considerably easier although, as it proved, hardly simple.

Acheson later phrased the effect directly: "As soon as we could get our breath from the immediate exigencies of Korea we reviewed the whole situation. . . . We all came to the conclusion that the ideas which Bradley had planted at the May meeting of NATO, of forces which should be considered as a whole rather than as separate national forces, had to be pushed forward." There was "substantial agreement on this by August," he noted. This agreement on new European forces and structures rose from two assumptions made by U.S. officials immediately after the 25 June invasion, assumptions that linked Korea and NATO. The first was that although the Communist use of force would probably remain localized, the entire collective security system of the United States was at stake. The second was that, as Pentagon officials told reporters on 26 June, "they were not losing sight of what they regarded as the larger theater of the 'cold war'—Europe." Midsummer polling by the State Department showed surprising public support for such a priority. Three of four Americans surveyed approved sending U.S. troops to Korea, but 51 percent believed it more important to stop an invasion of Europe than one in Asia, and only 17 percent put Asia first. Public approval for NATO itself rose from 81 percent before the Korean invasion to 87 percent shortly afterward. During that same time, approval for the creation of a West German armed force rose from 40 percent to 54 percent. As the Norwegian ambassador told Acheson on 30 June, "the small nations of Europe no longer doubted American determination to defend them under NATO."[25]

Assuming, in Acheson's words, that in Korea "we are fighting the second team, whereas the real enemy is the Soviet Union," the administration focused on European problems and dangers. Truman told correspondent Arthur Krock shortly after the invasion that he intended to hold Korea, but (as Krock recorded the conversation), "if any fire breaks out elsewhere . . . we will abandon Korea. . . . We want any showdown to come in Western Europe 'where we can use the bomb.'" To provide a more palatable alternative, Averell Harriman, Truman's diplomatic troubleshooter, told British officials in mid-July that although rearming West Germany was "premature," it was certainly time to begin discussing the problem, especially if the Schuman Plan continued to evolve satisfactorily and thus dissolve much of France's opposition. At NATO itself, the Standing Group began revising the Medium-Term Defense Plan. Truman cooperated by multiplying expenditures for U.S. armed forces and earmarking an additional $4 billion for military assistance, the large majority of it going to NATO.[26]

The meaning of the Korean outbreak for NATO ramified during the summer and early autumn of 1950. Acheson privately told the Foreign Relations Committee that the military demands gravely endangered West European recovery. The United States had to pour as much aid as possible, as rapidly as possible, into the region. Did that mean "another Marshall Plan?" Senator Claude Pepper (Dem.-Fla.) asked. "Yes," Acheson replied. Another area of expense appeared in mid-July when Congressman Jacob Javits (Rep.-N.Y.) suggested an Asian counterpart of NATO. This seminal idea for the future Southeast Asia Treaty Organization received unanimous endorsement from the House Foreign Affairs Committee. In October, the State Department announced that France would receive "by far the largest single part" of the new $5 billion Military Defense Assistance Program money for 1950–51, and tied the aid directly to helping France pay for its costs within NATO. In September, Truman announced additional U.S. divisions would be stationed in Western Europe. He expected the Europeans to reciprocate with military buildups of their own.[27]

These policies, Acheson remembered, settled the question of whether the United States would pursue an Atlantic or a West European policy. He recalled Kennan remarking in 1947 that "Maybe we'll have just to marry the British whether we like it or not," and how Kennan's interest in the courtship increased as he hoped Germany and the whole of Europe could somehow be pieced back together. The decisions of the summer of 1950, Acheson continued, settled the discussion and made them "a fairly important turning point in policy."[28] In perspective, however, the debate had no doubt been finally settled when Kennan decided to leave the State Department in late 1949. NSC-68, the initial commitment to French Indochina, the growing attractiveness of the Pentagon's plan for rearming West Germany, Acheson's and Bevin's anger over the Schuman Plan being created without sufficient consultation with Washington and London—all these events had helped decide where the heart, and thus the treasure, of U.S. policy would be located. The difference was the speed with which U.S. policies could move after June, a speed that worried some Europeans. Danish, Norwegian, and French ambassadors in London expressed concern to the Foreign Office that Truman was building up his military power so rapidly that a dangerous arms race could be starting. The French ambassador warned that "it was essential to avoid any step which would be likely to provoke the Russians. As our experience during the Berlin crisis had shown, the Americans were apt to be reckless."[29]

When Truman decided on 11 September 1950 to cross the 38th parallel and invade North Korea, and when waves of Chinese troops responded in November to drive the UN forces back towards the sea, the French ambassador's words seemed to be prophetic. In the eyes of some Europeans, Acheson's determination to push forward with German rearmament in September also made the ambassador a prophet. In a note passed to Byroade through Allen Dulles, Adenauer had asked on 6 September for a rapid buildup of conventional forces including as many as "13 armored divisions transferred to the Eastern borders of the Federal Republic." Otherwise, the chancellor worried, "the Soviets will take advantage of our defenselessness in order to begin a preventive [military] intervention in Germany." Within the week, Acheson, after top U.S. officials had dropped many hints in August that it was coming, proposed to the British and French that West German forces be created and integrated into a European army. At these New York City meetings, Secretary of Defense George Marshall, according to Bevin, "gave a verbal assurance" to British and French officials "that it was planned to send 5½ divisions" of U.S. troops "to Europe during 1951." Despite Marshall's offer, the French, with what Bevin privately termed "some half-hearted support from the Belgians and Luxembourgers," stood out firmly against the American plan for West Germany.[30]

Paris responded with the Pleven Plan that proposed integrating German forces at the smallest possible unit. The new force would be under a European minister of defense and responsible to a European assembly. British and American officials concluded that, in the words of the Foreign Office, "French policy is, in fact, directed against the North Atlantic Treaty organization." The Foreign Office noted a speech made by Schuman in Strasbourg on 24 November: "the Atlantic Pact has a temporary aim. The European Army in our view is a permanent solution and must ensure peace against all threats, internal and external, now and in the future." It needs to be underlined that U.S. policy was running in exactly the opposite direction. For example, three days after Schuman spoke, a special Presidential Commission reported in Washington that it was not only necessary to build rapidly "the defense capabilities of Western Europe" with full U.S. participation, but to reach that goal the United States had to ensure that the Europeans could obtain badly needed "raw material sources" and not "lose the sources of these needed raw materials to the forces of Communist aggression." Guaranteeing West European defense and making these new global commitments, the commission concluded, were "closely related."[31] Thus as Schuman tried to transform NATO into a European grouping, the Truman administration announced the need to place the NATO nations' future in a global context.

Truman and Acheson pursued that vision even during the worst days of the Korean War in December 1950 and January 1951. As the secretary of state told correspondent James Reston on 11 December, many "silly things" were being talked about in Washington. But, as Reston recorded Acheson's words, "We were going to keep our eye on the central issue, which was Germany, and not get diverted by anything from that." The administration's concern for European opinion might well have been crucial in preventing Truman from "hot pursuit" in to China. The British, Australian, Canadian, French, and other allied governments had strongly warned Washington against such a policy.[32]

Because NATO remained the top U.S. diplomatic priority, the Korean War remained limited. Paradoxically, because NATO required a rapid arms buildup and virtually unlimited confidence in the American willingness to use power, the Korean War's bloodshed became much extended. Truman and Acheson, moreover, could use the conflict as a rationale for both starting West Germany down the road to rearming and restructuring NATO's command under General Dwight D. Eisenhower. The prices paid to obtain these objectives were very high: ever-increasing U.S. involvement in Indochina, the heightening of French-U.S. tension, and the end of bipartisanship on foreign policy in Washington. Amid the swirl of these developments and the massive Chinese offensive into South Korea, Truman refused to rule out considering the use of atomic weapons. The next day, 1 December 1950, Colonel G. A. ("Abe") Lincoln, then professor at West Point, wrote columnist Joseph Alsop that "Historians may call this era the age of terror."[33]

Little evidence exists that Truman and Acheson viewed NATO as a bargaining lever to negotiate an end to the terror in the near future. When the Soviets asked for a foreign ministers conference in December 1950 to discuss the West German question, Acheson, in a heated discussion with Bevin, warned that there was nothing to discuss, at least not until Western powers had been built up. Bevin pointedly reminded Acheson of the summer of 1939, when the Western nations were slow to talk with Stalin about the German question. The secretary of state finally had his way, as he did again in 1952 when the Soviets reopened a bid to discuss a German settlement and Acheson refused to consider it seriously.[34] As NSC-68 urged, massive buildup had to precede diplomacy. Acheson never concluded that the buildup had become sufficiently massive. And it perhaps ran through his mind that if the alliance was arguing bitterly over the German question, it might break apart over the question of how to deal with the larger issue of relations between the Western nations and the Soviet Union. One wonders whether Acheson's mind pondered that point very long. After all, if the prize were Germany, then, as far as he was concerned, there was nothing to bargain or compromise.

The months between August 1949 and December 1950 held many revelations for those interested in NATO's development and the evolution of U.S. policy more generally. They learned that while it was not difficult to gain the attention of Americans and West Europeans when they were attacked or seemed threatened after late June 1950, it was difficult to build the alliance during periods of less or little tension. Such a problem, however, did not prevent Acheson and Pentagon military planners from pushing their programs for the alliance forward between August 1949 and June 1950, nor did the difficulty restrain Acheson and Truman from making a historic commitment in Indochina for the sake, in part, of NATO's cohesion. Additionally, during these months U.S. officials assumed that economic and political interests, especially as those interests became embodied in the integration of the Western European economies, assumed higher priority than did military interests. The economic integration of West Germany was the prerequisite for its military integration into Western Europe.

The massive U.S. military buildup after June 1950 has been viewed as a ready excuse for the Soviets, who accelerated their own armament programs; in that sense, the West's buildup was indeed self-defeating.[35] The roots of that buildup, it must be emphasized, formed not during the Korean War but especially in the ten months before the conflict when key Washington officials, led by Acheson, concluded that whether or not Stalin's armies threatened to march, the economic and political, as well as the military crises triggered by the events of late summer 1949 revealed fundamental problems in the American foreign policy system, and those problems required a restructuring of that policy. The restructuring had to occur, moreover, at a moment when there was little consensus that costly sacrifices and traumatic shifts in the system's relationships were needed. This was not the last time U.S. officials faced a set of problems that required the reshaping of NATO, but a set in which the debate over NATO was a manifestation of more fundamental problems within both the Western system and U.S. foreign policy.

ERNEST R. MAY

The American Commitment to Germany, 1949–1955

When the Atlantic alliance was conceived, its parents did not think much about how it might grow up. They were concerned mostly with a healthy birth. A formal treaty committing the United States and Canada to defend Europe was thought supremely important. Fear focused on residual American isolationism and possible crippling reservations. Officials in all alliance capitals celebrated the final ratifying vote by the U.S. Senate much as ordinary citizens had celebrated V-E Day. Only after the champagne bottles and caviar tins had been carted away did they begin to think about what the alliance might actually do.

The first noteworthy result of this thinking was adoption of a common strategic concept. Under the acronym DC-6 (short for Defense Committee paper number 6) this concept received unanimous approval, early in 1950, from the NATO Council. Originally drafted by a committee of American military officers reporting to the U.S. Joint Chiefs of Staff and amended slightly in the U.S. State Department, DC-6 was approved in other NATO capitals almost without alteration. It was an American product through and through.[1]

The strategic concept matched the language used by Secretary of State Dean Acheson and others when appealing for ratification. They had sworn that the treaty would entail no added expenditures for military forces and no significant changes in military deployments. Asked if it implied a long-term American troop presence in Europe, Acheson responded, "the answer to that question, Senator, is a clear and absolute 'No.'"[2] Consistent with these assurances, DC-6 said: "A basic principle of North Atlantic Treaty planning should be that each nation should undertake the task, or tasks, for which it is best suited. Certain nations, because of the geographic location or because of their capabilities, will be prepared to undertake appropriate specific missions."[3]

Existing U.S. defense budgets, approved—indeed shaped—by Congress, gave priority to strategic bombing. DC-6 said that, in NATO planning, preparation for strategic bombing would be "primarily a U.S. responsibility." It gave the United States and the United Kingdom joint responsibility for "the organization and control of ocean lines of communication." Otherwise, it put the onus of military readiness on the continental European allies. They were to provide "the hard core of ground forces" and "the bulk of the tactical air support and air defense."[4]

On almost any premise about international relations, the original NATO strategic concept is unsurprising. A great power extended protection to lesser powers strategically located. For protection—and money—the great power expected troops. So Britain had managed its affairs for three centuries. So other empires had trafficked with client states from at least the time of Cyrus the Great.

What actually developed is surprising, and hard to explain. The subsidies were paid. In the first half of the 1950s the United States provided its European allies with approximately $10 billion in military aid.[5] But the continental allies provided few soldiers. Making an independent survey in 1955, *Time* magazine found only ten effective divisions opposite the front line of the Red Army. Five were American; two were British.[6] Although Europeans provided a larger share of NATO's tactical air support, their most effective planes were American-built F-84s.[7]

In December 1954, moreover, the NATO Council adopted a new strategic concept. It was embodied in MC-48 (short for Military Committee paper number 48). The essence of the new strategic concept was an undertaking by the United States to defend the client states' frontiers with its own forces, no matter what the cost. MC-48 committed the alliance to "a forward strategy."[8] It implied that the United States would assume the onus for that strategy, for it said that the numerical superiority of the Eastern bloc was to be offset by Western nuclear weapons. Since existing or immediately prospective "tactical" nuclear weapons were American and only the president of the United States could authorize their use, this meant that U.S. forces assumed primary responsibility for coping with any attack on the alliance's front line. In other texts, many of them public, the United States had pledged also to answer an attack by strategic bombing—"massive retaliation"—against the Soviet homeland. As of late 1954, the Soviet Union was credited with a growing stockpile of nuclear weapons. The U.S. intelligence community estimated that before long the Soviet Union would be capable of "gravely" damaging the American homeland in event of a nuclear exchange.[9] In effect, the American government volunteered much of the population of the United States as hostages for the shelter of its continental allies.

Instead of buying protection, the great power seemed, through the alliance, to be taking on larger military burdens and increasing its own peril. How had this come about? Actions by the Soviet government obviously had some influence. So did actions by allies and associates. It is not easy, however, to argue that actions by other governments left the United States with no courses of action other than the ones it followed. The particular set of outcomes has to be explained at least in part in terms of factors peculiar to post–World War II Washington. Had Britain been the Western superpower (or France or Germany or Italy or Ruritania), it is unlikely that there would have been the same progression—from limited to sacrificial commitment—from DC-6 to MC-48.

Four features of the mid-twentieth century United States distinguished it from other great powers. First of all, its national government was new to governing and newer still to being a government organized to operate as a great power. A decade before World War II, the United States had had a national government exercising functions rather similar to those of the post-Stuart British monarchy. Before the Great Depression, Calvin Coolidge said, without much exaggeration, "If the Federal Government should go out of existence, the common run of people would not detect the difference in the affairs of their daily life for a considerable length of time."[10] It had taken the depression to break local and state monopolies in the exercise of public authority and to make departments of the national government forces in the lives of American citizens.[11]

The departments that mattered, however, were agriculture, labor, the interior, and the like. The State Department did little. The names of secretaries of war and the navy and the chiefs of staff were as little known to the public as are today the names of the secretaries of housing and veteran affairs. Apart from attachés and cryptanalysts in the army and navy, the United States had no intelligence service. Only with World War II and the Cold War did foreign-oriented and security-oriented components of the U.S. government become prominent and important and begin to attract ambitious and energetic men and women comparable to those traditionally drawn to "high politics" in European capitals.

A second distinguishing feature was that the United States had a government of much-divided mind. There was a split between, on one hand, elected officials and their intimates and, on the other, appointed officials and members of career services. This split resembled that in Britain between "ministers" and "officials" but with so many differences that the terms cannot be invoked. American counterparts for British ministers included not only elected presidents and members of Congress but presidential and congressional staffers, would-be presidents and their advisers, and many others professionally or semiprofessionally concerned with elections or with the public side of governance. American counterparts for British officials were less often civil servants than lawyers, bankers, or others brought in from private life, often for brief spells, to head executive departments, agencies, or bureaus, or to serve in advisory posts.[12]

The basic distinction between minister and official in Britain nevertheless applied to "politician" and "official" in America. Politicians tended to judge policy primarily in terms of public approval. Although they did not necessarily bend according to the most recent public opinion polls or election results, they tended to assume that, at least in the long run, the crucial test of a decision or course of action would be the express satisfaction of the electorate. Officials tended to be skeptical about the wishes of the populace, whether in the short or long run. They assumed, as a rule, that there were national interests, discernible by a knowledgeable elite, and that the test of policy was whether it protected or advanced those interests. Officials tended to be scornful of politicians precisely on the ground that they were likely to sacrifice national interests for the sake of votes or other signs of popularity. This basic division was complicated by the existence of other divisions, some with, but some without, counterparts in other political systems. The sharing of powers by the separated branches of government is the most obvious. Ministries of the U.S. government answer to a hierarchy of presidential appointees. They also answer to an array of congressional committees and subcommittees entirely independent of the president and his appointees. This complicates the lives of officials. Secretaries of state have estimated that they and their principal advisers spend half their working hours preparing for or delivering testimony before Congress. Half of their remaining hours go to thinking about what to say to the press, partly with thought to how their words may echo on Capitol Hill. In better funded agencies, such as the Defense Department and the Atomic Energy Commission (now the core of the Department of Energy), relations with congressional committees are more important than relations with the White House. As a result, nearly all elements of the American government live in year-to-year uncertainty. At the same time, many of them have a degree of autonomy not matched in most other developed nations since the suppression of feudalism.[13]

A third feature was that the American government—politicians and officials alike—suffered in the early postwar decades from collective feelings of both guilt and fear. In the first, they were not alone; in the second, they were more so. Americans were nearly unanimous that the "isolationism" of the interwar years had been wrong and had contributed to, perhaps even caused, World War II. Staple lines in official speeches expressed shame for American policies prior to the war and determination that the mistakes not be repeated. In this respect, American, British, and European rhetoric ran parallel. Among Americans, however, there was also pervasive fear that the mistakes would be repeated. Politicians worried, and officials worried even more, lest the public be seduced into some new isolationism. Even Jeffersonians like Truman, Arthur Vandenberg, and young J. William Fulbright believed that unremitting campaigns of education were needed to guard against this peril.[14]

Finally, the American government was one extraordinarily open to foreign influence. In the American federal system there was no barrier to citizens of one state meddling in the affairs of another. A long history of hospitality to immigration had made it not uncommon for foreign politics to become American politics and vice versa. After World War II, these traditions, combined with the newness of high politics and the overlap and rivalry of branches that so fragmented decision making, opened for interested noncitizens uncommon opportunities for effectively inserting their opinions and recommendations.[15]

Even in 1950, at the time of the adoption of DC-6, these peculiar characteristics of American government were already producing some movement toward a voluntary increase in the extent to which the United States would assume military costs and risks that another great power would probably have pressed on its clients. Some of this movement stemmed from elements of the armed services attempting to protect or advance their own parochial interests.

At the time, most politicians agreed that unpreparedness had been one of the mistakes of the interwar years. Consequently, they were ready to spend much more for defense. They were not ready, however, to fund all or even most of the programs proposed to them by the armed services. One reason, among many, was that spokesmen for each service and for many service branches frequently belittled the programs of others. Late 1949, for example, had seen admirals before Congress trying to condemn the air force's long-range bomber, the B-36, as a "billion dollar blunder." Air force representatives had countered with accusations that most money spent on navy aircraft carriers was wasted.[16]

Truman and Congress set ceilings that they believed generous and pressed the services to live within them. The services could not accommodate this demand. Differences between and among them were unbridgeable. Devotees of the land-based long-range bomber and the aircraft carrier were as firm in their different faiths as were inquisitors and heretics in sixteenth-century Spain. Faith equally pure pervaded parts of the services committed to tactical aviation, air defense, surface and subsurface sea warfare, armor, artillery, and infantry (the latter seaborne and airborne as well as mudborne). With new technologies multiplying, unit costs skyrocketing, lead times lengthening, the experience of the last war becoming more remote, and images of a future war consequently growing ever more cloudy, responsible leaders in the armed services felt more and more desperate about their inability to persuade politicians that spending for military force should be increased.[17]

After the North Atlantic Treaty was signed, army officers found in it a new argument for why their service should get more money or at least a larger share of existing money. Heretofore, the president—and Congress even more—had given marginally more to air power, especially to the air force's Strategic Air Command, or SAC. The army officers now pointed out that SAC, at its most extravagant, boasted only of being able to obliterate the Soviet Union. It could make no claim of being able to prevent the Red Army from occupying Europe. Army officers argued for an *American* strategic concept, entailing defense of Europe on line as far east as feasible. They gained support from navy officers animated at least in part by simple hatred of the air force. They also gained quiet support from the air force's Tactical Air Command. The army concept then became the organizing principle for war planning in all parts of the military establishment except SAC. Army, navy, and Tactical Air Command officers used this concept as a basis for arguing for more *American* troops, tactical aircraft, and naval vessels. Toward that end, it was useful for these officers to emphasize the limitations on what Europeans could do for themselves.[18]

Other movement centered in the State Department. In November 1948 Truman had been elected president in his own right—a surprise to everyone except possibly Truman himself. He then made some cabinet changes. At State, Dean Acheson replaced General George Marshall. By 1950, Acheson's chief planner was Paul Nitze, and Nitze proved an extraordinarily effective ally for the armed services.[19] When working earlier on European and economic affairs, Nitze had developed several strong convictions. He had concluded that the Soviet Union would seize any opportunity, and use any means, to extend its domain. He further believed that the Soviets would be deterred from moving against Western Europe only if sure they could not succeed. Visits to Western Europe in 1949 persuaded Nitze that the Europeans could not and would not do what was necessary to this end. If they created strong military forces, the momentum of economic recovery would die. Governments would lose popular support. The Soviets might be encouraged to act rather than the reverse. In Nitze's mind, it followed ineluctably that the rich and powerful United States should fill the breach by building up its own military forces and interposing them between the Russians and the Europeans.[20]

Nitze began quickly to work with like-minded military officers. The effort had some qualities of a conspiracy, for it went on behind the back of the civilian secretary of defense. Truman, believing that adequate preparedness could be achieved with defense spending around twice its prewar level—2½ percent of GNP instead of only 1¼ percent—had appointed a tough, ambitious fellow politician, Louis Johnson of West Virginia, to preside over the Pentagon. Realizing that dissident military officers might get aid and comfort from the State Department (not least because he and Acheson loathed each other), Johnson ordered that there be no Pentagon-State consultation without his personal approval. Consultation with Nitze involved, to say the least, evasion of these directives.[21]

A man of rare intelligence, industry, and cunning, Nitze devised a strategy whereby he and his bureaucratic allies could put the politicians in a corner. He developed the now-famous NSC-68. This document portrayed the East-West contest as one between slavery and freedom. It argued that decisive struggles were close at hand. Combining close reasoning, moral fervor, and urgency of warning, it appealed both to Wilsonian moralism and legalism and to memories of Pearl Harbor. Drafted after consultation with scores of eminent private citizens, it carried the authority not only of officialdom but also of the nascent American foreign policy establishment. Although the document was technically secret, its power derived in large part from the embarrassment it could cause if made public. If Truman continued to push down military spending and NSC-68 got into the hands of Congress, it would become the occasion for speeches, hearings, and anti-administration resolutions. Either way, Nitze and his fellow officials would probably win some increase in defense spending.[22]

When Truman received NSC-68, he sensed the danger. He ordered that it *"be handled with special security precautions . . . [and] that no publicity be given this report or its contents without his approval."* He asked the secretary of the treasury, the budget director, the foreign aid administrator, and the chairman of the Council of Economic Advisers to comment, expecting that they would at least provide counterarguments.[23] He evidently hoped thus to escape the trap Nitze had laid, for he said to reporters, off the record, that he counted still on being able to have a smaller defense budget in 1951 than in 1950.[24]

Chances are, however, that Truman would not have been able to make good that promise. Nitze's trap was too ingenious. Officialdom was too fervent and too much of one mind. Moreover, the mass public to which the politicians answered was too volatile. Truman and his congressional allies were already seeing signs that they had misjudged the popular temper. The China white paper had not produced its intended effect. Instead of persuading the public that the United States could not have rescued Chiang Kai-shek from defeat by the Chinese Communists, the white paper had greatly increased the numbers suspecting that the blame lay with covert Communists in the American government. Truman and his allies were shortly to learn that they were even more mistaken in assuming that a hearing or two would discredit the irresponsible junior senator from Wisconsin, Joe McCarthy. Come November, McCarthy and his friends would win elections. Their critics would not.[25]

What accounted for the trends in public opinion remains in debate. It has been argued that the Truman administration set them off, partly by trying to outdo the Republican right in anticommunism, partly by deliberate overstatements when selling the Truman Doctrine and the Marshall Plan. It has also been argued that the public was ripe for one of its periodic spells of paranoia, perhaps in part because of cyclonic social changes resulting from the depression and the war. Not wholly out of the question is the simple hypothesis that the mass mind was seeking escape from fears engendered by the Soviet atomic bomb and publicity concerning the new hydrogen bomb.[26] In any case, there was enough tinder about to make it difficult for politicians to preserve calm if officials began publicly crying alarm.

The North Korean attack on South Korea in late June 1950 made it unnecessary for Nitze and his associates to test the effects of leaking NSC-68. Seeing events of the 1930s repeating themselves, Truman unhesitatingly rallied the United Nations and sent in American troops. At the same time, he endorsed NSC-68 and asked the armed services to tell him what he should request from Congress in the way of supplemental appropriations. With Americans actually at war and almost everyone assuming that the Russians were the North Koreans' puppetmasters, congressmen of both parties indicated readiness to vote for whatever the president asked.[27]

The actual increases came in stages, partly determined by the pace of bargaining within and among the services, ensuring that new funds were allocated in the same proportions as the old. The first supplemental, a $10.5 billion add-on to the pre-Korean $13.3 billion budget, was designed largely to pay for operations in Korea; a second, which totalled $16.8 billion, drew its rationale from NSC-68. It was designed to pay for an overall increase in military readiness. Against the possibility that the Soviets might try in divided Germany what they had tried in divided Korea, the second supplemental provided specifically for augmenting American forces in Europe.[28]

While the Pentagon and budget bureau negotiated the second supplemental, General MacArthur effected a surprise landing at Inchon, athwart North Korean supply lines. The North Koreans beat a retreat, with UN forces on their heels. Congressmen became less enthusiastic about defense spending. The president advised the chiefs of staff not to be too ambitious when putting together a budget for the next fiscal year. Then Chinese "volunteers" appeared in mass in North Korea. It was the turn of UN troops to beat a retreat. General Marshall was now secretary of defense, Truman having fired Johnson as a symbolic way of repudiating the policy he had

Table 1
Forces Projected in Truman Administration Budgets

Before Korea		FY 1951	FY 1952	FY 1953	FY 1954
Army					
divisions	10	18	18	20	20
manpower	630,000	1,353,000	1,550,000	1,552,000	1,540,000
Navy					
carrier task forces	9	14	14	16	16
total vessels	618	1,161	1,161	1,191	1,200
Marine					
divisions	2	2+	2⅓	3	3
manpower	460,605	887,000	980,516	1,079,605	1,048,612
Air Force					
wings	42	80	95	126	143
manpower	419,000	971,000	1,061,000	1,061,000	1,061,000
Total					
manpower	1,506,605	3,211,000	3,591,516	3,692,605	3,649,612

Source: Condit, *Test of War,* 240, 255, 278, 301.

commissioned Johnson to carry out. On Marshall's advice, Truman asked Congress not only for the second supplemental but soon afterward for a third supplemental, this of $6.4 billion, to send additional forces to Korea. With Congress approving all these supplementals, defense spending for the current fiscal year reached three times the pre-Korea level.[29]

For the next fiscal year, the military establishment recommended spending even more; Truman accepted the advice, asked Congress for $56.2 billion, and got appropriations of $55.5 billion. The services were on their way to explosive across-the-board expansion. The table above shows the basic numbers projected. The table is, however, partially misleading, for it does not reflect the reequipment central to the new preparedness effort. The additional units were to have new model planes, ships, tanks, guns, etc. Approximately half the budget was for procurement, in many instances of items not to be delivered for years. Consistent with the argumentation in NSC-68, the buildup was intended not just for the emergency but for the long term.

Also consistent with NSC-68, the buildup gave priority to defense of Europe. Truman announced in December 1950 that four first-line army divisions would be sent to Europe. A large proportion of American tactical aircraft would accompany them. American warships on duty in the Mediterranean and elsewhere around Europe would be increased. General Eisenhower, currently in retirement and president of Columbia University, would return to active duty as supreme allied commander, Europe, commanding all military forces assigned to NATO.[30]

These sudden American force commitments lend themselves to several different explanations. These explanations are hard to separate from one another or to evaluate independently. One is, of course, the contemporaneous explanation that the United States was responding to evidence concerning the potential Soviet military threat. Intelligence estimates conventionally credited the Soviets with 175 active divisions and spoke of their being able to mobilize three hundred divisions in emergency. These numbers were probably inflated. For reasons not all of which are foolish, order of battle estimates ordinarily err on the high side. Planners in the NATO military establishment seem in practice to have been concerned chiefly by indications that the Soviets had about forty-five divisions positioned and equipped much as had been forward units of the Wehrmacht in the era of the 1940 blitz against the Low Countries and France.[31] Increasing numbers of these divisions had new tanks and motor transport. Soviet tactical air forces had been acquiring jet fighters and fighter-bombers at a much more rapid rate than Western forces. The Soviet Long-Range Air Force had TU-4 bombers, which were exact copies of the U.S. B-29. They could fly round trip missions delivering up to ten tons of bombs on base systems, industrial facilities, or population anywhere within an arc from the north central Atlantic to the Sahara. The Long-Range Air Force was estimated in 1950 to have five hundred of these aircraft. By 1954 it had twelve hundred.[32] This represented a far greater threat to Western Europe and the United Kingdom than any ever posed by the bombers of Hitler's Luftwaffe.

Hard intelligence data about Soviet military capabilities was thus enough in itself to create apprehension. Softer accompanying data, particularly in the form of rumors reaching Russian émigrés, enhanced this apprehension, for it whispered of Kremlin conferences contemplating offensive military operations and of exercises in Eastern Europe consistent with offensive planning.[33] An American official acquainted only with intelligence concerning the Soviet Union could quite rationally have concluded that there was an immediate Soviet threat to Western Europe and the United Kingdom calling for some exceptional America response.

A second explanation for these sudden American force commitments would emphasize European appeals to Washington. Konrad Adenauer was head of the German regime brought in to being by the Western occupying powers. He repeatedly spoke to American high commissioner John J. McCloy not only about the Soviet armies just across the German border but also about the light infantry units being formed among East Germans under the guise of "people's police" (Volkspolizei).[34] In seeming doubt that McCloy appreciated the depth of his concern, Adenauer talked also with American newspapermen in Bonn. In one such interview, he used language not very different from that contemporaneously being framed by Nitze for NSC-68. "[A]ny war would be worth while for Soviet Russia which left Europe in her hands," he said. "Hence I believe that the incentive to make war is greater for Soviet Russia than is generally assumed. In these circumstances peace can only be secured if the Soviet leaders are convinced of the hopelessness of conquering Europe."[35] American correspondents in Germany reported that Adenauer's feelings were widely shared. They told, for example, of German families packing up and going westward on foot so as not to be in the immediate paths of a Russian advance. In France, Americans were exposed to signs of nervousness reminding many of the 1930s. During the initial period of the Marshall Plan, French Communists had organized or capitalized on a wave of strikes and riots. French officials sought out not only Americans in the embassy and the aid mission but even journalists, such as young Theodore White, then in Europe for the left-wing American Overseas News Agency, to tell them how close run was their effort to keep France out of Communist hands.[36]

By 1950 French officials had learned from their American contacts and from French reporters in Washington that additional American economic assistance would be meager at best. With the same fervor, Frenchmen now made a case for America's providing military aid. France had the only effective army on the Continent, they said. It was weakened because so many French volunteers were fighting Communist guerrillas in Indochina. The alternatives to building up French military forces were all thought to be distasteful, perhaps unacceptable, to the United States or Britain or both:

arming West Germans, committing British troops to the Continent, or committing American troops there. It was argumentation such as this that Nitze had heard when touring France in 1949.[37]

After the beginning of the Korean War, American missions in Western Europe observed near panic. McCloy reported (in cablese) that in West Germany he perceived "acute realization threat to Germany implied in Kremlin decision resort 'hot war' Korea, eliminating German hope that Soviet fear US potential would suffice deter overt military action by Soviet or orbit governments. Generally realized now that Germany defenseless." He said that some business firms and well-to-do individuals had begun making secret contributions to the German Communist party in anticipation of having soon to come to terms with it.[38] David Bruce, the ambassador in Paris, not typically an alarmist, wrote, "The Communist invasion of the Republic of Korea constituted a traumatic experience of the first order for the collective mind of France.... [A] feeling of extreme nakedness overcame the French at the thought that Russia, having shown that it was willing to risk war, might next attack in Europe."[39]

The American chiefs of staff had already begun to argue for creating a new German army. The army–navy–Tactical Air Command prescription for active defense of European territory had called for enlisting German troops. Especially given the French war in Indochina, arming Germans made sense militarily. In view of what appeared to be rocklike opposition by Truman and American public opinion, it made even more sense as a supporting argument for more money for American military forces.[40]

With Korea, however, the case for arming Germans suddenly became one that politicians would accept. Truman made a complete about-face. He first agreed to the principle that German soldiers should participate in defense of Western Europe. Soon afterward, he came all the way around to endorsing re-creation of a German army on whatever terms were agreeable to the other allies.[41]

This was more than Adenauer had proposed. He had called for nothing more than a West German national militia counterpart to the East German Volkspolizei. After the shock of Korea, he was prepared to think in somewhat more ambitious terms, but the last thing Adenauer wanted was a new Wehrmacht. He was afraid of Russian reactions. He was equally afraid of awakening dread and hostility among the French and other Western Europeans. He thought West German public opinion antimilitarist. A Catholic Rhinelander through and through, he had deep personal misgivings about restoring any of Germany's character or image as a greater Prussia. Many of his fears and feelings were shared by the Social Democratic minority in the new Bundestag. Through McCloy, through American correspondents in Bonn, and through private channels, Adenauer and other Germans advised Washington to think less in terms of German military formations than in terms of reassuring Germans, the French and other Western Europeans by stationing more American and British troops along the West German–East German frontier.

The French, not surprisingly, reacted with alarm to evidence that the United States was coming to favor German rearmament. They argued that whatever forces France could not provide should be American and British. Both via the American and British missions in Paris and in face-to-face ministerial meetings, French officials were presented arguments they found hard to answer. The French themselves insisted that NATO strategy should aim at holding a defense line as far east as possible—as far away as possible from France's own soil. Were Germans to be required or allowed to make no contribution to defending their own territory? The French acknowledged that they could not field many divisions in Europe unless they received much larger subsidies from the United States. General Marshall, the new American secretary of defense, asked them softly how they expected him to obtain those subsidies from Congress if he had to say that France was insisting that American soldiers man lines that might be manned by German soldiers. With evident anguish, the French retreated. Their eventual compromise took the form of the Pleven Plan—for a European Defense Community, with a European army including units of many nationalities.[42]

With West Germany given permission to form its own Volkspolizei (though in individual states, on the model of the American National Guard, not under the central government), Adenauer indicated a willingness to negotiate about participation in a European Defense Community, should one materialize. The American and British governments, though skeptical, concluded that they should let the issue be debated in Paris in terms of Pleven's EDC. This, it was thought, would prevent a hardening of division in the French National Assembly. It would protect the French leaders most likely eventually to engineer a workable solution—Pleven; his mentor, Jean Monnet; Robert Schuman; and their like. Since McCloy advised that preparatory work in Germany would take at least a year,

Washington and London agreed that it would be possible to wait until 1951 before pressing the French for that workable solution.[43]

In the meantime, the American government yielded to the urgings of its allies. Truman announced the dispatch to Germany of four additional army divisions. With two divisions already there doing occupation duty, this brought the total to six divisions. Since a full-strength U.S. division had three to four times as many men as a standard division in either the Red Army or most NATO armies, this was the rough equivalent of twenty Soviet, French, or British divisions. Only later did Truman add the announcement that, at the request of the allies, Eisenhower would be named supreme commander. This announcement was delayed so that Acheson and Marshall could use Eisenhower's nomination as a chip in their game with the French.[44] It was made only after the decision not to oppose the Pleven Plan. The initial commitment of American forces to front-line duty in Europe can thus be seen as a response to a Soviet military threat reinforced by pleas from allies, or vice versa, a response to pleas from allies reinforced by evidence that the allies were not simply imagining or inventing an Eastern bloc threat.

Yet another explanation of the American action could emphasize a force at work within the United States, namely the need and desire of various service elements to justify their budgetary claims. As noted earlier, ground forces and tactical air forces and certain elements of the navy had made use, well before June 1950, of the rationale that they would be needed to hold a line somewhere on the Continent. This had been the central argument for the army's getting 34 percent of $13 billion allocated to defense before the Korean conflict. It was equally central to the army's argument for getting 38 percent of the $49 billion eventually allocated for that fiscal year and 36 percent of the $55 billion allocated for the year beyond.

In the new atmosphere, army officers tried briefly to revive the idea of universal military training. Congress and the public showed no more enthusiasm than earlier. The army could use the Korean War bonanza only to expand its regular establishment. Within its approximate third of the new money, the army could go from ten divisions under strength to eighteen divisions at full strength. Less than half of this force could be engaged in Korea. The army had to put the other divisions somewhere. If they were all in training at home, they would be easy marks the next time budgets began to shrink. The army *needed* to deploy divisions to Europe and to prepare arguments as to why those divisions could not easily be dismantled and brought home.

These observations may seem cynical. They are not. Ground force officers believed in their service. They believed that wars were won in the mud. They believed that the next war could be lost if the public and the politicians let themselves neglect ground forces in favor of the fancy technologies of SAC or the flying navy. Any argument that persuaded the public and the politicians to invest in foot soldiers was therefore an argument in a good cause. The ground force faithful had every incentive to believe—and none to disbelieve—that there was an imminent Soviet threat and that forward-deployed American troops constituted an answer to allies' prayers.

And the ground force faithful included a significant proportion not only of the nation's leadership but also of its pantheon. Marshall, Eisenhower, and Omar Bradley were not just officials, they were heroes. If they said American forces should be stationed on the front lines, it was not easy for ordinary citizens to express doubts. In January 1951, when former president Herbert Hoover and Senator Robert A. Taft questioned both the constitutionality and wisdom of the policy, they were branded mossback "isolationists." Even though Taft was minority leader and a likely 1952 presidential candidate, the Senate repudiated his views.[45]

An explanation in terms of interservice politics cannot stand on its own, for one cannot imagine six American divisions and eight tactical air wings being posted to Germany had there not also been intelligence about the Soviet military buildup—put in bold relief by events in Korea—and indications of European alarm. It is equally hard, however, to imagine that particular outcome absent the iron percentages arrangement giving each service and each service branch a more or less fixed proportion of the defense budget, whatever its total size.

With the American force commitments went comparable commitments by Britain. This was in part because London and Washington were subject to identical pressures. In addition, London felt pressure from Washington. The American government asked the British to join in augmenting their occupation forces, promised to pay a substantial part of the costs, and warned gently that, absent such action, it might be difficult or impossible for the United States to help Britain escape the new dollar gaps into which it had fallen. In larger part, probably, it reflected a feeling in London that, if there were to be a continental commitment, it had to be British *and*

American. It could not be American alone. Otherwise, Britain might cede her place as *secundus inter pares*.[46]

The American troop and aircraft commitments of 1950–51 were represented as emergency measures. Truman, Acheson, Marshall, and Eisenhower all said publicly that these forces would come home once Europeans were able to put in place their own ground and air forces. How far in the future that day might be remained unclear. Whether some American units would stay indefinitely also remained unclear. The official assurances were not, however, disingenuous. Almost everyone felt, as Eisenhower was to say years later, that American troops were only in Europe on "temporary or emergency" basis and that the United States could not and would not man "a Roman wall" in Germany.[47]

Two developments after the winter of 1950–51 reduced the likelihood that either American or British forces would soon leave their exposed positions. The first was interallied accord on the force levels needed to safeguard Europe against the Soviet menace. The second was failure by the European states either to create a common army or by other means to reach or even approach the agreed-upon force goals. The result was to keep both the United States and Britain in the position of not being able to pull back their forces without radically revising their estimates of either the threat or the interests in jeopardy. A change in posture would involve, as Secretary of State John Foster Dulles would later say, "agonizing reappraisal."

Each of these developments had a complex history, the course of which can only be summarized here. The estimate of NATO force requirements took fixed (though not immutable) form at the North Atlantic Council meeting at Lisbon in February 1952. The council agreed to the goals shown in Table 2. Just how the Lisbon goals were calculated remains a mystery. The NATO Defense Committee had in circulation even before the Korean War documents with numbers in the Lisbon range. Partly, no doubt, these numbers were a function of the 175 to 300 divisions ascribed to the Russians. The traditional rule of thumb says that defense needs a one to three ratio against the offense. Probably, the totals resulted simply from adding together the wish lists of military services in all the NATO capitals. American and British documents suggest such a process. The American and British chiefs of staff made the most of "NATO requirement" as one more band of armor against penny pinchers from the budget bureau or the appropriations committees or, in Britain, the treasury.[48]

Table 2
Lisbon Force Goals

	Dec. 1952	Dec. 1953	Dec. 1954
Ground force divisions			
M-Day	25	36⅔	41⅔
M + 30	51⅔	72⅓	89⅔
Combat vessels			
M-Day	461	470	504
M + 180	834	848	941
Aircraft			
M-Day	4,067	7,005	9,965

Source: Condit, *Test of War*, 377.

What gave this cumulative wish list a special sanctity was the endorsement of Eisenhower. As SACEUR, he had periodically pushed up the estimate of how many divisions and air wings NATO would need to cope with the Soviets. Officials in the State Department interpreted this as a tactical maneuver. Wrote one of them: "Eisenhower has masterfully impaled our allies on the horns of a dilemma—military v. political. They can assume an intolerable military burden or they can agree to accept Germany as a political equal. . . . Since SACEUR's judgment on what he needs can hardly be challenged successfully, our allies must inevitably be tempted by the reduction in their obligations which his plan offers."[49] Eisenhower's prestige and authority were such that hardly anyone at the time dared question his pronouncements.

The ministers at Lisbon who might have asked if the force goals were realistic were not of a mind to do so. Acheson was preoccupied with getting the French to take the first practical step toward legitimizing German contributions to European defense—signing the contractual agreements that would give the Federal Republic many of the attributes of independence. If part of the price was a set of force goals seeming to necessitate a longer-term American and British military presence in Germany, he had no hesitation about agreeing. His attitude was reflected in a preconference letter to Schuman and in a midconference letter to Truman. The former, written against the advice of Bruce, warned gloomily that if the conferees did not make progress toward giving Germany a role in European defense, the Truman administration "would have little chance of saving policies and programs on which all of us have worked for years and which are right." The latter exulted that the only open question was whether the conference "will be a success or a great success."[50]

Robert A. Lovett had been Marshall's deputy and was now secretary of defense. He shared Acheson's view. In addition, he shared the interests of his chiefs of staff. Truman had begun once again to press for reductions in military spending. Lovett had worked hard to stretch out procurement so as to get the total budget down from the previous year's $55.5 billion to a proposed $48.6 billion, but he wanted every penny. His original request to Truman had been for $51.6 billion.[51] The Lisbon force-goal statement helped him.

Attitudes within the British delegation were similar. Though some Foreign Office officials thought the force goals "manifestly impossible" and blamed the American delegates, they remained quiet. Churchill, recently reinstalled as prime minister, attached overriding importance to unity with the United States, not least because he perceived Britain as "a broken and impoverished power, which has cast away a great part of its Empire and of late years has misused its resources."[52]

The Lisbon force goals became and remained NATO's benchmark. Every shortfall had to be justified or at least explained. Since preferred force levels were never to match the Lisbon goals (and actual levels, usually detectable to the press, rarely matched preferred levels), the American government was never able to say that conditions had become propitious for drawing down forces in Europe.[53]

That the EDC would never materialize had been foreseen. The American and British governments had acquiesced in the Pleven Plan on the assumption that debates in France would lead to some more practicable scheme. Within months, however, American officialdom, or at least a large part of it, had made the EDC its own. It had, moreover, become optimistic about the EDC's prospects. The processes producing this result had started much earlier.[54]

Jean Monnet, the author of France's economic recovery plan, had been one of the earliest "Europeans." Traveling in Canada and the United States for his family's cognac firm, Monnet had become convinced of the advantages of federalism. With an emphasis more on economic than on political institutions, he became an advocate of Aristide Briand's "United States of Europe." Venturing successfully into international high finance, Monnet in the interwar years developed friendships with a large number of Americans, McCloy, Lovett, Acheson, and the Dulles brothers among them. As head of a wartime purchasing mission for Free France, Monnet had opportunity to make these friendships stronger. He worked tirelessly at doing so, also preaching to each such friend the gospel of European unity. Over and over he said that Europe must never again endure a civil war; the great, disinterested United States must use its influence to that end.[55]

Back in France after the war, Monnet built close ties with senior civil servants and with leaders from all the non-Communist parties. His inner circle included Schuman, a Christian Democrat (MRP); Pleven, of the moderately left UDSR; and Maurice Petsche of the right-wing Peasant party. Georgette Elgey, the chronicler of the Fourth Republic, says that only one prime minister counted himself at odds with Monnet. That was Socialist Paul Ramadier.[56]

As Monnet and his circle perceived the resurgence of Germany in 1949 and afterward, they tried to come up with practical formulae for knitting Germany to France and the rest of Europe. One of the most dramatic was that proposed and effected by Robert Schuman when foreign minister—for the creation of a European Coal and Steel Community.[57] When the question of German rearmament came to the fore, it was Monnet and his friends who came up with the concept of a European army.

The concept was adopted more or less simultaneously by Monnet and several of his friends, including McCloy and Bruce. In part jointly but in part also from independent sources, Monnet and Bruce argued that, in some form, the EDC would eventually win acceptance in France. Building upon these seemingly separate estimates, McCloy and Adenauer then reinforced in each other hope that the prophecies of Monnet and Bruce would prove accurate. Monnet's advocacy of and optimism about the EDC was thus heard by his friends in the United States, such as Acheson and Foster Dulles, with seeming substantiation from the American missions in Paris and Bonn. (And, in some degree, London; for the American ambassador there was McCloy's brother-in-law, Lewis Douglas.) In intelligence analysis, this is described as an echo effect. Acheson et al. did not perceive it as such. The whole circle fell victim to Monnet's tendency to be overhopeful about anything "European."[58]

In mid-1951, in the course of a single long lunch, Monnet made an even more important convert, Eisenhower. At home, Eisenhower had heard Bradley and other former army colleagues argue that the

EDC was a chimera and that it would be preferable simply to have Germany a member of NATO. Over the one lunch, Monnet convinced Eisenhower that the European army held much greater promise. Afterward, Eisenhower became as ardent as Monnet in championing the EDC. Since Eisenhower had more credit with Congress and the American public than any member of the Truman administration, his advocacy of the EDC constrained every official in Washington and every politician not on the Democratic left or the Republican right. If Ike said it was a good thing and would work, who could oppose it or express doubts?[59]

In fact, as would eventually become evident, the EDC never commanded adequate support in France. Communists decried German rearmament in any way, shape, or form, and even after the elections of June 1951, they still had 16 percent of the seats in the National Assembly. Supporters of de Gaulle, accounting for another 19 percent, scorned the notion of the French army's abandoning its national identity. In the center-right parties led by Schuman, Pleven, and their like, enthusiasm for the EDC never ran high. Socialists with slightly more strength than the Communists (107 seats to 101) would not for the most part reconcile themselves to again seeing Germans in uniform.[60] As defense minister for Pleven, Socialist Jules Moch let himself be party to the plan, but he manifested misgivings from beginning to end. As he was to write later: "In those days, I had a tendency to take all Germans for henchmen of Hitler. I could not see one without asking myself, 'What did he do? What crimes did he commit before 1945?'"[61]

The history of the EDC in France became a history of postponements. Time after time, prime ministers said to Monnet or to Americans or to Adenauer that, in another few weeks, the time would be ripe for a favorable assembly vote. That time never arrived. Usually the ministers excused themselves by pleading need for some new concession. Not infrequently they asked for something they knew to be out of the question, such as British participation or Germany's permanent renunciation of the Saarland or a formal American pledge always to maintain large forces in Germany. Fruitless haggling would ensue. Finally, in the spring of 1954, Pierre Mendès-France ended the charade. He let the issue go to a vote. It lost 319 to 264. Within a matter of months, with surprisingly little resistance, even from French Socialists, it was agreed that the German Federal Republic could become a member of NATO and, in that capacity, create and contribute complete German divisions and tactical air wings.[62]

AMERICAN COMMITMENT TO GERMANY 73

The long delay and accompanying uncertainty had had three effects. First, it habituated Americans—politicians, officials, and the public alike—to having a large garrison in Germany. Second, it habituated Europeans to that particular solution for the European dilemma. The American and British forces in Germany protected Germans not only against Russians but also against everyone else, themselves included. They reassured the French and others who had suffered Nazi occupation. (Probably, though there is no supporting evidence, the presence of American and British armies in Germany also reassured the Russians.)[63]

Third, the prolonged EDC debate exposed to Americans, Europeans, and the English how relatively limited was Washington's menu of alternatives. Hoping to shock the French into action, Secretary of State Dulles tried to sketch what the United States might do if no EDC were created. It was in a secret speech to the NATO Council that he employed the phrase he was to use more vaguely in a subsequent press conference. He said:

> If . . . the European Defense Community should not become effective, if France and Germany remain apart so that they will again be potential enemies then there would indeed be grave doubt as to whether Continental Europe could be made a place of safety. That would compel an agonizing reappraisal of basic United States policy. . . . Unless unity is achieved soon different and divisive forces may take command. These separatist forces will also be found in the United States. It may never again be possible for integration to occur in freedom although it might be that West Europe would be unified as East Europe has been unified in defeat and servitude.[64]

The substance of Dulles's statement immediately leaked. From right to center left, French politicians protested Dulles's interference in French domestic affairs. Correspondents for CBS News and the *New York Herald Tribune,* both ordinarily strong supporters of both the Eisenhower administration and Dulles, sent home dispatches asking if the secretary were signaling a shift to "isolationism." At a press conference, Eisenhower said he had not read Dulles's statement but that he believed it said nothing more than that "a greater unification of Europe, politically, economically, militarily, will greatly add to the safety of the Western World."[65] Pro-administration newspapers and magazines hastened to print assurances that Dulles had merely been "talking tough" to a laggard ally, and "agonizing reappraisal" became one of several phrases cited thereafter as evidence of an inclination by Dulles toward hyperbole.[66]

After Eisenhower's tactful repudiation of Dulles, it was more than two years before any American official again suggested that the commitment of American forces to Germany might be reexamined. The suggestion then came from joint chiefs chairman Admiral Arthur Radford. It was a suggestion not for "agonizing reappraisal" but merely for a rationalized reduction in deployed forces. It was probably not meant for public venting, at least not by Radford. The leak almost surely came from someone who opposed the "Radford Plan." The reaction, at home as well as in Europe, resembled a firestorm. The administration denied that anything of the sort was in contemplation. Reappraisal, agonizing or otherwise, had become heresy.

This might not have been the case had nuclear weapons not become an integral part of the American commitment. The costs of the military establishment had begun to cause concern in the last year of the Truman administration. Since Eisenhower came into office committed to cutting back all government spending, these costs seemed to him and his economic aides to be intolerable. The curve of cost for new technology seemed to be shooting due north. A great deal more money bought a great deal less in the way of deployed military forces. A P-38 fighter-bomber of World War II had cost less than $135,000. Its early 1950s replacement, the F-84, cost five times as much. The mid-1950s successor, the F-105, came in at $2.2 million a copy.[67] The British had concluded during the first year of post-Korean rearmament that they could not keep up the planned pace. Trying to do so while maintaining the new welfare state led them, in the phrase of a left-wing member of the cabinet, to "the arithmetic of Bedlam."[68] Eisenhower, as president, could have concluded that the United States simply could not afford the forces and commitments for which Eisenhower, the supreme commander, had been partly responsible.

Nuclear weapons saved Eisenhower from such a choice (or seemed to). Back in the year before Korea, when the Soviets exploded their first fission device, American officialdom had gone through its debate about whether or not to develop a fusion weapon, a hydrogen bomb. Truman had decided in favor of proceeding. He had also decided to give the Atomic Energy Commission more money so that it would not have to cut back on production of fission weapons. The opponents of the hydrogen bomb had argued, among other things, for a priority effort to develop fission weapons suitable for tactical use. The enlarged AEC budget made it possible to pursue simultaneously research on both big weapons and small weapons. Research along both lines sped up when, as part of the Korean rearmament program, Truman authorized a near tripling in AEC production facilities, enlargement of existing weapons laboratories, and creation of a new laboratory at Livermore, California.[69]

Technical breakthroughs enabled the weapons laboratories to tell the services that they would eventually be able to provide nuclear weapons in almost any desired shape, size, yield, or quantity. This promised to solve everyone's problems. The president and Congress could cut defense spending on the argument that nuclear firepower compensated for having fewer men and fewer deployed units. Officials in the State Department and in American missions in Europe could invoke the same argument to explain how the alliance could achieve deterrence without coming close to fulfilling the Lisbon force goals. And the services were comparatively content because they could maintain their relative percentages, pare back on expensive and bothersome ready forces, and invest where they preferred to invest—in force structure and advanced weaponry. Earlier, many service elements had expressed skepticism about the military utility of nuclear weapons. That had been when big, clumsy atomic bombs seemed usable only by the Strategic Air Command. Now, however, there seemed to be nuclear roles for everyone—even the infantry.[70]

In 1954–55 the army and the Tactical Air Command boasted that they were beefing up elements in Europe with nuclear firepower. MC-48 provided alliance endorsement to a voluntary American commitment not only to defend the front line in Germany with American troops but to make any war that began there a nuclear war, whatever the consequences.[71]

This last adaptation was made without serious high-level consideration either by politicians or by officials in Washington. It is explicable only as a product of a combination of optimism and ignorance. Decision makers did not possess much technical understanding of nuclear weapons. They relied either on technicians or on junior staffers. For whatever reasons, the latter let the former believe that weapons promised for the distant future were actually available in the present and that "tactical" nuclear weapons were simply more efficient forms of familiar weapons, involving, therefore, no particularly difficult new operational problems.[72]

The truth was that "tactical" nuclear weapons of the 1950s were grossly unsuited for any battlefield use, and Americans at NATO headquarters, cleared for access to nuclear weapons data, could not figure out what possibly to do with the weapons actually deployed in the theater. But that is another story, not to be told here.[73]

To conclude: It is the premise of this paper that the American commitment to Germany, in the particular form that it had by 1955, needs to be explained—that it involves action by a great power not to have been predicted easily by any general theory of international relations. That premise is not unchallengeable. One might point to many examples of great empires placing soldiers of their own on distant marches—Romans in Britain; Spaniards in the Netherlands; Britons in Afghanistan; or, for that matter, the Group of Soviet Forces in Germany. But, in all such examples that come to mind, the soldiers were policing as well as protecting. In Greece and the Levant, where the Romans had allies, the garrisons were mostly Greek. The Spaniards did not station *tercios* on the Danube. The British made an art of enlisting local princes. Outside of Germany, the Russians have usually put upon their allies as much of the burden of local defense as possible. The American (and British) posture in Germany after 1949 seems an exception.

For explanation, one must look in part to the evidence of mounting Soviet offensive military power, made suddenly more ominous by events in Korea; to the exigencies of European allies; and to peculiarities of the American political system. Without all three factors, the actual outcome would have been less likely.

The peculiarities of the American system particularly in play were the newness of the apparatus of national power, the inherent fragmentation of the governmental apparatus as a whole, the burden of lessons drawn from recent history, and an extraordinary openness to influence from sources outside the nation.

The effects of newness in the national security apparatus were evident in jealous, sometimes mindless guarding of turf by elements of the bureaucracy. Here, the armed services are particularly conspicuous. No service or service element would give up a fraction of what it had won in the struggles over defense organization and service roles and missions during the postwar transition. As service chiefs, even the most statesmanlike of generals and admirals—Omar Bradley and Forrest Sherman, for example—looked at foreign commitments in terms of their effects on budgets and force structure, not the other way around. They tended not to ask, "What does a commitment to defense of Germany imply for the American military establishment?" Instead, they asked, "How can a commitment to defense of Germany benefit my service?" While such behavior was not unknown in other, older governments, it was usually subject to correctives. In the United States, correctives would eventually begin to develop, particularly as the office of the secretary of defense enlarged its functions. In the period considered here, there were none.[74]

The varieties of fragmentation ticked off earlier were all in play. Politicians responded to swings in public mood. Officials exerted themselves so to maneuver the politicians as to make them act in the supposed national interest. The Lisbon force goals, for example, owed something to the fact that Truman and Congress had begun to lean toward reducing defense expenditures. Officials hoped to lock them into comparatively high levels of spending. At every step, American policy (when it can be called such) resulted from complex interplay between and within the executive and legislative branches. When Marshall or Dulles warned Europeans that Congress might withhold aid, they were not conjuring up entirely imaginary risks. When Eisenhower began in 1951 to increase his estimate of the numbers of divisions needed on the central front, he did so knowing that, at that moment, Congress was disposed to give the U.S. Army whatever it asked.

The weight of history was omnipresent. Truman and Eisenhower, Acheson and Dulles, and most of their colleagues worried constantly lest "isolationism" revive. Dulles probably meant sincerely his warning to the NATO Council about "separatist" tendencies in the United States. At the time, Robert Taft was majority leader in the Senate, and Joe McCarthy still rode high. Responsible American politicians and officials worried not only about what actually might happen but about what Europeans thought might happen. American officials spent a lot of time assuring Europeans that the United States would not abandon them. Sometimes they were whistling in the dark; sometimes they felt that reassurance had to go beyond words.[75]

Finally, one cannot leave out the roles within the American political system of Britons and of Europeans such as Monnet and Adenauer. The British record of influencing American governmental action was by no means one of uniform success. Congress had been slow to vote postwar credits. A few key Senators frustrated the British desire—widely shared among American officials—for a nuclear partnership. But the record certainly had its plusses. The Truman Doctrine was a triumph for the Foreign Office. The North Atlantic Treaty had its origins at least as much in London and Ottawa as in Washington. Despite the breakup of the Combined Chiefs of Staff organization, British influence on American military thinking remained strong. The "New Look" doctrine adopted by the Eisenhower administration as a general rationale for reduced defense spending apparently had its origins in earlier British air staff and chiefs of staff committee papers. At many levels, British officials worked with American officials much as they might have worked had the two nations formed a union. But this collaboration usually concerned American policy, not British policy. In papers of the cabinet, the Foreign Office, and other British government departments, one seldom sees evidence of Americans taking part in decision making. The systems worked differently.[76]

Except for Monnet and a few of his associates, the French were slower to note and take advantage of the openness and fragmentation of American political life. They had great potential leverage, for Americans preferred Paris to other European capitals. There were always many more diplomats, economic aid officials, and journalists in Paris than even in London or Rome, let alone Bonn. And junketing congressmen usually scheduled long stopovers there. But French politicians and officials found it hard to make use of these assets. While a reputation for being able to get something out of Washington could be useful to a French politician, it all too easily turned into a reputation for being an American pawn. Frenchmen who might have learned to work Washington as British officials learned to work it were simply not long enough in office.[77]

The Germans adapted more readily. Despite his advanced age and his seeming simplicity of mind, Adenauer learned quickly the complex rules of the American political game. Through reporters in Bonn, he used the American press to provoke debate within the United States. He seemed instinctively to understand what questions, if posed publicly to presidents or members of Congress, created a likelihood of yielding the answers he wanted. He did not say to American reporters, for example, what he said to McCloy. He did not tell them he wanted a West German militia. He simply talked about the East German Volkspolizei. These reporters then caused questions to be asked at home about what the Americans and West Germans should do in response. Possibly Adenauer had coaching from acquaintances who understood American politics. Possibly he benefited from long experience as mayor of Cologne, seeking to affect decisions in the distant, somewhat alien, capital, Berlin.[78] In any case, Adenauer had become by the mid-1950s one of the individuals most influential inside the American government.

Participation in the American political system was neither painless nor cost free. Britons and Europeans often had to make sacrifices in order to gain, within the United States, the allies they needed for a coalition that could move a president or pass a piece of legislation. They were often frustrated. The history of British efforts to improve nuclear relationships, and of German efforts to regain the Saarland, serve as examples.

But the experiences of America's allies were not the experiences of colonial subjects or of people in *dependencia*. They were, rather, the experiences of Americans. The same kinds of sacrifices were made, the same kinds of frustrations were suffered by politicians or officials acting in the interests of New York or Texas or in the interests of the Department of the Interior, the Economic Cooperation Administration, or the navy. The major allies of the United States under the North Atlantic Treaty had not become elements in an empire—even, in Geir Lundestad's nice phrase, "an empire by invitation."[79] They had become, at least temporarily, part of an organic federal system.

And that, more than anything else, may explain the American commitment to Germany as of the mid-1950s. American institutions were in flux. The many-sided bargaining within the American government easily included—indeed reached out for—new participants. History gave Americans feelings of guilt and obligation toward Europeans. Europeans needed American aid and protection. The American republic, as a result, embraced Britain and Western Europe as if they had become equal states in the American union. In this framework, the American commitment to Germany seems less surprising. If foreign armies had menaced New York or Texas, Americans would have posted troops and been prepared to assume mortal risk. Why not for Germany?

This was a perspective of Americans, of course, not of Germans. Officials and analysts in the German Federal Republic continued to look upon the United States as a separate foreign power. Their operating assumption was that the United States acted on its own conceptions of its own distinguishable national interests. Some difference in perspective has persisted; thus far it has produced no harm. During the Cold War, it manifested itself chiefly in cross-purpose exchanges concerning "burden sharing"—who was to pay for what within the NATO tent.[80] As developments in Europe bring nearer a benign version of the New Order, continuing differences in understanding of the history and nature of the relationship may have more serious consequences.

SAMUEL F. WELLS, Jr.

Charles de Gaulle and the French Withdrawal from NATO's Integrated Command

American specialists on international affairs tend to see the French withdrawal from the military command of NATO as a vivid illustration of the exercise of power by a willful French leader. The general view is that Charles de Gaulle waited until the political situation in France became so disorganized and unpleasant that he was returned to power with vastly expanded authority and given a mandate to restore his country to international prominence. This view holds that de Gaulle sought to do this by vigorously protecting French economic interests, by developing an independent nuclear force and emphasizing its reflected power and glory for all aspects of French national life, and by standing up to the domineering Americans and ultimately forcing American and Canadian troops, as well as NATO headquarters, off French soil.

In reading much of the secondary literature and some of the primary material that is available, and in interviewing a number of participants from those years, a somewhat different view emerges today. This evidence indicates that well before de Gaulle returned to power in 1958, many French political and military leaders objected strongly to United States policies for NATO and those policies calling for an elimination of colonialism, but that support for the Atlantic alliance was sufficiently strong that de Gaulle's continuation in power and his firm insistence on his policies were essential to their successful implementation. It also shows that, despite the willingness of a significant number of U.S. officials to make significant concessions to accommodate de Gaulle, no compromises possible for Washington would have satisfied the French leader.

Immediately after the end of World War II, France was in an extremely difficult position. Heavily damaged by the war, politically fractured by the experience of occupation and widespread collaboration and the presence of a large Communist movement, the nation labored under the cloud of defeat by the Germans in the initial phases of three wars. For such a France the main problem became how to restore national vitality and resist the challenge of Soviet power while making sure that Germany did not become a threat again.

The basic solutions to these problems came in careful state management of economic recovery and participation in the North Atlantic Alliance and the European Coal and Steel Community as the instruments for developing and coordinating the power of the West and binding Germany tightly to these institutions. The central role of the United States in each of these aspects of recovery and reconstruction was essential and generally welcomed by the French.

In the 1950s new challenges to the French power developed from two sources. Colonial wars, first in Indochina and then in Algeria, cost a great deal in money and manpower and, in each case, ultimately proved unwinnable. Further complicating the situation in the perception of the French nationalists was the domination of the international system by the United States. French leaders of all political persuasions became increasingly uncomfortable under the long shadow cast from Washington. They felt marginalized by American nuclear power, constrained by the hegemony of the dollar, and intensely irritated by the American opposition to colonialism as manifested in refusal to support the French at Dien Bien Phu and in Algeria, as well as Washington's opposition to the Anglo-French-Israeli intervention at Suez. Embittered by what they saw as American opposition to French interests, many colonial administrators and military officers would have agreed with the judgment of Foreign Minister Christian Pineau about Suez: "The main victim of the affair was the Atlantic alliance. . . . If our allies have abandoned us in difficult, even dramatic, circumstances, they would be capable of doing so again if Europe in its turn found itself in danger."[1]

Many French leaders wanted to achieve a high degree of autonomy from American direction for their military forces well before de Gaulle returned to power in 1958. As early as 1951, this trend was evident when the NATO Council asked the "three wise men," Sir Edwin Plowden, Jean Monnet, and W. Averell Harriman, to develop proposals to reconcile the vastly increased military needs of the alliance during the Korean War period with the budgetary constraints faced by each nation. At this time the NATO representatives met with the highest levels of the French military. During these discussions they learned that the French government would make every effort to increase its spending for defense, but the military leaders insisted that the French forces would not be amalgamated within any European Defense Community or within NATO and that French command would have to be retained. In 1953, when General Alfred Gruenther as SACEUR began staff planning for NATO's use of nuclear weapons, the French took full part in the planning effort known as the New Approach Group but showed a distinctly independent approach. Former SACEUR General Andrew J. Goodpaster was a member of the group and recalls that in the midst of their work they received news of the successful detonation of a fusion device, or hydrogen bomb. He and a number of his colleagues, later to include President Eisenhower, concluded that the hydrogen weapon was not really usable as a military weapon and that planning should take this into account. The seeds of significant future differences were sown at this point because the French rejected this distinction and proceeded to make the hydrogen bomb the centerpiece of their emerging strategy of dissuasion.[2]

French leaders greatly resented Anglo-American cooperation on security issues that appeared designed to exclude France. In 1957 Paris tried to link the proposed deployment of U.S. IRBMs on French territory to U.S. nuclear-weapons aid. When this failed, French officials were all the more wounded when the United States revived nuclear cooperation with the British in 1958 as part of a bargain that included stationing American missiles in the United Kingdom. Political and military leaders in France also objected strongly to the dominance of American and British officers in the NATO military organization. In the early days of the alliance, France had been pleased to participate as part of a three-member Standing Group with Britain and the United States. But when this group was replaced by SACEUR and SHAPE as the focal point of allied military planning, the French became increasingly resentful of Anglo-Saxon dominance, especially on matters of nuclear weapons and strategy.

By the time Charles de Gaulle returned to power in June 1958, the stage was set for a fundamental change in French policy. Many of de Gaulle's views had been established during World War II, and he had refined them in the period he had been out of power. His assessment of France's international situation in 1958 contained a number of key elements. He believed the problem in Algeria had to be resolved and was prepared, if necessary, to withdraw from that important colonial territory in order to restore political unity and revive the economy at home. As a result of crises in the summer of 1958 in both Lebanon and the Formosa Straits, the new French leader believed that problems in the Third World would heavily involve the resources and attention of the United States and, more seriously, could drag France into an unwanted clash between the superpowers.

In the international system, de Gaulle believed that the growth of Soviet nuclear power would increase strategic stability by making each superpower vulnerable to the other. The Soviets had tested a hydrogen device in August 1953 and successfully orbited *Sputnik I* in October 1957. With the foreseeable balance in nuclear weapons between the superpowers, de Gaulle was convinced that nuclear war was not likely. He believed further that a Soviet attack on Western Europe was highly improbable and that, in its own interests, the United States was committed strongly to the security of Western Europe. The Berlin crises beginning in November 1958 served to confirm his estimate of the U.S. commitment to Europe.

From this evaluation de Gaulle concluded that France, as part of its national renewal and as a central part of his own policy, should chart its own course. After several speeches indicating that he thought France should play a larger role in the direction of Western strategy, he made a formal proposal on 17 September 1958 for a tripartite directorate for global policy by France, Great Britain, and the United States. When several negotiating sessions between representatives of the three countries made no progress, he announced on 7 March 1959 the withdrawal of the French Mediterranean fleet from NATO command as a first step of putting pressure on his negotiating partners. In this initiative, de Gaulle was also motivated by the desire to gain a free hand to use these naval forces in the Algerian war without any alliance constraints. His second major initiative was to advance full speed in the development of a French nuclear weapons program. He requested support from the United States at a time when Washington had agreed to give renewed nuclear assistance to Britain. The United States was able to give some enriched uranium (U-235) but did not provide the technology to construct the submarine nuclear reactors that de Gaulle wished to obtain. With the U.S. rejection in large measure of each of these requests, the process of French withdrawal from NATO had begun.[3]

A steady series of French initiatives and negotiations continued for about three years after the initial tripartite directorate proposal of September 1958. Following the withdrawal of the French

Mediterranean fleet from NATO command in March 1959, de Gaulle sent private letters to President Dwight Eisenhower about the need for joint planning and control of nuclear weapons. Although Washington did not discuss this idea with French representatives, General Lauris Norstad as SACEUR began to move supplies and equipment into northern France during the Berlin crisis early in 1959 and began construction of igloos for housing nuclear weapons. In June 1959 the French government announced that no U.S. or NATO nuclear weapons could be based on French soil unless de Gaulle's conditions were met for joint decision on their use and for French control of the warheads. In response, General Norstad decided several weeks later to move from France to bases in Britain and West Germany some 250 U.S. fighter-bombers with nuclear weapons capability. This was the first withdrawal of NATO forces from French territory.

On 3 November 1959 Charles de Gaulle made a speech at the École militaire stating several important points of policy. He made a strong case for autonomous French control over national defense, announced that a nuclear *force de frappe* would be available in the near future, and strongly implied that the integration of French military forces within NATO could not last much longer. In his complex, orotund style the President declared:

> The defense of France must be French. This is a necessity which has not always been familiar in these recent years. I know that. It is indispensable that it become familiar again. If a country like France must make war, it must be her war. Her effort must be her effort. If it were otherwise, our country would be in contradiction with everything which it has been from its beginnings, with its role, with its esteem for itself, with its soul. Naturally, the defense of France, in the event, would be joined with that of other countries. That is in the nature of things. But it is indispensable that it be ours—that France defend herself by herself, for herself and in her way.

After insisting that national defense had been the central purpose of the government of France for centuries, he turned to nuclear issues:

> In consequence, it is evidently necessary that we be able to provide ourselves in the coming years with a force that can act on our account, with what is customarily called a *force de frappe*,

able to be deployed anywhere at any time. It goes without saying that the basis for this force will be nuclear armament—whether we make it or buy it—which must belong to us. And, since eventually France can be destroyed from any point in the world, our force must be designed to act anywhere on earth.[4]

Within a few weeks after this speech the first French nuclear test occurred slightly ahead of schedule in the Sahara desert on 13 February 1960.

The speech at the École militaire reflected a clear choice for an independent French defense posture. While not obvious at that time, this presentation is now widely accepted as the essence of Gaullist defense policy. The present French ambassador to NATO, Gabriel Robin, recently identified the École militaire speech as the basic statement of de Gaulle's defense autonomy. Robin, who has been characterized by a colleague in the French diplomatic service as "an archeo-Gaullist" because of the purity of his views, said that "the general direction of de Gaulle's policy was set by 1959, but its actual terms were not set and responded to events as they developed." Several other French specialists on defense and foreign affairs have independently stated the same view.[5]

The rapid progress of the French nuclear weapons program did not surprise President Eisenhower. He had always felt, General Goodpaster remembers, that the United States could not expect any other result if it refused to share nuclear technology and rejected the French proposal for a NATO triumvirate. Eisenhower understood de Gaulle's desire for French autonomy and the role that nuclear weapons played in achieving that goal, and at a press conference in February 1960 he expressed a willingness to help the French. With regard to providing nuclear technology and possibly the custody of nuclear weapons to allies including the French, Eisenhower said:

> From the very beginning, from what I knew about allied cooperation . . . I have always been of the belief that we should not deny to our allies what your potential enemy already has. We do want allies to be treated as partners and allies, and not as junior members of a firm who are to be seen but not heard.
> So I would think that it would be better, for the interests of the United States, to make our law more liberal, as long as we classify our countries as those that we are confident, by our treaties and everything else, they'd stand by us, and stand by us in time of trouble.[6]

But opposition in the State and Defense Departments and in the Joint Committee on Atomic Energy of the Congress was too strong, and only very limited assistance was provided to France.[7]

The administration of John F. Kennedy produced a different relationship with France. Whereas Eisenhower had sought to go as far as he could to satisfy French demands, Kennedy was more insistent on American leadership of NATO and on a revised form of nuclear strategy. Kennedy refused to consider the tripartite directorate proposal; he linked any provision of U.S. nuclear aid to a French commitment to forego the development of an independent nuclear force, and he had sharp disagreements with France over the Berlin crisis. In addition, Kennedy insisted on centralized control over both strategic and theater nuclear weapons in the process of developing and imposing his administration's strategy of flexible response. Although Kennedy was somewhat sympathetic to de Gaulle's nuclear ambitions, he ultimately adopted the policy urged by Secretary of Defense Robert S. McNamara and his civilian strategists. McNamara summed up his attitude toward the French nuclear program in his speech at Ann Arbor, Michigan, on 16 June 1962, when he said, "In short, then, limited nuclear capabilities, operating independently, are dangerous, expensive, prone to obsolescence, and lacking in credibility as a deterrent." By the summer of 1962 an unpleasant antagonism had developed between the Kennedy administration and President de Gaulle as a result of differences on a wide range of defense issues.[8]

Along with the progressive disengagement from NATO functions, de Gaulle kept certain connections with the alliance that served practical French interests. Even though American nuclear weapons could not be based on French soil, French forces in Germany were allowed to accept them in order to gain experience in handling atomic warheads and delivery systems. France also agreed to place its first Tactical Air Command (CATAC) within SACEUR's extended air defense command in order to gain access to NATO's new early-warning system, NADGE (NATO Air Defense Ground Environment). And despite the fact that the French fleet in the Mediterranean was withdrawn from NATO, it participated in the usual NATO maneuvers in the summer of 1959.

Resolution of the Algerian war and French recognition of the independence of Algeria on 3 July 1962 accomplished one of de Gaulle's principal tasks. He was now able to concentrate more fully on restoring French unity and prestige and on expanding its role in

Europe. In an important statement at a news conference on 15 May 1962, de Gaulle announced that the three principal objectives of France in coming months would be to free herself of the obligations of colonial administration, to participate fully in the construction of Europe, and to create "a modern national [defense] force" to allow France, "whatever happens, to play our own part in our destiny."[9]

In response to a question asking if France intended to modify the terms of its participation in NATO, the president described how conditions had changed since France first joined the integrated alliance military structure. He emphasized how the growth of Soviet nuclear power and the mutual vulnerability of the superpowers placed in question when they would use their nuclear armaments and whether they would be used in the defense of Europe. Then he showed how the circumstances for France had also changed:

> On the other hand, a French atomic deterrent force is coming into existence and is going to grow continuously. It is a relatively modest force, it is true, but one which is changing and will completely change the conditions of our own defense, those of our intervention in faraway lands and those of the contribution that we would be able to make to safeguard our allies. Furthermore, a gradual return of our military forces from Algeria is enabling us to acquire a modernized army; an army which is not, I daresay, destined to play a separate or isolated role, but one which must and can play a role that would be France's own. Finally, it is absolutely necessary, morally and politically, for us to make our army a more integral part of the nation. Therefore, it is necessary for us to restation it, for the most part, on our soil; for us to give it once again a direct responsibility in the external security of the country; in short, for our defense to become once again a national defense. It is indispensable, I repeat, both morally and politically.[10]

To satisfy the requirements of "a national defense," de Gaulle reorganized French defense forces to fulfill new missions under national command. The two divisions that came back from Algeria did not return to the NATO command, and in 1964 they joined with tactical air units to form the First Corps. The next year all tactical air forces were put under national command. The First Corps was to be the main intervention force in a European war (referred to as *la corps de bataille*), and it was designed to work closely with the warning-shot mission of tactical nuclear weapons. Early in 1966 the

Mirage IV fighter-bomber was deployed, and the *force de frappe* became an operational reality.[11]

While defense reorganization proceeded, de Gaulle pursued a set of parallel diplomatic policies aimed at creating a European confederation of nations as an alternative to NATO and the European Economic Community (EEC). An early version was the Fouchet Plan for political and security cooperation. Under negotiation in 1961–62, this proposal lost virtually all support outside France when Paris insisted on adding economic affairs to the authority of the group. De Gaulle then worked to expand his warm, personal relationship with Konrad Adenauer into a broader Franco-German entente. The military staffs of the two states had worked together closely during the stages of the Berlin crisis, and this cooperation was expanded and formalized in the Élysée Treaty of 22 January 1963, which provided for regular security consultations, exchanges of personnel, and joint arms production. The West German Bundestag thwarted French hopes for this treaty by attaching a preamble that declared the Federal Republic's close association with the United States and its strong support for "common defense within the framework of [the] North Atlantic Alliance and the integration of armed forces of members of that Pact."[12]

At the same time that he was working to build a continental coalition, de Gaulle took several steps to exclude Great Britain from participation in European institutions. Viewing Britain as a Trojan horse filled with American values and policies, de Gaulle had limited the Fouchet Plan to continental states. When Prime Minister Harold Macmillan and John F. Kennedy negotiated a deal in Nassau to share American Polaris missiles with Britain and offered to make similar missiles available to France for use within a multinational nuclear force, de Gaulle seized the opportunity. At his press conference on 14 January 1963 he rejected the Polaris offer and announced that France would veto Britain's application for membership in the EEC.[13]

Although his efforts to create a European alternative to NATO achieved no success, the stage was set by the end of 1965 for the completion of the process of withdrawing from the military structure of the alliance. The military reorganization was complete, and the *force de frappe* was operational. France was increasingly critical of the expanding American war effort in Vietnam and its potential complications with the Soviet Union. De Gaulle had won reelection on 19 December to a second presidential term of seven years and would not have to be concerned about the possibility that a successor might modify or revoke his policies on NATO before they could be fully implemented. Some evidence suggests that the French leader wanted to present a bold example of national independence before his scheduled visit to Moscow in June 1966.[14]

By February 1966 de Gaulle was ready to implement his plan for France's withdrawal from the military structure of NATO. On 21 February he announced at a press conference that from that date he planned to alter France's relationship with the alliance in order to restore "a normal situation of sovereignty" in which France would command all forces and equipment on French territory as well as all French forces outside France. He further spelled out the implications of this decision in messages to each allied government in March, concluding with a memorandum on 29 March in which he set 1 April 1967 as the deadline for all NATO personnel and equipment to be out of France. Allied governments held a series of discussions about how to respond to this dramatic change, and they decided essentially to accept it with minimum fanfare and try to keep the French military as involved within the alliance as possible.[15]

In order to evaluate the capacity for compromise on each side, it is useful to engage in some counterfactual analysis and speculation. A different outcome would have required a fundamental change of policy in either Paris or Washington, and ultimately a change by either Charles de Gaulle or by one of three U.S. presidents (Eisenhower, Kennedy, or Johnson). Given the ego and certitude that characterized each man and the complex range of problems facing each nation, we are talking about prospects for change that are a very low order of probability.

With regard to France, scholars and European integrationists have long speculated about another path that might have been taken. This would have been the route favored by Jean Monnet and his colleagues of building an integrated Europe, including economic, military, and political institutions. Given the problems posed by the Algerian war and the whole range of political and military attitudes held by General de Gaulle, it is not possible to make a case for this policy option in the years of his presidency. Had de Gaulle not come to power, France would not have been able to make such a change of course regarding NATO. And with de Gaulle in power, a policy that subordinated France to Europe was unthinkable.

The other logical alternative for France would have been for de Gaulle to compromise his demands. No participant in those decisions and no scholar since that day contends that this was possible. French participants of quite different political views agree that de Gaulle was firm in his objective. Gabriel Robin, the Gaullist ambassador to NATO today, contends that compromise by de Gaulle was neither possible nor desirable. A highly respected diplomat, François de Rose, who spent 1962–63 without assignment, presumably for entertaining unorthodox ideas about the planned cooperation of French forces with NATO forces, agrees that compromise was not possible. De Rose argues that once French nuclear weapons became operational, the general would never accept another nation having a voice in their use. "Pulling out of NATO was the decision he wanted, and the rest was pretext," he declares. Jean Laloy, a distinguished diplomat and specialist on the Soviet Union, whose career was damaged by standing up to de Gaulle, points out that a number of American officials, especially President Eisenhower, tried without success to satisfy de Gaulle's demands. Laloy insists: "De Gaulle was a very difficult man. He was very intelligent, but his decisions were not always based on reason. He had an immense ego and a long memory. Many of his actions were based on passion, not reason. When one told him something he did not want to hear and made a very strong case for it, he, generally, made an ugly face and did not answer. He was very unpredictable."[16]

American officials involved in shaping policy for France basically agree about de Gaulle's inflexibility. Robert R. Bowie, a former head of the planning staff and counselor of the Department of State, argues that "de Gaulle had a view of France's role and of the need for France to be an equal partner in any cooperative venture that made it impossible for France and the United States to cooperate. Since America was so powerful compared to France, any cooperation would be between unequal partners and was therefore unacceptable to de Gaulle." A foreign service officer specializing in French affairs, Edgar J. Beigel, put it in less personal terms: "De Gaulle had his mind set on a series of objectives for France which the United States could not accept."[17]

The possibilities of a different policy in the United States were higher. Eisenhower clearly was more willing than Kennedy to compromise and go as far as he could to meet de Gaulle's demands, and it became clear in 1966 that a number of European specialists in the Defense Department, the National Security Council, and some junior officers at the State Department were more willing to compromise than were the senior leadership at the State Department, especially those around Under Secretary George Ball and the senior civilians at the Defense Department.

Among American participants in these affairs, General Andrew Goodpaster is the strongest supporter of the possibility of a different outcome. Goodpaster was defense liaison officer and staff secretary to President Eisenhower from 1954–61 and later supreme allied commander in Europe. For him the principal obstacles to compromise were Secretary of Defense Robert McNamara and his civilian analysts who wanted to rationalize U.S. strategy into a series of steps on an escalation ladder and control all types of nuclear weapons from Washington. Goodpaster emphasizes the need for military commanders to have operational flexibility. He declares: "It is simply impossible to predict how a war will develop or how nations will choose to use their forces. It cannot be planned out in every detail and controlled from a great distance." He also believes that keeping the alliance together is more important than any item of doctrine, and he contends that a compromise could have been offered to the French that might have been acceptable to de Gaulle. He explains General Eisenhower's attitude toward de Gaulle:

> On numerous occasions General Eisenhower said that you always had to realize what type of man you're dealing with in de Gaulle. He will go his own way. Eisenhower had a very high regard for de Gaulle and felt that he was just what France needed at this point in its history. But he would always add that we will pay a large price in our relations with France and in alliance unity for de Gaulle's restoration of French self-esteem. Nevertheless Eisenhower wanted to do everything possible to keep France within the alliance.[18]

Other Americans are less sanguine about the possibility of an American compromise that would have satisfied the French. Eisenhower's compromises up through 1960 had not been sufficient to change de Gaulle's mind. Robert Bowie points out that his 1960 proposal for a multilateral nuclear force (MLF) had as one of its goals to head off national nuclear forces. He believed that a combination of pressure and persuasion might have brought the British into such a force and feels that France might have joined after de Gaulle left office if other NATO members had participated, and especially if the European Economic Community had made significant progress. But, acknowledging that the MLF proposal was always a long shot, he concludes that he "does not believe that there was a course of action we could have chosen which would have prevented de Gaulle from taking the course he did."[19]

The prospects for any different outcome under Lyndon Johnson were extremely remote. While not averse to compromise, Johnson needed an assurance that concessions would bring personal advantage later. His fundamental concern was winning election as president in his own right in 1964, and to this end he concentrated on domestic issues and on standing up to international communism in foreign affairs. After his election, he proceeded to expand the war in Vietnam in a quest for victory. Although he did not want a confrontation with de Gaulle, Johnson was unwilling to alter American strategic and alliance policy to satisfy the French leader. There is no evidence to suggest that compromise was possible as late as 1965.[20]

The foregoing analysis forces one to conclude that, within the feasible policy choices, the United States could not have satisfied French demands. Charles de Gaulle wanted a degree of independence in national defense that could only be achieved by harshly rejecting the NATO military structure and the leadership of the United States. He also wanted to make France the dominant nation in Western Europe and was willing to ruin the EEC if he could not turn it to his own use. De Gaulle had visions of a special French relationship with the Soviet Union, and he wanted to establish firm control over his own generals as an additional goal. A dramatic withdrawal from the military components of the Atlantic alliance advanced all of these interests and enhanced his reputation as a powerful, independent leader.

Analysis of de Gaulle's relations with NATO shows a few points where time could have been bought and tactics modified. The United States could have accepted the directory proposal in some form and could have provided nuclear assistance in greater amount to France.

But nothing done by American leaders would have changed de Gaulle's objective of separating France from a NATO dominated by the United States. It is hard to avoid the acerbic conclusion of John Newhouse, who wrote as early as 1970 that "whatever the mistakes of the American and British leaders of the period—and these were numerous—there never was a possibility of doing serious business with de Gaulle on reasonable terms. Still, in both Washington and

London, numerous thoughtful men devoted much of their time, often the better part of it, to trying to find the key to a productive relationship, or *any* relationship, with de Gaulle." Despite divisions between people who wanted to compromise and those who wanted to be "hard-nosed," Newhouse argues that "the heavy investment in effort and time made by so many sensible and well-intentioned Americans and Britons—Presidents and Prime Ministers among them—was wasted. It was a tragic waste; de Gaulle was a tragic figure."[21]

Many political and defense leaders in France felt in 1966 that de Gaulle went too far. Even more feel that way today. Indeed, a number of steps have been taken between Washington and Paris to develop liaison and joint plans, to share technology—even nuclear technology, and to cooperate politically. As conflict between the two blocs wound down at the end of the 1980s, it is now possible that new bridges may be built between Washington and Paris and between Paris and the North Atlantic Alliance.

JOAN HOFF-WILSON

"Nixingerism," NATO, and Détente

At first glance Richard M. Nixon and Henry A. Kissinger appear to be an odd couple—an American Quaker and a German Jew—to collaborate in the formation of U.S. foreign policy. In fact, however, by the time they met in 1968 they shared many similar viewpoints and similar operational styles. Both thrived on covert activity and decisions reached in private, both distrusted the federal bureaucracy, both resented any attempts by Congress to interfere with their diplomatic initiatives, and both agreed that the United States could impose order and stability in foreign affairs if the White House controlled policy by appearing conciliatory but acting tough. Neither man had previously headed any complex organizational structure, but both thought that "personalized executive control" and formalistic procedures and structures would enable them to succeed in the area of their greatest combined experiences; namely, foreign policy.

Most important, Nixon and Kissinger each had a history of previous failure and rejection by academic peers or government officials that made them very sensitive to protecting themselves and their positions of power from public and private criticism. Often their concern for self-protection was reflected in their obsession with all types of eavesdropping, whether in the form of wiretaps or reconnaissance flights over Communist territory. They even eavesdropped on themselves: Nixon by installing an automatic taping system at the White House and Kissinger by having some of his meetings and all of his phone conversations either taped or transcribed from notes.

Little wonder that the president and his national security adviser developed a "special relationship."[1] However, their partnership went beyond the collaboration on foreign policy that existed between

Woodrow Wilson and Colonel Edward M. House or between Franklin D. Roosevelt and Harry Hopkins. Characterized by excessive meetings and telephone calls, it became a relationship that brought out the worst characteristics of both men, especially the paranoid and dark sides of each.[2] Nonetheless, it was a relationship that appeared capable of significantly changing the conduct of U.S. foreign policy in a time of transition. Despite structural reforms[3] and their combined personal determination and expertise, Nixon and Kissinger were never able to institutionalize their "grand design" approach to foreign affairs. Instead, their special relationship only temporarily succeeded in appearing to transform "the conduct of diplomacy into a perpetual *tour de force*."[4] Like the concept of détente itself, "Nixinger" foreign policy proved more tenuous and ephemeral than either man has yet to admit.

Through a Byzantine public and private diplomatic process, détente came to represent as much symbol as substance of the Nixon administration's evolving foreign policy. Détente's literal French and Russian meaning (for the word *razryadka*) as a "relaxing or easing of tensions between nations," has no precise English equivalent. Even if there were an equivalent, it would pale beside the complexities involved in realizing it, however imperfectly, between 1967 and 1975. At one level détente became more important as a domestic political struggle between the president and Congress than as a debate over the actual details of either the ABM agreement or Strategic Arms Limitation Talks (SALT I); at another level it was symptomatic of the covert modus operandi of the president and his national security adviser;[5] and at still another level it symbolized White House control of foreign policy above and beyond Congress and the State Department. As an executive branch creation, détente also became associated with both the Nixon Doctrine, and Kissinger's convoluted concept of "linkage," which the Soviets refused to accept as part of détente.[6]

Finally, détente reflected Nixon's belief that "there could never be absolute parity between the U.S. and the U.S.S.R. in the area of nuclear and conventional weapons," it was time for the United States to seek *sufficiency* rather than *superiority* in describing its arms control goals. This acceptance by the president of "strategic parity" as a basis for negotiating a détente with the Soviets is all the more remarkable in light of the fact that "there was virtually no national public discussion of the issue in the United States." On 16 June 1969, Nixon simply informed Kissinger that he wanted the State and

Defense departments, as well as the CIA, to provide him with "their best judgment as to what our force level should be . . . in order to provide sufficiency." Then he added: "These recommendations should be made to me personally, on an eyes only basis, and will not be disclosed in an NSC meeting." In this fashion a great opportunity was lost to educate the American public with respect to the "real" meaning of détente within the context of sufficiency, as opposed to unnecessarily raising popular expectations by concentrating on its more simplistic and symbolic aspects. It should be remembered, however, that the very nature of American foreign policy formulation requires a certain amount of "overselling." And détente was no exception.[7]

In reality détente from a Nixinger perspective represented nothing more or less than a political and economic means or strategy or process (as opposed to an actual goal or condition) for: (1) avoiding nuclear war, (2) "building a network of mutually advantageous relationships," and (3) a way of modifying Soviet behavior by gaining its de facto acceptance of international cooperation and competition (sometimes referred to as "competitive coexistence") in order to preserve international stability by according the Soviet Union a greater stake in the status quo. Moreover, détente was very dependent on the personal interactions between individual leaders and their perceptions of their respective nation's relative strengths or of any tangible benefits accruing from "relaxed tensions."[8] To a lesser degree than some have argued, détente also reflected the domestic and international economic problems the United States faced as a result of the impact of the Vietnam War. At the time, the one thing détente did not represent under the Nixon administration was a continuation of traditional Cold War policy of containment, although the former president has equivocated on this point since resigning from office.[9]

During the summer of 1969, as U.S. foreign policy was being formulated largely in secret (including the secret bombing of Cambodia), congressional opposition loomed large in the president's mind. The ways in which he and his aides tried to outmaneuver diplomatic initiatives on the part of the U.S. Senate forced Nixon into a delicate political balancing act that ultimately shaped his and Kissinger's "grand design" more than they wanted at the time and more than they have admitted since. Their "grand design" thus became more a "balancing act" than a blueprint for U.S. diplomacy; and, much like détente, its centerpiece, remained a process rather than a fixed policy.[10] It is in these ever-shifting sands of domestic political considerations (which increased after details of the Watergate break-in and cover-up became known in 1973 and 1974) that one must look for both the strengths and weaknesses of Nixon's NATO and détente policies—rather than in the lofty realms of pure theory, as apologists for Kissinger are apt to do, or in the murky realm of the president's psychological makeup, as so many Nixon critics are prone to do.

Even before his formal inauguration as president, Nixon wrote to the secretary general of NATO: "There will be no diminution of America's commitment to the defense of Western Europe or to the Organization you so ably serve.... The North Atlantic Treaty Organization will continue to be a cornerstone of our foreign policy." He also took advantage of the twentieth anniversary of NATO on 4 April 1969 to issue a proclamation praising the organization and calling for the creation of a new Committee on the Challenge of Modern Society so the Atlantic alliance could begin to address common environmental issues. During the same time, Kissinger was privately assuring congressmen that the president wanted to "widen and improve the consultative role of NATO."[11]

Nixon was not pleased, however, by the response to his proclamation and subsequent address to the foreign and defense ministers of the fifteen NATO nations on 10 April in which he insisted that détente with the Soviet Union was possible, but that it was "not enough to talk of détente, unless at the same time, we anticipate the need for giving it the genuine political content that would prevent détente from becoming delusion."[12] The president complained to his top foreign policy advisers that the NATO representatives and members of his own administration had paid little attention to either address. "During the past 8 years Kennedy or Johnson could burp and the whole administration establishment went into action saying what a 'great and imaginative proposal' this was," Nixon privately noted. "I want some action taken immediately to see that [my] three recommendations are implemented by NATO. I think taking some rather strong positions, going beyond the toasts, the nice dinners, the 'consultations ad infinatum' [sic] might bring us a little respect in the organization which we currently do not seem to enjoy."[13]

Long before Nixon and Kissinger formally adopted the word détente to describe their diplomatic strategies and goals,[14] the president's use of the term in early foreign policy statements and in private notes for speeches clearly indicated that he thought the relationship between NATO and détente with the U.S.S.R. problematic. This uncertainty was considerably exacerbated when the bilateral, "back-channel" methods used to achieve détente first with China and then the Soviet Union bypassed the North Atlantic Treaty countries. In particular, both the ABM and SALT I agreements were negotiated with a minimum of consultation with NATO nations. The same was true of the New Economic Policy (NEP) announced by Nixon in August 1971. Among other things, the NEP unilaterally "floated" the U.S. dollar on international financial markets, setting the stage for its subsequent devaluation, and ending the post–World War II Bretton Woods international monetary system.[15] Moreover, none of the recently released Nixon presidential papers indicates that he relied extensively on the 1967 Harmel Report in formulating NATO or détente policies. That report on "The Future Tasks of the Alliance" not only called for a "détente in East-West relations," but also specifically argued that "military security and a policy of détente are not contradictory but complementary." A decade later, Kissinger repudiated this basic premise of the Harmel Report, claiming that "NATO is not equipped to be an instrument of détente." Little wonder that their respective memoirs do not focus on this significant NATO document. Nonetheless, both men were clearly aware of the European and Warsaw Pact moves toward détente that had produced the Harmel Report; Nixon, in particular, was a strong admirer of Charles de Gaulle, one of the earliest advocates of European détente.[16]

In preparation for his first presidential trip to Europe in late February (scarcely a month after assuming office), Nixon's private handwritten notes convey the distinct impression that while he recognized the complex relationship between adequate NATO defenses, disarmament, and détente, he thought that U.S. relations with Europe stood "at a great watershed. Now is the time to move. We must seize the moment. I shall do it." Moreover, in his predeparture notes Nixon repeatedly reminded himself to stress that the United States was initiating "a new era of consultation" with its European allies and that "no demonstrations shall deter me at home or abroad. . . . the demonstrators cannot hurt me—only themselves and the cause of peace . . . [which is] too important to be derailed by irresponsible [demonstrators]."[17]

It would also appear, however, that by the spring of 1969 Nixon thought that the 1968 intervention into Czechoslovakia by the U.S.S.R. made continued European and Soviet proclamations favoring détente somewhat hollow, even though he believed that up to then moves toward "détente [had] produced less fear." Upon his return from Europe, Nixon told legislative leaders that he recognized how "dangerous" détente would be if it were not based on something "real," and that there could be no reduction of U.S. support to NATO or arms negotiations between America and the Soviet Union until there had been "progress on political issues... because most wars start as [the] result of political issues." In the interim, however, talks "should go forward on all fronts."[18] According to these private notes, Nixon also returned from his first trip abroad as president ostensibly convinced that the alliance should be consulted "in advance of East-West negotiations," but at the same time more selective about dealing with individual NATO nations. In a 2 March 1970 "eyes only" memorandum, for example, Nixon outlined his priorities in foreign policy indicating that with respect to Western Europe he would direct his attention only to those problems "where NATO . . . and where major countries (Britain, Germany, and France) are affected. The only minor countries in Europe which I want to pay attention to in the foreseeable future will be Spain, Italy, and Greece. *I do not want to see any papers of the other countries unless their problems are directly related to NATO.*"[19]

Nixon and Kissinger's official involvement with NATO began at a crucial time in the arms control talks left over from the Johnson administration. LBJ had already signed the Treaty of Nonproliferation of Nuclear Weapons. Even though the president and his national security adviser were not particularly enthusiastic about this treaty, because they believed that technical knowledge about nuclear power could not be contained or limited only to major powers, the far more important issues they inherited from the previous administration were deteriorated relations with NATO and inconclusive disarmament talks with the Soviet Union.

According to a February 1969 issue of *U.S. News and World Report*, Nixon came into office determined to repair the damage that President Johnson and his secretary of defense Robert S. McNamara had done to the alliance by not consulting with its members and by opposing the development of British and French national nuclear deterrents. Their policy of negotiating secretly with the Soviet Union over terms of the nuclear nonproliferation treaty had "generated resentment and confusion" among alliance members that this national news magazine predicted would be remedied during the Nixon administration because it would not "doctor" intelligence information about the relative strengths of NATO and Warsaw Pact forces as had the Defense Department "whiz kids" under Johnson to rationalize bilateral talks.[20] Ironically, Nixon and Kissinger continued to bypass NATO as it pursued private conversations with the U.S.S.R. and used CIA reports about Soviet nuclear buildup to win support for the ABM. Unlike under their Democratic predecessors, Nixingerism proceeded under the more acceptable rhetorical guise of consultation, cooperation, and competitive coexistence—all of which were later to be summed up with the word *détente*. Actually, however, Nixon and Kissinger had to start where Johnson left off.

In the summer of 1967, the United States was on the verge of developing an anti-ballistic missile system just as LBJ and Soviet premier Alexei Kosygin had agreed to discussions about reducing their countries' respective nuclear arsenals.[21] It was obvious to both Nixon and Kissinger that the ABM might prove counterproductive if it resulted in an increased number of missiles (as did indeed occur later with the MIRVs), but the president, in particular, was convinced that he had to have the ABM as a "bargaining chip." Consequently, Nixon viewed any opposition from Congress to the ABM system as not only a threat to the possibility of détente, but also to continued U.S. conventional arms support for the North Atlantic Treaty nations because liberal, Democratic senators who opposed ABM tended to be the same senators who wanted to reduce U.S. troop contributions to NATO through what was known at the time as the Mansfield amendment.[22]

The administration also did not place as much emphasis as its opponents within Congress and the arms control community that the ABM would endanger the ongoing negotiations between Gerard C. Smith, head of the U.S. Arms Control and Disarmament Agency (ACDA), and his Soviet counterpart Vladimir Semenov, who were meeting in Vienna. As head of the U.S. SALT delegation as well, Smith also wanted the development and deployment of multiple independently targetable reentry vehicles (MIRVs) limited along with ABM systems. This placed him immediately in opposition with Nixingerism on two counts because the administration was in the process of striking a private bargain with the Joint Chiefs of Staff (JCS), trading no ban on MIRVs for their agreement to limit ABM sites. (Smith was to add a third count against himself later on in 1972 when he disagreed with aspects of SALT I.)[23]

Faced with Smith's outspoken opposition to the ABM, difficulty with the JCS, and convinced by intelligence reports that the U.S.S.R.

was deploying more ICBMs and building its own ABM system around Moscow, Nixon decided that he had to initiate back-channel talks directly through Kissinger with Soviet ambassador Anatoly Dobrynin. This approach would outflank not only the State Department bureaucracy (of which he considered Smith but the tip of the iceberg) but Congress in the formulation of foreign policy. Arms control, like all other diplomatic endeavors, was to be the preserve of the White House, even if this meant avoiding needed expert advice on this technically complicated topic. Nixon's only public concession on the issue was to downgrade the "extensive ABM coverage," known as Sentinel under the Johnson administration, to a "reduced version" he called Safeguard. As with so many other of Nixon's foreign policy initiatives, Kissinger, who had never been an advocate of arms control because he thought that nuclear weapons had both a strategic and tactical usefulness, became the secret conduit between Dobrynin and the president and, paradoxically, between the president and the arms control community with whom the professor had been at odds since the 1950s.[24]

During the spring and summer of 1969, Nixon dealt publicly and privately with NATO nations and his gradually emerging détente policy, while battling the U.S. senators over the ABM. The president's handwritten comments and memoranda testify to his personal involvement in the domestic political fight over the ABM issue. From telling his staff to "raise hell with CBS" for its anti-ABM coverage when polls showed 64 percent of the American public in favor, to criticizing members of his own cabinet, such as Secretary of Defense Melvin Laird, for not "doing enough," he alternately cajoled his supporters and berated his opponents. After informing Congress on 14 March of his decision to go forward with a "substantial modification in the ABM system submitted by the previous administration," Nixon privately called Senator Edmund Muskie's proposal to use the $6.6 billion proposed for the ABM on hunger and poverty at home and abroad, "unbelievable nonsense from a national leader!" When he read that former astronaut Senator John Glenn had called the ABM a "false hope" because "no one knows if it works," the president sarcastically asked: "Did he know the first space shot would absolutely work?" These private outbursts notwithstanding, Nixon, always the consummate politician, issued practical orders to his staff to "concentrate on those [Senators] who are on the fence and only on those where we have a chance to win." On 6 August the president narrowly won this battle in three separate amendment votes on this anti-ballistic missile system, when Vice President Spiro Agnew broke a tie on the crucial amendment providing "spending for Safeguard deployment."[25]

While carefully monitoring and refusing to compromise on his basic ABM proposal, Nixon authorized the secret back-channel meetings between Kissinger and Anatoly Dobrynin, garnered support for the ABM from NATO nations, and decided to go ahead with MIRV testing despite the opposition of nonmilitary experts—all before leaving for his 8 June meeting with South Vietnamese president Nguyen Van Thieu on Midway Island in the Pacific.[26] On his way there, Nixon stopped over in Guam and unexpectedly presented the Nixon Doctrine to a group of reporters attending a background press briefing. When I asked Nixon why he had announced this important doctrine in such an offhand manner, he said that it was for the same reasons that a year later he introduced his five-power or "pentagonal" global economic concept: (1) to avoid having it leaked in advance by State Department bureaucrats; and (2) to avoid telling Kissinger, which would have entailed National Security Staff Memoranda (NSSMs) on the subject and, in turn, would have entailed a National Security Council discussion before his proclamation. In both instances he has also specifically denied "getting" these particular diplomatic ideas from Kissinger; they "originated in the bureaucracy" and simply had been presented to him like choices on a menu.[27]

While the Nixon Doctrine was initially aimed at "southern tier" Third World countries in East Asia, it came to represent the formal institutionalization of the policy of Vietnamization; that is, U.S. support for regional security and local self-sufficiency in the Far East. It also had important international implications for the Atlantic alliance because, like détente, it embodied "a genuine American acceptance of the implications of nascent multipolarity—the so-called 'new pluralism.'" The Nixon Doctrine was, in fact, the corollary, in particular, to détente between the U.S. and U.S.S.R. and, in general, to the president's pentagonal approach to world affairs. As such, it allowed the United States to begin to resolve the contradiction that had plagued its foreign policy throughout the Cold War containment years: how to maintain its commitments abroad while reducing its direct military involvement. "The local efforts suggested by the Nixon Doctrine were not narrowly conveyed as an adjunct to the global modus vivendi achieved at the super power level," according to Robert S. Litwak. "Rather, they were to serve as a kind of regional safety-net, presumably consonant with American interests should there develop a local crack in the stable structure."[28]

The Nixon Doctrine also "repudiated the rationale under which the United States had first become involved in Vietnam." It therefore transformed that conflict from a "strategic contest between the proxies of two great powers—the United States and China—into a dirty little war that could ... be lost or settle in a way that would not gravely damage American interests or increase threats."[29] Hence, the Nixon Doctrine was more necessary, from an American perspective, as a foundation block upon which to build the later détente agreements with the Soviet Union (and China) than the ABM legislation, despite the greater domestic attention that the latter received in the United States during the spring and summer of 1969.

As a defense system, the ABM was more important to Soviet foreign policy than it was to the American "grand design." The relative unimportance of the ABM issue for Nixingerism became more evident after Kissinger and Dobrynin agreed to divide the issues of the defensive weapons (the ABM) and offensive weapons (ultimately SALT I) in May 1971. By that time, the president and his national security adviser had decided that it would be easier to come to an agreement over future deployment of their respective ABM systems, which primarily existed only on paper, than it would be to conclude a treaty limiting the deployment of existing nuclear weapons. It was at this point in the spring of 1971 that Nixon also decided that it was time to "break the back of the establishment and Democratic leadership ... [and] then build a strong defense in [our] second term." When the president wrote this to Kissinger, he faced stiff opposition in Congress over three issues: U.S. NATO troop commitments, suspicion about a Soviet ABM system and, of course, the ongoing Strategic Arms Limitation Talks. Even when under such domestic political duress on these questions, the president did not forget the dual nature of détente; namely, that from his perspective, despite détente's public call for arms limitations and economic exchanges, it privately meant continued military buildup—except in Vietnam. Nonetheless, Nixon was forced by the perennial Mansfield amendments, calling for the reduction of U.S. NATO troop strength, to deal publicly with disarmament, even though it was not part of his "grand design." The other two issues he chose to have Kissinger negotiate privately and directly with Dobrynin, telling his cabinet not to "speculate on where" the negotiations might go now that the two basic issues had been separated. "The less said regarding what is going on the better," Nixon warned members of the cabinet. "The more we talk, the less chance of an agreement."[30]

In Kansas City on 6 July 1971, Nixon announced his five-power or "northern tier" strategy, which he hoped would replace the bipolar, confrontational aspects of the Cold War since 1945. Instead of continuing to deal only bilaterally with the Soviet Union, Nixon wanted to bring the five great economic regions of the world— the United States, the U.S.S.R., mainland China, Japan, and Western Europe—into constructive negotiation and mutually profitable economic competition. Admitting that the United States could not long maintain its post–World War II position of "complete preeminence or predominance," Nixon outlined a pentagonal strategy that would promote peace and economic progress among the major regional powers. Kissinger never officially endorsed this five-power geopolitical strategy, preferring his more exclusive "trilateral" approach that included only the U.S., Japan, and the Common Market nations of Western Europe (including England), augmented by a strategy of linkage.[31] However, their respective geometric divisions of the world were not incompatible. Both carried the responsibility to keep order in its sphere of influence and not to intrude in areas dominated by others. Thus Nixon thought that détente would prevent small Third World nations from setting the great powers against one another by making the possibility of outside aid more remote. He and Kissinger also thought that détente would help the United States deal simultaneously with the U.S.S.R. and the People's Republic of China by taking advantage of their differences with one another to create a triangular relationship in which American leverage could be exerted. Circumstances in all five (or three) areas of the world (and as reflected in the Harmel Report) simultaneously favored détente between 1969 and 1972.[32] Consequently, the United States and the Soviet Union capitalized upon the favorable international atmosphere that developed during the first Nixon administration to improve Soviet-American relations.

While the European and Soviet conditions favored détente during Nixon's first administration, an unfavorable congressional climate toward continued U.S. troop support of NATO complicated things for Nixon. Beginning in 1966, Montana senator Mike Mansfield had periodically introduced "a sense of the Senate resolution" to reduce substantially the number of American soldiers stationed in Europe. Support for the Mansfield NATO Troop Reduction Amendment to the Military Selective Service Act grew during the last half of the 1960s in direct proportion to the increase of the antimilitary sentiment associated with the anti-Vietnam / peace movement. Thus, two years into his presidency Nixon faced the distinct possibility that the Mansfield amendment, calling for an outright U.S. troop reduction of one-half or 150,000 by the end of the year, would pass.[33]

The president's staff closely monitored all of the various troop reduction amendments, in addition to Mansfield's, during the spring and summer of 1971. The president himself personally made telephone calls to individual senators to ensure a negative note, and even wrote to former occupants of the White House to have them reassert their support for NATO, while Kissinger desperately drew upon the support of such notables of American foreign policy as Dean Rusk. When all of the votes on the different amendments are considered, "a majority of the Senate [was] on record as supporting some type of positive action with respect to NATO," Senator Charles Mathias, Jr., gravely informed Kissinger, as he complained about the way the administration had handled his substitute for the Mansfield amendment, calling for "balanced force reduction."[34]

The 1967 Harmel Report produced the first NATO studies on mutual force reductions, which by the early 1970s had turned into a formal NATO call for negotiations on mutual and balanced force reductions (MBFR). During the same time, the Warsaw Pact nations began advocating a conference on European security. Both sides were aware (and wary) of the other's proposal, and reciprocal acceptance was considerably delayed by the intervention into Czechoslovakia by the U.S.S.R. and some of the Warsaw Pact nations. Then in the course of 1970–71, West Germany's Ostpolitik gave new life to these mutual proposals and to détente in general. Nixon and Kissinger were already worried that West Germany would achieve détente with the Soviet Union before the United States did, and so when Mansfield used Brandt's Ostpolitik (in addition to the U.S. balance of payments problem) to justify his 1971 amendment, they tried to thwart both. Because Nixon and Kissinger understood that NATO support of MBFR was designed to guarantee the existence of a large number of American troops in Europe, they made sure that at a 19 November 1970 meeting of the National Security Council (NSC) a decision was reached not to reduce U.S. forces in Europe, "except in the context of mutual reductions negotiated with the East."[35] In addition, the administration was prepared to prevent passage of the Democratic Mansfield amendment (which required unilateral withdrawal of American troops from NATO) with a Republican counteramendment introduced by Senator Mathias that requested the president to negotiate a MBFR "consistent with balance of payments situation and to report to Congress the results every six months commencing September 15, 1971." Mansfield had already accepted a friendly amendment to his resolution saying that his called-for U.S. troop reductions would "become inoperative if prior to December 30, 1971, representatives of the Warsaw Pact countries . . . entered into negotiations, or . . . entered into formal discussions, regarding a mutual reduction by such organizations of their military forces stationed in Europe."[36]

Before the final vote on the Mansfield amendment in May 1971, the administration received some unexpected help toward its defeat from Soviet Premier Leonid Brezhnev—for which Kissinger later tried to give the administration credit. In March, and again in May 1971, Brezhnev indicated that the Soviet Union was willing to begin discussing mutual arms reductions in Central Europe. While the administration took advantage of especially the May statement to undercut support for the Mansfield amendment by arguing that a unilateral withdrawal of U.S. troops would prevent taking Brezhnev up on his MBFR offer, there is no documentary proof for Kissinger's assertion that "carefully calibrated measures of the Administration toward the Soviet Union . . . [and] our willingness to discuss détente had lured Brezhnev into an initiative about mutual force reductions that saved our whole European defense structure from Congressional savaging." For his part, Mansfield tried to downplay Brezhnev's announcement by saying the proposal was similar to one made a year earlier, but at the time he, too, grudgingly gave the administration credit for the Soviet initiative. In fact, Soviet officials were more concerned about the "unpredictable consequences of a sudden massive American military withdrawal [from NATO]" than with the back-channel contacts between Kissinger and Dobrynin.[37]

Contrary to Kissinger's claims,[38] therefore, what is significant about this Mansfield amendment defeat, and subsequent ones until 1973, was Nixon's ability to outmaneuver a Democratically controlled Congress between 1969 and 1971—not his (or Kissinger's) ability to outmaneuver the Soviet Union which, after all, had been pursuing détente longer (and ultimately would do so more consistently) than the United States. When next the Mansfield or similar resolutions, such as the Jackson-Nunn amendments to the 1973 1974 and Defense Appropriations Authorization Acts, became a problem for the administration's foreign policy, the president's political power in Congress had been so weakened by the unfolding Watergate scandal that his arguments about the debilitating effects on "the confidence of our allies in the U.S. [NATO] commitment and the likelihood of further progress in SALT, European Security and MBFR negotiations" no longer carried the day. Thus, in March 1973 NSC staffers were frantically pointing out to Kissinger that "we are behind the eight ball once again on the NATO Troop Cuts," and Nixon was privately admitting to his national security adviser that NATO GIs in Germany were so expensive that "we can't stay forever" at current military levels. So the Nixinger 1973 "Year of Europe" ended, even by Kissinger's admission, with "the effort to revitalize America's alliances with its fellow democracies... run[ning] into unexpected obstacles," including the uncooperative attitude of most NATO nations during the October war in the Middle East.[39]

By May 1974, Kissinger submitted to Nixon the second report "pursuant to the Jackson-Nunn Amendment" requiring written information at ninety-day intervals "on the progress that has been made... to have our Allies fully offset the balance of payments deficit incurred as a result of our troop deployment in NATO Europe." (The Jackson-Nunn amendment called for mandatory unilateral cuts of U.S. troops designed to go into effect automatically if full offset of U.S. NATO balance of payments was not achieved and was in keeping with the previous sense of the Congress resolutions passed in 1973 calling for NATO allies to contribute more to the cost of their own defense.)[40] Before Nixon resigned from office in August, he reported to the NATO Council on its twenty-fifth anniversary in June that he had succeeded in maintaining U.S. forces in Europe and would continue to do so until there was a reciprocal reduction in troop force on the part of the Warsaw Pact nations. He also affirmed that without the alliance he doubted that détente would have begun or continued. Otherwise, his remarks echoed those he had uttered on the twentieth anniversary—a tacit indication that not much progress had been made toward cementing better NATO relations through consultation.[41]

Nevertheless, Nixon's most lasting foreign policy achievements remain improved relations with China and the Soviet Union, including a strategic arms limitation agreement with the latter. Normalization of U.S. relations with China was part of the "grand design" to bring this giant Communist nation into the ranks of the superpowers. Long before Nixon sent Kissinger on a secret mission to Peking in July 1971 to arrange the details of his own visit there the following year, the administration had been indicating to the Chinese through various unilateral gestures of reconciliation that it wanted to make fundamental improvements in economic and scholarly exchanges.[42]

Although various government officials denied Nixon courted China in order to bring pressure to bear on the Soviet Union, the president's highly publicized visit to the People's Republic of China in February 1972 (with its attendant joint communiqué) was clearly part of the Nixinger triangularization policy and did not go unnoticed by Russian leaders. While the Sino-American rapprochement made the Soviets more amenable to moving ahead with détente, it is usually forgotten that the original purpose behind improved relations with China (and the U.S.S.R.) was to bring leverage to bear on both nations to *improve the military situation for the United States in Vietnam.* This particular attempt at linkage did not prove successful.[43] Because of the Soviet concern over the results of Nixon's trip to China, however, it became indirectly linked to the success of negotiations leading to the ten formal agreements signed in Moscow between the United States and the U.S.S.R. in May 1972. These agreements provided for: prevention of military incidents at sea and in the air; scholarly cooperation and exchange in the fields of science and technology; cooperation in health research; cooperation in environmental matters; cooperation in the exploration of outer space; facilitation of commercial and economic relations; and most important, the Anti-Ballistic Missile Treaty, the Interim Agreement on the Limitations on Strategic Arms (SALT I), and the Basic Principles of U.S.-Soviet Relations.

In the area of arms control, Nixinger détente strategy contained the potential not only to substitute for containment (the standard way the United States had fought the Cold War against the Soviet Union since the late 1940s) but also to transcend the procrustean ideological constraints which were at the very heart of the post–World War II conflict between these two nations. This potential was never fully realized in large measure because Nixon and Kissinger chose to give priority to SALT talks over MIRV talks. It also was never realized in part because their successors proved unable (or unwilling) to build upon the delicate distinction between containment and détente that they left behind; and in part because there was no changed leadership or structural base in the U.S.S.R. to reinforce the concept inside or outside its borders during the last half of the 1970s, as there now appears to be under Gorbachev.

Nonetheless, the Strategic Arms Limitation Talks (SALT I) conducted in Helsinki in 1969 and Vienna in 1970 led to the two arms control documents at the 1972 Moscow summit. These included a treaty limiting the deployment of anti-ballistic missile systems (ABMs) to two for each country, and an agreement freezing the number of offensive intercontinental ballistic missiles (ICBMs) at the level of those then under production or deployed. Unlike SALT I, the ABM treaty was of "unlimited duration . . . and not open to material unilateral revision," regardless of attempts by the Reagan administration to do just this beginning in 1985. Until the SDI efforts in the last half of the 1980s, however, the ABM treaty essentially succeeded in relegating deployment of conventional ballistic missile defense systems to minor strategic significance.[44]

SALT I, on other hand, was an agreement of limited, five-year duration that attempted to establish a rough balance, or parity, between the offensive nuclear arsenals of the two superpowers, despite the "missile gaps" that continued to exist between them in specific weapons. For example, when Nixon signed SALT I, the United States had a total of 1,710 missiles: 1,054 land-based ICBMs and 656 on submarines. The U.S.S.R. had a total of 2,358 missiles: 1,618 land-based ICBMs and 740 on submarines (SLBMs). SALT I not only recognized the strategic parity of the U.S.S.R. but gave it a numerical edge in missiles and a slight throw-weight advantage. The U.S. retained a numerical advantage in warheads and a superiority in strategic bombers—460 in 1972 to 120 for the Soviets. SALT I by no means stopped the nuclear arms race, but it recognized that unregulated weapons competition between the two superpowers could no longer be rationally condoned. By freezing further missile buildup, SALT I meant that by the time SALT II was signed in 1979, total American-Soviet missile strength remained essentially unchanged: 2,283 to 2,504, respectively. From 1972 until the mid-1980s, therefore, SALT talks have been regarded as a barometer of relations between the two countries, even though the MIRVing engaged in by both sides has tended to obscure their generally parallel buildup since 1972, contrary to the claims of critics.[45]

While it is relatively easy to generalize about the meaning of SALT I almost two decades after its announcement, there was much controversy and confusion over specific terms at the time. The controversy was largely partisan, but the confusion was legitimate because in terms of sheer complexity and scope this summit meeting between Nixon and Brezhnev was unprecedented by contrast to the previous five summits following World War II. Complicating matters, we now know from those who participated in the multilevel negotiations and in drafting the various technical provisions that Nixon and Kissinger did not completely understand all the terms, let alone the implications, of arms control, especially the SLBMs sections of the interim agreement. Among other things, the protocol had to be rewritten and signed again by Nixon and Brezhnev after the formal ceremony.[46]

Despite the semantics and interpretation problems of the arms control sections of the signed agreements that made up détente, economic relations between the two countries almost immediately improved. While Soviet trade with the United States remained relatively small except for the World War II period of lend-lease, considerable improvement had been made by the end of 1972. Even before a trade agreement was signed on 18 October 1972, as payment by the U.S.S.R. of $722 million on its lend-lease debt over the next three decades, the Nixon administration promised to seek Export-Import Bank credits to finance Soviet purchases in the United States and to extend most-favored-nation (MFN) treatment to imports from the U.S.S.R. In 1972 the Soviet Union purchased 25 percent of the American wheat crop in what became a very controversial deal because it raised American consumer prices. By mid-1973 a number of major American corporations, including Pepsi-Cola and Occidental Petroleum Company, had signed major contracts with the U.S.S.R and other Communist nations of Eastern Europe. When Nixon visited Moscow for a second time in June 1974, trade between the two nations had doubled to $1.5 billion— far exceeding the increase that had been predicted. At the end of 1976, the Soviet bloc trade deficit with Western nations hovered around $40 billion. Four countries held up to 87 percent of this debt: West Germany, 40.4 percent; America, 25.3 percent; France and Japan approximately 10 percent each.[47]

This improvement in trade suffered a setback in 1975 when the Soviets rejected a U.S. congressional trade bill that had been under discussion since 1972 because certain members of Congress insisted that in return for increased trade and credit arrangements, Soviet emigration policies should be liberalized. While American wheat exports to the Soviet Union erratically continued, no way was found to overcome the insistence of conservatives in Congress that détente should not only change relations between the U.S.S.R. and the U.S. but that conditions inside the Soviet Union should also change in exchange for most-favored-nation treatment. Once again, as on NATO troop reductions and arms control, Senator Henry "Scoop" Jackson orchestrated the Senate amendment to counter the Soviet-American trade agreement signed in October 1972 as part of the Moscow summit. After two and one-half years of haggling over various versions of the Jackson-Vanik amendment, which was extended in 1974 to include a ceiling on loans to the Soviet Union from the Export-Import Bank, Ford signed the Trade Reform Bill on 3 January 1975, with the amendment, and the Soviet government officially refused to comply with it on 10 January. That same month the president withdrew his support for the MFN treatment of the U.S.S.R. because of Soviet actions in Angola. Thus ended the move toward liberalizing trade with the Communist world (at least as represented by the Soviet Union) that had begun so optimistically under the Nixon administration with the passage of the Export Administration Act of 1969, liberalizing export controls.[48]

Such improved trade relations as did result, however, tended to be viewed ambivalently by American leaders. In June 1976, for example, even Kissinger warned the Organization for Economic Cooperation that the fast-growing trade with Soviet bloc nations could be used by Moscow for political leverage against Western nations; in contrast, the Joint Economic Committee of Congress issued a report later that same year indicating that increased trade would make Moscow more dependent upon Western goods and technology, thus lessening the danger of war and weakening centralized pricing policies and other internal Communist structures. The latter has been the most commonly held American view about the U.S. / U.S.S.R. trade since the Bolshevik revolution.[49] As noted, however, since 1917 the Soviet Union has steadfastly refused to relax internal controls in order to obtain external benefits, regardless of chronic economic difficulties stemming from demands for more consumer goods and the growing gap between advanced Soviet and Western technological and managerial skills.

With American-Soviet trade relations temporarily on hold, and U.S. NATO allies restive over having been bypassed at the Moscow summit, and faced with uncertainty over how the United States was going to respond to talk of increasing Soviet military strength, the long awaited Conference on Security and Cooperation in Europe

(CSCE) began in July 1975. The declaration of ten principles signed by thirty-five nations at Helsinki on 1 August was important to the United States and the Soviet Union for at least two basically different reasons. Consequently, their interpretations about how best to implement the final act of the CSCE are not in agreement because they each emphasize different sections of the Helsinki Accords.

Helsinki was primarily a Soviet triumph because of the recognition of the post–World War II boundaries of Eastern Europe that Moscow had long sought. In the face of this reality, and to mitigate mounting political criticism at home, Kissinger supported the human rights declaration at Helsinki, even though he had always eschewed moral restraints in the pursuit of détente. He has since rationalized his position by saying that he thought it would encourage the Soviets to be more forthcoming in SALT II talks. This was risky for a variety of reasons, not the least of which was the fact that Kissinger was much less intimately involved in the writing of the Helsinki texts than in the earlier ABM and SALT ones. The American government, especially since President Carter's election in 1976, has stressed the human rights provision of the CSCE and used it as a standard by which to measure the treatment of citizens within foreign countries, including the U.S.S.R. and its satellite nations. To the United States, this seventh principle of the declaration "became the major problem area" between it and the Soviet Union. On the other hand, Moscow has logically preferred to focus on those segments of the final act which granted implied recognition of Soviet hegemony in Eastern Europe. A major legacy of Nixinger foreign policy from 1975 to the present has been manifested by the U.S. and U.S.S.R. agreement to disagree over the importance of the Helsinki Accords.

In truth, President Ford and Kissinger were defensive about Helsinki from the very beginning. Philip Buchen, counsel to the president, and other Ford staff members immediately announced that the Helsinki Accords were "not legally binding."[50] Kissinger also found upon his return that Congress no longer responded positively to his imperious ways on SALT talks. "Your persistent failure to appear before [the armed services] committee in the face of Soviet deployments is inconsistent with your assurances," Senator Jackson sarcastically informed the secretary of state in August 1975, "raises serious doubts about the manner in which that agreement was negotiated." To add insult to injury, Kissinger found that the dual nature of détente came back to haunt him from inside the Ford administration. Secretary of Defense James Schlesinger began to hawkishly lobby Congress for more defense appropriations in the face of "the largest [Soviet] deployment of improved strategic capabilities in the history of nuclear competition," and Kissinger was left to pursue the more dovish arms control and economic and cultural aspects of détente. Minimizing benefits from strategic arms agreements and noting the drastic decline in real dollars (some 42 percent) of the U.S. defense budget since it peaked in 1968, Schlesinger bluntly told Congress: "Despite détente and its opportunities, the need for steadfastness is no less great than it was a decade or more ago. Putting aside the shibboleths of the cold war era, it is nonetheless the case that the world remains a turbulent place."[51]

Ford resolved this conflict between Kissinger and Schlesinger in October 1975 by relieving them both of their respective positions as national security adviser and secretary of defense, leaving Kissinger still secretary of state. Additionally, the president reduced Kissinger's visibility nationally and restricted his access to the Oval Office, sending him off, instead, to spend 30 percent of his time conducting "shuttle diplomacy." Most indicative of Kissinger's loss of power and stature, however, was the Ford administration's decision first to deride the term détente and then to discontinue its use when it began to sound too much like "appeasement" as it headed into the 1976 presidential election.[52] This linguistic "backtracking" was easy enough to implement given the amorphous nature and internal contradictions that the term had come to represent under Nixingerism. Détente to a large degree had always been a matter of perception and individual leadership on both sides. By 1975 these had changed.

Nixon and Kissinger returned from the Moscow summit meeting in May 1972 triumphant, but more vulnerable than ever on three fronts. The first was military, the second was economic, and the third was morally ideological. All three boded ill for the SALT II talks that began six months after the Moscow summit. Critics immediately asserted the United States had been "hoodwinked" by the Soviet Union into a disadvantageous military deal with respect to SLBMs. With Helsinki and CSCE agreements still three years away and no MBFR in sight, as negotiations over SALT II dragged on over the course of a decade, an additional military criticism became that the Soviets were violating the terms of both the ABM and SALT I agreements. Trade arguments against détente were ultimately translated into congressional legislation in the form of the

Jackson-Vanik amendments to the Trade Reform Bill in the course of 1973 and 1974. Moral criticism of Nixingerism based on ideological hostility to the U.S.S.R. became more credible in the wake of Watergate, but it had always been strong particularly with Republican and Democratic conservatives in Congress and the country. It was this criticism that Nixon and Kissinger found the hardest to answer because their approach to détente had not, in fact, been based on moral or ideological considerations but on very pragmatic ones. The situation did not improve with Nixon's resignation in August 1974. In the summer of 1975, with Gerald Ford as president, Kissinger went on a national speaking tour to convince people that détente was more important than "blind assertions of moral absolutes."[53] But the Camelot days of détente had long since passed. In fact, 1972 to 1974 saw declining rather than rising popular support for détente despite all the "hard sell" tactics used to promote it.

One of the greatest ironies of Kissinger's career is that he assumed the height of his power within the Nixon administration, just as Watergate was undermining the president's ability to command respect and confidence at home and, to a lesser degree, abroad. As special adviser to the president on national security affairs (a position he had held since January 1969), he became secretary of state in September 1973, during the crisis in the Middle East. While Watergate resulted in Kissinger uniquely occupying two major foreign policy positions until December 1974, when President Ford replaced him as national security adviser, it did not give him any more personal or official power and influence than he had exercised during the brief period of the October war when Nixon was preoccupied with Watergate. Although Kissinger remained secretary of state until 1977, he was unable to initiate any major foreign policy moves from 1974 because he was without the unquestioned position of international authority that Nixon had provided for their joint attempts to restructure U.S. diplomacy. Moreover, the professor's esoteric sentences and logic, as well as his macho, pseudo-swinger image, had always impressed members of the American press corps more than foreign heads of state who were looking for foreign policies and actions they could understand.

To a less obvious, but significant degree, therefore, Watergate proved Kissinger's Waterloo as well as Nixon's. Nixingerism thus disintegrated in the wake of this unprecedented national constitutional scandal. Aspects of détente survived as, of course, did NATO, but without the illusion of the "grand design."

GADDIS SMITH

The SS-20 Challenge and Opportunity: The Dual-Track Decision and Its Consequences, 1977–1983

Professor Kaplan originally proposed as the title of this paper "The SS-20 Challenge: The Dual-Track Decision and Its Consequences, 1977–1983". That title suggested the following simple story of linear causality. The Soviet Union in 1977 challenged NATO by deploying the new, triple-headed, nuclear, mobile intermediate-range SS-20 missiles aimed militarily at Europe and politically at producing discord within the Atlantic alliance. NATO responded, after some internal recriminations, with the dual-track decision of December 1979. American Pershing II and cruise missiles would be deployed in Europe and, concurrently, the United States would seek to engage the Soviet Union in negotiations aimed at limiting intermediate-range nuclear weapons on both sides. Various consequences then followed one by one until the first American missiles became operational in late 1983 and the Soviet Union in retaliation broke off all arms-control negotiations.

The foregoing summary is not so much wrong as incomplete and oversimplified. The Soviet deployment of the SS-20 was as much an opportunity for the accomplishment of several purposes in the West as it was a challenge. The dual-track decision responded to more than just the presence of the SS-20s. The consequences produced a dramatic chapter in the history of arms control, extended into the domestic political arena of all countries involved, and stimulated the intense and loosely connected antinuclear movements on both sides of the Atlantic. The open sources now available reveal that the story was complex indeed. They also point to questions that cannot be answered until that day when, should fortune shine on posterity in general and historians in particular, archives are open for those years in both the Soviet Union and the West.

Under different circumstances the deployment of the SS-20s, the Pershing IIs, and the cruise missiles and the call for arms control discussions might have passed almost unnoticed by the general public. Here were modern additions to nuclear arsenals that increased by only a few percentage points the number of nuclear warheads and the throw weight deployed on both sides. Both the Soviets and the West claimed that their own weapons in question were entirely defensive and were designed to maintain or restore a stable balance. They represented normal modernization, not threatening innovation. The call to arms-control negotiation had a familiar, ritualistic sound. The negotiations were likely neither to produce radical agreement nor cause turmoil if they yielded no agreement at all.

Why then did the dual-track decision become the focal point for a crisis which, while it lasted, seemed to threaten the future of NATO as had few others in the alliance's history? The answers are to be found in the characteristics of individual leaders, in domestic and alliance politics, in the global deterioration of Soviet-American relations, in the technology of weapons and the complexities of arms control, and above all in the sense among political elites and the public that the danger of nuclear war was higher than it had ever been and was continuing to increase.

For several reasons the new administration of President Jimmy Carter was handicapped at the outset in dealing effectively with Western Europe. For more than a decade the United States had been preoccupied with the Vietnam War and its aftermath. The foreign policy elite, the press, and the general public had been paying relatively less attention to European issues than at any time since the 1930s. Henry Kissinger's "Year of Europe" had been an embarrassing joke, which only underlined his focus on the Washington-Moscow-Beijing triangle. The SALT process was the heart of Nixon's and Kissinger's policy of détente with the Soviet Union and European theater. Weapons were almost irrelevant for SALT. Cyrus Vance, who would become Carter's secretary of state, reflected widespread attitudes in the long memorandum he wrote in October 1976 for candidate Carter: "Overview of Foreign Policy Issues and Positions." What little he wrote about Europe was banal. For example: "Our approach should be low-key and should be worked out in conjunction with European leaders." He did not mention nuclear weapons in Europe and considered the Greek-Turkish conflict the most urgent single issue.[1]

Issues involving Western Europe and NATO played almost no role in the 1976 presidential campaign, while Jimmy Carter concentrated on criticizing the alleged immorality of American foreign policy in the Nixon-Ford years. His heaviest emphasis was on Vietnam, Latin America, and the exclusion through secrecy of the American people from participating in decisions. His call for a foreign policy as morally sound as the American people was politically appealing but had no connection to relations with Western Europe where allegations of immorality were not an issue.

Europe was notably absent as a factor in Carter's education and experience, as were international issues as a whole. But as a devout Bible reader he felt a special empathy toward the Middle East and his humanitarian impulses stimulated an interest in the Third World. Carter mixed sincere conviction and shrewd calculation in his politics of guilt and repentance. His claim was that if the United States would repent for past sins, foreswear its evil ways, be open and honest and generous, and make an absolute commitment to human rights, then all would be well with the world. As I have argued elsewhere, Carter was propounding another version of the myth of American omnipotence: Omnipotence expressed not through overwhelming material power but through spiritual regeneration.[2] President Carter's most important foreign speech during his first months in office was given at Notre Dame University in May 1977. Note the core sentences, both because they epitomize Carter's initial approach to international issues and because of their almost total lack of meaning for the American role in NATO.

> Being confident of our own future, we are now free of that inordinate fear of communism which once led us to embrace any dictator who joined us in that fear.... For too many years, we've been willing to adopt the flawed and erroneous principles and tactics of our adversaries, sometimes abandoning our own values for theirs. We've fought fire with fire, never thinking that fire is better quenched with water. This approach failed, with Vietnam the best example of its intellectual and moral poverty. But through failure we have now found our way back to our own principles and values, and we have regained our lost confidence.

President Carter did believe in the importance of continuing the strategic arms control talks and he was sincerely committed to trying to reduce the level of armaments in the world, strategic and tactical, nuclear and conventional. He wanted his administration to make bold proposals quickly. But with little sense of history, he did not appreciate how connected different issues were. His style was to focus on each issue and do the right thing. Confident of his own good intentions, he did not understand that others would not necessarily see his actions as he did.

Carter's approach to the Soviets on strategic arms was in character. He began by surprising the Soviets in March 1977 with a proposal that departed from the provisional Vladivostok Accords of 1974 and that, from Moscow's point of view, would give unilateral advantages to the United States. This initiative produced a dramatic, humiliating, and public Soviet rejection. Within weeks of his inauguration, the president's competence was at issue. He had suffered the diplomatic equivalent of a Bay of Pigs invasion.[3]

Then, in June 1977 Carter cancelled production of the B-1 bomber, a move which Secretary of State Cyrus Vance called "one of the most courageous and politically costly defense decisions of his presidency."[4] Carter had sound technical reasons for abandoning the B-1. It was very expensive, rapidly improving Soviet air defense might well prevent its assigned penetrating mission, and existing B-52s equipped with air-launched cruise missiles could maintain the airborne segment of strategic deterrence at much lower cost. Furthermore, Carter saw himself as a St. George standing up to the "live and writhing" dragon of the B-1 lobby.[5] The decision, however, gave effective ammunition to those who would portray him as weak on defense and a unilateral disarmer.

Late in 1977 the Soviet Union began to deploy the SS-20 missiles targeted on Western Europe, allegedly as a normal modernization, replacing the obsolete SS-4s and SS-5s. The SS-20 was a formidable weapon: mobile not fixed, triple not single warheaded, solid not liquid fueled (and thus capable of being launched on a few minutes notice rather than hours as with the missiles it superseded). The SS-20 could strike all of Western Europe but lacked the range to reach the United States. The Carter administration was worried by the appearance of the SS-20s, but the concern was not primarily over its impact on Europe but over the ease with which it could be converted to an intercontinental missile, by the addition of a third stage. American SALT negotiators pressed the Soviets hard on this point and in October 1977 won a concession that the components for such a conversion would not be built. Carter was euphoric and with characteristic exaggeration declared that a SALT agreement would be completed in a few weeks.[6]

The connection between American satisfaction over blocking the possible conversion of the SS-20 into a weapon capable of striking the United States and the growing apprehension of European leaders, especially Chancellor Helmut Schmidt, over the SS-20 in its unconverted state needs to be emphasized. It is no coincidence, as they say, that Schmidt's endlessly quoted remarks in the Alastair Buchan lecture of 28 October 1977 came immediately after the nonconversion agreement on the SS-20:

> SALT codifies the nuclear strategic balance between the Soviet Union and the United States. To put it another way: SALT neutralizes their strategic nuclear capabilities. In Europe this magnifies the significance of the disparities between East and West in nuclear tactical and conventional weapons.... Strategic arms limitations confined to the United States and the Soviet Union will inevitably impair the security of the West European members of the Alliance vis-à-vis Soviet military superiority in Europe if we do not succeed in removing the disparities of military power in Europe parallel to the SALT negotiations. So long as this is not the case we must maintain the full range of deterrence strategy.[7]

Those remarks bear the stylistic hallmarks of a last-minute insert, for the theme of the speech as a whole emphasized arms control and economic questions as fundamental elements of security. And much of what the chancellor did say about weapons dealt with the imbalance of conventional forces. The SS-20s were not mentioned by name, but Schmidt's reference to "the full range of deterrence strategy" left no doubt as to his meaning—a meaning put in bold face when, before the end of 1977, the Soviets deployed the first ten SS-20s aimed at Europe.

Chancellor Schmidt's speech added a political urgency to working-level discussions already under way within NATO on the issue of deploying new land-based intermediate-range nuclear missiles. The instrument of greatest interest to European defense ministries at this stage was the modern unmanned cruise missile equipped with the ability to navigate at treetop level and, by reading land contours, to follow a zigzag course thousands of kilometers and strike targets with only a few feet margin of error. It was small, completely mobile, and very cheap (about $1 million each). The European fascination with the cruise missile had been stimulated and maintained by the assiduous and persuasive lobbying of several American aerospace companies who had developed the device. According to a high German defense ministry official at the time, "the U.S. manufacturers badly wanted a European endorsement of the cruise missile. They even offered the opportunity to cooperate in production, in hopes that certain European nations would then pressure the United States to produce it in large numbers."[8] Here we have a question that cannot be fully answered, a marker for the next generation's research. Defense contractors and their uniformed friends, Eisenhower's famous "military-industrial complex," are much discussed by journalists and the Left. They are frequently accorded determinative power over basic foreign policy and national security decisions. Common sense tells us that contractors were part of the equation—but how large and precisely how that part played is now impossible to measure. If and when correspondence between contractors and governments and internal company archives are ever open to historians, there will be much interesting research to undertake.

President Carter was also enamored of the cruise missile, but in its air-launched (ALCM) rather than ground-launched version (GLCM). The Soviets for their part were apprehensive. The cruise missile's flight time was hours rather than minutes as with ballistic missiles, but its accuracy and capacity for evasion meant it had a very good chance of getting through. Furthermore, with small size and mobility it could easily be hidden and thus could escape existing means of verification in an arms control agreement. Carter's preference for the ACLM and Soviet fears produced an agreement in the SALT talks that once again seemed to subordinate the Western European interest to the American objective of reaching a strategic accord. The Soviets wanted to limit the range of American GLCMs to six hundred kilometers and the range of ALCMs on U.S. bombers to twenty-five hundred kilometers measured as straight flight. The U.S. military said the allowable range for the air-launched cruise missile had to be far greater because it flew a wiggly path. The agreement was that there would be no deployment of land- or sea-based cruise missiles with a range in excess of six hundred kilometers (insufficient to strike the Soviet Union) before 31 December 1981. In return the Soviets said they would not require a range limit on American air-launched cruise missiles. "You can fly your air-launched cruise missiles around the world if you like," Soviet foreign secretary Andrei Gromyko said to President Carter.[9]

Meanwhile, the egregiously mismanaged controversy over the production and deployment by the United States of enhanced-radiation warheads—popularly known as "neutron bombs"—on battlefield nuclear weapons in Europe had further damaged President Carter's reputation and soured European-American defense relations. Enhanced-radiation warheads, under development for almost twenty years and under discussion within NATO since 1973, were designed to be used in Germany in short-range missiles, such as the Lance, and artillery against invading Soviet tanks and infantry. They produced as much killing radiation as existing battlefield nuclear weapons but with approximately one-tenth the blast and heat effect. Their purpose was to limit somewhat the collateral damage to civilian population and structures in the event of a nuclear barrage.[10] Whether the enhanced radiation weapons would work as designed is another matter, but they were described by proponents as reducing collateral damage by 90 percent below that of existing tactical warheads while maintaining equal battlefield effectiveness. Logically, an individual strongly opposed to nuclear weapons but admitting their tragic necessity as deterrents could find the enhanced-radiation weapons marginally less horrible than their ordinary nuclear cousins.

The enhanced-radiation warheads became a public international issue after a June 1977 article in the *Washington Post* by Walter Pincus. The headline read: "Neutron Killer Warhead Buried in ERDA Budget."[11] Soon the press in America, Europe, and the Soviet Union was full of hyperbolic accounts and condemnation of a satanic device which irradiated people while leaving property unscathed. The critics on the political Left described it as a particularly fiendish invention of capitalism. Carter was affected by the criticism and felt a personal emotional repugnance at the thought of the neutron bomb. But the president directed his administration to press ahead with research and planning as part of a general modernization of NATO forces. He insisted, however, that the German government ask publicly and specifically for the enhanced-radiation warheads. This insistence, designed to avoid the appearance that the United States was forcing the neutron bomb, ironically had the opposite effect of making it appear that the United States was dictating what the German government must decide. Chancellor Schmidt, in a move that anticipated the dual-track decision of 1979, proposed that the United States produce the enhanced-radiation warheads and use them as a bargaining chip to negotiate a reduction in Soviet tank forces; meanwhile, a decision on deployment would be deferred. Carter was interested in the two-track approach. He suggested that the enhanced-radiation warheads might be bargained for a reduction of Soviet SS-20s—an idea that made less sense than linking them to tanks—but that did introduce the idea of bargaining down the number of SS-20s. Carter, however, continued to insist on an unequivocal German request for deployment in the absence of an arms-reduction agreement.[12] By the end of 1977, as Secretary Vance has written, "the ERW controversy had become a test of the alliance's ability to make hard and politically sensitive decisions. Worse, for many allies, the issue was becoming a test of the president's ability to lead the alliance."[13]

Early in 1978 an American team of negotiators produced a face-saving scenario whereby NATO collectively (although no government individually) would endorse deployment if the arms-control approach failed, and the United States would proceed with production. A North Atlantic Council meeting was scheduled to ratify the arrangement. Vance and National Security Adviser Zbigniew Brzezinski believed the president was aware of the plan and that he approved. At the last minute the president said no. He found the European posture too ambiguous to support a decision. Months of NATO diplomacy collapsed. Vance and Brzezinski, for once in agreement, criticized Carter more sharply than on any issue in his presidency. Your decision will "contribute to a sickness and then weakening of the alliance," said Brzezinski.[14] And Vance concluded that Carter "appeared not to appreciate the enormous damage to his prestige and the U.S. that would result from backing away from the alliance consensus that had been worked out in his name."[15] Carter's mind was made up. He announced that production of ERWs would be deferred.

Raymond L. Garthoff, the preeminent scholar of Soviet-American relations in this period, agrees with Vance and Brzezinski. "The principal effect of the neutron weapon affair," he writes, "was to reduce Western confidence in American leadership, and later to lead the U.S. to seek to undo that effect by another new arms initiative for NATO."[16] The new initiative, of course, was the first track of the dual-track decision: the deployment of new intermediate-range weapons, to be announced as a necessary counter to the SS-20s. By the end of 1978, the Soviets had deployed seventy SS-20s—capable of hitting 210 separate targets—and were bringing them on line at the rate of one a week.

American leaders still did not see the SS-20s as a threat to the military balance. Thousands of American nuclear weapons were targeted on the Soviet Union. But by pretending to see a threat and joining the Europeans in declaring that something must be done, they could use the SS-20s as an opportunity to display leadership, to repair the frayed political fabric of NATO. That is how the SS-20s were as much an opportunity for the United States as a challenge. Substance was less important than the fact of doing something, anything at all to demonstrate leadership. But by declaring that the security of the alliance depended on meeting the SS-20s, a failure to respond would be a grievous defeat. In that sense the SS-20s were a threat, or challenge, because they were described as such.

The first weapon under discussion in working-level NATO discussions of a new generation of intermediate-range nuclear weapons was the ground-launched cruise missiles—deployable under the emerging SALT II agreements beginning in 1982. Development and production schedules would not allow them to be deployed before that date in any event. But in 1978 the Pershing II was added to the equation. Routine modernization plans had long called for the replacement of old Pershing IA missiles in Germany with new weapons of comparable range, i.e., about six hundred kilometers, capable of reaching western Poland but falling far short of Soviet territory. The U.S. Army and the manufacturer of the Pershing IIs proposed, however, that by adding a second stage the improved missile could hit targets in the Soviet Union. According to the subsequent testimony of several participants, the NATO group working on the issue embraced the idea without thinking of how the Soviet Union might react. "What we all missed at the time was the profound difference between a weapons system that reaches the Soviet Union and one that doesn't," said a German Defense Ministry official.[17]

Were the Americans and their NATO colleagues so innocent and oblivious? Although the two-staged Pershing II was not intercontinental and thus not "strategic" under the definitional rules of the SALT negotiations, it was certainly strategic from the Soviet point of view. It was highly accurate and had a flight time of between six to twelve minutes, compared to thirty minutes plus for missiles launched from the United States. From Moscow, the Pershing II looked like a deliberate attempt to upset the balance, a European equivalent of the missiles in Cuba in 1962. Here is one of many critical junctures at which we need the archival record opened. Were the Pershing IIs, like the ground-launched cruise missiles, primarily the product of enthusiastic defense contractors unconnected to far-reaching political and strategic concepts? Or were they envisioned from the outset as instruments of special pressure on Moscow and components in new potential types of nuclear war? And how did Soviet leadership truly see them?

Again it was Chancellor Schmidt who introduced track two, as he had already done in the abortive neutron bomb affair. In January 1979 at the informal Guadeloupe summit conference with Carter, Prime Minister James Callaghan of the United Kingdom, and President Valéry Giscard d'Estaing of France, Schmidt argued that deployment of the weapons should be linked to an effort to negotiate mutual limits with the Soviets. This not only made good sense to Schmidt in terms of alliance security, but it was also a political necessity if Schmidt were to keep control of his own party in Germany. Carter agreed on the desirability of a negotiation track, and in April 1979 a NATO working group on the arms control issue was established. After some anxious moments over whether an agreed program were possible, the two tracks were brought together at a special meeting of NATO foreign and defense ministers in December 1979 in Brussels, where the famous decision was formally made and announced. The communiqué of 12 December, a piece of sacred NATO scripture, emphasized the provocation of the SS-20s (about 125 were then in place) as part of a dangerous Warsaw Pact nuclear buildup. Were these trends to continue, said the communiqué, "Soviet superiority in theatre nuclear systems could undermine the stability achieved in inter-continental systems and cast doubt on the credibility of the Alliance's deterrent strategy by highlighting the gap in the spectrum of NATO's available nuclear response to aggression." Accordingly, 108 Pershing II missiles would be deployed as replacement to existing Pershing IAs in Germany and 464 ground-launched cruise missiles would be installed. The communiqué also announced that one thousand U.S. nuclear warheads "would be withdrawn from Europe as soon as feasible." It then discussed the arms control track, emphasizing the goal of using limitations to achieve equal, verifiable ceilings of Soviet and American intermediate-range missiles.[18]

During the remaining thirteen months of the Carter presidency, the preparations for installing the 572 American Pershing II and cruise missiles proceeded. Late 1983 emerged as the target date for deployment. The Soviets continued installing the SS-20s at an unabated rate. About 225 were operational when Carter left office. But events outside of Europe prevented the pursuit of track two except in the most perfunctory matter in the final weeks of the administration. Five weeks before the dual-track decision, Iranian militants had seized the American Embassy in Tehran. They would hold fifty-three Americans hostage throughout the rest of the Carter presidency. Three weeks after the dual-track decision, the Soviets invaded Afghanistan and President Carter professed to see a threat to world peace greater than any since 1945. He withdrew the signed but unratified SALT II treaty from consideration by the Senate, instituted a range of sanctions against the Soviet Union, and tried with only limited success to get other nations to join in making the Kremlin feel the cost of aggression. Iran and Afghanistan took European issues off American front pages and focused the administration's thinking on the Persian Gulf region.

Iran and Afghanistan completed the transformation of the administration's approach to the Soviet Union from negotiation, symbolized by Secretary Vance, to confrontation, symbolized by National Security Adviser Brzezinski; from trying to change Soviet behavior through patient exploration of common interests, to military buildup, strident rhetorical denunciation, to making the Kremlin apprehensive, and to trying to inflict pain rather than signaling reassurance. The transition from Carter's emphasis on quiet confidence and moral values in the first year of his administration to the tough military posturing of the final year was far greater than the transition, soon to take place, between the Carter and Reagan administrations. The first and last years of the Carter presidency had one common characteristic: slight attention to Europe and NATO.

Afghanistan also was an irritant to American relations with European governments, because the Europeans took a less cosmic and alarmist view of the implications of the Soviet military presence in a remote and barren region. Acrimony over trade sanctions against the Soviet Union and the boycott of the 1980 Olympic Games in Moscow infected the tone of NATO discussions. As Brzezinski has written of the year: "The Europeans, particularly Schmidt, grew more anxious, and their reluctance to take firm steps on sanctions quickly became clear. We pressed and pulled and prodded, but with limited success."[19]

In June 1980 there was a minicrisis. Chancellor Schmidt suggested publicly that there might be a moratorium on the deployment of theater nuclear weapons. Brzezinski, who had come to see the Pershing IIs and cruise missiles as important in themselves, was appalled. He persuaded Carter, who was about to meet with Schmidt in Venice, to write a letter of reprimand. Schmidt was furious. Here is Brzezinski's diary account of the Venice meeting:

> All last week he, Schmidt, has been fuming over Carter's letter on TNF. He started the meeting by loudly proclaiming that he had never let us down, and he repeatedly described the letter as an insult. The President was rather conciliatory, tried to calm him down. However, Schmidt persisted, and at some point I weighed in, pointing out that at least we never engage in personal recriminations.... Schmidt was somewhat taken aback by this and said, "Well, I don't mind a fight. If necessary, one has to criticize."[20]

The Venice meeting was the lowest point in a generally abyssmal relationship between Carter and Schmidt. This raises the question of the importance of clashing personalities. It is hard to find an American president and the leader of an allied country who disliked each other with quite the intensity of Carter and Schmidt. Each considered the other unreliable. Schmidt did little at the time, and has done nothing since, to conceal his contempt for Carter, and for many of Carter's aides and advisers. A novelist might make the whole affair of the SS-20s and the dual-track decision hang on this clash of personalities. Both men bear responsibility for exacerbating difficulties inherent in the situation. Carter deserves to be faulted for his penchant, hardly unique among Americans, for unilateral decisions made with little thought to the consequences for NATO partners. And Schmidt is guilty of going out of his way to put Carter in an unfavorable light.

In November 1980 Jimmy Carter was soundly defeated in the presidential election by Ronald Reagan, the first elected incumbent to lose since Herbert Hoover in 1932. So many factors were working against Carter's reelection that a change in one or two probably would have made no difference. The "loss" of Iran and the hostage crisis reinforced his public image of weakness, as had the decisions to cancel the B-1 bomber and neutron bombs, and the post-Afghanistan posturing did not reverse existing public impressions. Carter was also vulnerable for having "given away" the Panama Canal and for permitting the leftist Sandinista regime in Nicaragua to gain power. The economy was sliding into recession with double-digit inflation and paralyzing interest rates. The SALT II treaty was on the shelf and, in any event, could not have been ratified. Reagan and his supporters considered it "fatally flawed." Carter's difficulties with Europe were little mentioned in the 1980 campaign. They did not hurt him politically. On the other hand, given all his other difficulties, a flawless record on NATO questions probably would not have helped.

To this day Carter remains understandably obsessed with the hostage issue to the exclusion of much else, including problems within NATO. In April 1989, in response to a question about what he would do differently if he had the opportunity to replay his presidency, he answered, "One more helicopter." The reference being to the April 1980 military attempt to rescue the hostages, an attempt that was cancelled in its first stage because mechanical failure had reduced the number of helicopters below the minimum deemed necessary for success.

Ronald Reagan was inaugurated in January 1981. His administration embraced the first part of the dual-track decision, deploying the Pershing II and cruise missiles, but initially seemed indifferent, even hostile, to the second track. That indifference, combined with the rapidly approaching time when the new missiles would be in place, and above all with the perception that Reagan and his aides were viewing the possibility of nuclear war with frightening equanimity, produced the second frenetic and spectacular chapter in the SS-20 affair. It was a chapter filled with strident rhetoric, gigantic public demonstrations against nuclear weapons that seemed capable of overthrowing not only individual governments but NATO itself, and with an acrimonious end, for the time being, of the negotiating track.

Time and space permit only some broad comments. Strobe Talbott has in two books presented informed accounts of the internal American bureaucratic battles and the negotiating phase of the story.[21] First came the new administration's initial antipathy to any sort of arms control. Then the belated opening of discussions in November 1981 on track two, not out of belief in the process, but in response to domestic and European public opinion. Reagan proposed the zero/zero option—if all Soviet intermediate missiles were withdrawn, the U.S. would not carry out the deployment of missiles that did not yet exist—a proposal that most observers considered patently absurd because of its unacceptability by the Soviet side. Zero/zero at the time appeared to be an onus-shifting gimmick of the most unsophisticated sort. Then the repudiated efforts of Paul Nitze and Yuli Kvitsinsky, the American and Soviet negotiators walking in the woods, to reach a compromise that would trade the Pershing IIs for a large reduction in the number of SS-20s; and the fulfilled Soviet threat to break off negotiations if the American deployment actually began at the end of 1983.

Rather than retrace that ground, let me focus in closing on how the dual-track decisions influenced and mingled with the brief but remarkably intense popular antinuclear movement in Europe and America during those years.

Without the conjunction of Ronald Reagan and the pending deployment of the cruise and Pershing II missiles there would not have been an antinuclear movement of such breadth and intensity. The discussions and controversies surrounding the deployment of missiles in the Carter years had evoked professional interest among specialists in and out of government. The journals dealing with security and international affairs ran scores of articles on the subject. But there was no broad popular interest and virtually no mass criticism or protest. Even the increasing militarization of Carter's foreign policy in 1979–80, including signs that the actual waging of nuclear war was becoming more "thinkable," failed to stir much public response. For example, Carter's hint in his "Carter Doctrine" speech of January 1980 that nuclear weapons might be used against a Soviet move in the Persian Gulf; Presidential Directive 59 of July 1980, with contents substantially leaked, discussed the need to maintain nuclear superiority up every step of an escalation ladder; and the announcement of the "Stealth" bomber program in August 1980 all looked toward war fighting, not simply deterrence against the use of nuclear weapons by the Soviet Union. But the antinuclear movement, quiet since the late 1950s, continued to slumber. One explanation may be that just as the hard-line supporters of Ronald Reagan and members, for example, of the Committee on the Present Danger, did not believe that Carter had been converted to their kind of president, so potential members of an antinuclear movement, what there was of it, still saw Carter as a sympathetic figure.

But with Reagan's inauguration, scores of voices in or close to the administration began to suggest publicly that nothing good ever came out of arms control, that the first priority of the United States must be a crash program to close a supposed window of nuclear vulnerability, that nuclear wars might be fought and won, that with evacuation of cities and shelters dug with enough shovels there would be sufficient American survivors of a nuclear war to reconstruct the country, that nuclear war might actually be confined to Europe in any event, and that there were worse things than nuclear war, especially when the foe was communism. There was public discussion of nuclear strategies of "decapitation" and of exploiting the nationalities problem in the Soviet Union with a deliberate policy of ethnic targeting. One theorist, with influence on the Reagan circle, had publicly asserted that "Victory Is Possible" in nuclear war. "The United States," wrote Colin Gray, "should plan to defeat the Soviet Union and to do so at a cost that would not prohibit U.S. recovery. Washington should identify war aims that in the last resort would contemplate the destruction of Soviet political authority and the emergence of a postwar world order compatible with Western values."[22]

The result in the United States of Reagan's apparent readiness to engage in nuclear war was the revival of an antinuclear movement, but on a scale far larger than ever seen before. Leaders who had learned the techniques of protest during the Vietnam War returned to action. Thousands who had never joined a protest organization immersed themselves in the statistics, terminology, and consequences of nuclear war. The freeze movement—calling for a mutual, verifiable freeze by both the Soviet Union and the United States—was born and rapidly gained adherents in Congress.[23] Four eminent senior national security managers from previous administrations publicly called for the United States to adopt a declared policy of no first use of nuclear weapons.[24] Books and movies on the horrors of nuclear war, rare on publishers' lists or the screen for two decades, appeared by the dozen. Jonathan Schell's emotional best seller *The Fate of the Earth* (1982)—hailed at the time as an equivalent in the opposition to nuclear weapons of Harriet Beecher Stowe's antislavery novel, *Uncle Tom's Cabin*—was the most famous.[25]

President Reagan invigorated the antinuclear movement by his open disdain and his suggestion that it might be made in Moscow. His fervent denunciation of the "evil empire" of the Soviet Union drew acclaim from the Right and frightened others. His strongest statement was the March 1983 speech to a convention of Evangelicals. It contained the oft-quoted phrase about the Soviets being the "focus of evil in the modern world"—but more important was the embrace of an idea once called "better dead than red."

> A number of years ago, I heard a young father, a very prominent young man in the entertainment world, addressing a tremendous gathering in California. It was during the time of the cold war, and communism and our own way of life were very much on people's minds.... And ... I heard him saying, "I love my little girls more than anything—" And I said to myself, "Oh, no, don't. You can't. Don't say that." But I had underestimated him. He went on: "I would rather see my little girls die now, still believing in God, than have them grow up under communism and one day die no longer believing in God."
> There were thousands of young people in that audience. They came to their feet with shouts of joy. They had instantly recognized the profound truth in what he had said, with regard to the physical and the soul and what was truly important.
> Yes, let us pray for the salvation of all those who live in that totalitarian darkness—pray they will discover the joy of knowing God. But until they do, let us be aware that while they preach the supremacy of the state, declare its omnipotence over individual man, and predict its eventual domination of all peoples on the Earth, they are the focus of evil in the modern world.

The immediate purpose of Reagan's speech was to combat the freeze resolution, then nearing a vote in the House of Representatives. Listen to a few more sentences:

> I urge you to speak out against those who would place the United States in a position of military and moral inferiority.... In your discussions of the nuclear freeze proposals, I urge you to beware the temptation of pride—the temptation of blithely declaring ... both sides equally at fault, to ignore the facts of history and the aggressive impulses of an evil empire, to simply call the arms race a giant misunderstanding and thereby remove yourself from the struggle between right and wrong and good and evil.

In 1981 and for much of 1982 the antinuclear movement in the United States paid scant attention to intermediate-range missiles in Europe. And here I speak with the personal knowledge of one who participated fairly actively at the local level. SS-20s and cruise missiles and Pershings II were just items on the long list of terms for people to study. The emphasis was first on simply teaching as many people as possible the meaning of the alphabetical and euphemistic terms that comprised the vocabulary of nuclear weapons; and second, on portraying as vividly as possible the consequences of nuclear war on American towns, states, and the United States as a whole. The antinuclear movement at first, like the American government's approach to weapons and their control, comprehended only the United States and the Soviet Union at best and was self-centered and isolationist at worst.

The antinuclear movement in Europe—especially Germany, the Netherlands, and the United Kingdom—involved more mass demonstrations and civil disobedience and was far more sharply focused on the pending deployment of the cruise and Pershing IIs. Those devices were direct and visible symbols. The European movement, as so many observers have commented, combined resentment against environmental degradation, nuclear war, the United States, and Ronald Reagan individually. "Reagan go into a home for the aged so that we can get as old as you are" read a banner seen by journalist Henry Brandon at a giant rally in Bonn.[26]

Gradually the European movement began to be noticed in the United States, and by 1983 the freeze campaign and other groups in the United States took a closer look at the Euro-missiles question. The rapidly approaching date of deployment had an impact and so did President Reagan's unveiling in March 1983 of his dream of a strategic defense initiative, a supposedly impervious bowl of defense against ballistic missiles striking the United States. From the perspective of some critics, SDI was as isolationist as the most parochial segment of the antinuclear movement in the United States. Other critics denounced it as a hypocritical device behind which plans for launching nuclear war could be incubated. All critics saw it as an obstacle to arms control.

Did the antinuclear movements have an impact? They did succeed in educating and sensitizing millions of citizens to nuclear issues, teaching them the vocabulary, the euphemistic acronyms, and endless numbers. They showed that nuclear strategy is not a mystery accessible only to a priesthood with super clearances. They created a constituency of potential activists who might grow tired and withdraw when a particular moment for protest had passed, but who were a latent political force that no democratic politician could ignore. But the antinuclear movements failed to achieve specific objectives. The U.S. House of Representatives did pass a freeze resolution, but the chances that the Senate would do the same or that a presidential veto could be overridden were nil. Nor did the U.S. government respond with any sympathy to the idea of renouncing first use of nuclear weapons. And the schedule for bringing the first Pershing IIs and cruise missiles on line proceeded inexorably. The Soviet government sustained its deployment of the SS-20s and produced a crescendo of propaganda against the Pershing IIs and cruise missiles, against SDI, and against Reagan. It all may have been counterproductive from Moscow's point of view. The Western missiles went in and all arms-control negotiations stopped. By the end of 1983, commentators, especially those unenthusiastic about the Reagan administration, saw a bleak future of an escalating arms race, end to negotiation for the foreseeable future, and injury to the Atlantic alliance.

By 1989, the opinions of six years earlier appeared singularly overwrought and inaccurate, but curiously the Pershing II–cruise missile issue was replayed in the debate over whether to introduce a modernized Lance missile with a range approaching the lower limits of the banned intermediate-range devices. The Soviets saw the Pershing II as circumventing the intent of SALT II. Now they see the proposed longer-range version of Lance as circumventing INF.

In closing, let me mention again some tasks for future historians, who will return to this topic when there is an archival record available. The first and most obvious questions to ask and answer concern the Soviet Union. Did the Soviets have definite objectives that they expected the deployment of the SS-20s to fulfill? Or were these weapons an ordinary and quite predictable modernization, new technology in place of obsolete, the result of the natural ambition of designers, manufacturers, and the military? Or were the SS-20s intended to do what many Europeans feared: upset the balance of deterrence in Europe, further enhancing Soviet superiority in conventional weapons, loosening the coupling between the United States and the European members of NATO?

We know, of course, how the Soviet government reacted to the dual-track decision—with denunciation, encouragement of the antinuclear movement, and offers of small numerical reductions in return for nondeployment by the United States. And then—after the parade of the dying leaders (Brezhnev, Andropov, and Chernenko) had at last been replaced by Gorbachev—we saw what no one had predicted: Gorbachev's acceptance of the zero/zero option and the INF treaty of December 1987. But what hopes, fears, and possible internal disagreements were behind this behavior?

The record in the West is relatively open. We can follow the domestic politics of the issue. The negotiating positions within the alliance and with the Soviet Union are quite clear; so too are the bureaucratic struggles within the Carter and Reagan administrations. But for understandable reasons, the nuclear war planning documents are closed, as are records of defense contractors who lobbied for their particular weapons systems. Someday perhaps we will be able to measure the influence of particular contractors, of specific officers, and of specific military scenarios. We will then be able to say whether some of the wilder open commentary on how to fight nuclear wars was no more than the infatuated musings of theorists or whether it had close connections to real planning. We may be able to find out, in short, whether the SS-20 affair was at all times only a political struggle over military symbolism or whether the contending forces in Europe in those years came close to accepting the use of nuclear weapons. Was 1977 to 1983 a time of real danger, greater than in previous or subsequent years, or just a time of fear and shouting?

LAWRENCE S. KAPLAN

The INF Treaty and the Future of NATO: Lessons from the 1960s

As the North Atlantic Treaty approached its fortieth anniversary, the United States and the Soviet Union signed an Intermediate-Range Nuclear Arms Reduction Treaty in December 1987. On one level this action represented a striking triumph for the West, and a vindication of the promise inherent in the North Atlantic Council's dual-track decision of 1979. America's firmness over deploying the cruise and Pershing II missiles in Western Europe led initially to a confrontation with the Soviet adversary in 1983, when its delegates walked out of the arms talks in Geneva. But it ultimately led to an agreement that would remove both the newly deployed American missiles and the Soviet SS-4 and SS-5 as well as the SS-20 missiles. An elaborate system of verification would follow over the next thirteen years. The signing of this treaty, with its Memorandum of Understanding and Protocols, and its subsequent ratification in 1988, seemed to testify to the validity of a major NATO assumption: that a strong defensive posture was a prerequisite to genuine détente with the East bloc.

On another level, however, the INF treaty raised a host of new questions about the future of the alliance that could lead to its dissolution if its members could not respond to new challenges:

1. Would the new agreement produce a normalization of East-West relations that would permit American troops to be returned to the United States? If so, there might not be a further need for the alliance to continue.

2. Would the new agreement be a prelude to denuclearization of Europe, which would leave the allies vulnerable to the Warsaw bloc's superiority in conventional arms? If so, the treaty would have produced less rather than more stability in Europe.

135

3. Would the new agreement become a symbol of superpower collaboration at the expense of the European allies? If so, longstanding suspicions of American commitment would rise again, to the detriment of the alliance's solidarity.

In short, a détente between the United States and the Soviet Union could carry in its wake the decoupling of America from Europe. If this were to be the result, the treaty of Washington of 1987 could lead to the dissolution of the treaty of Washington of 1949.

Predictions of NATO's demise had been abundant in the late 1980s, even before the INF treaty was signed. Some of the commentators coming from the neoconservative Right, such as Irving Kristol and Melvyn Krauss, cite the lack of support given by the allies to American efforts on their behalf. Rather than carry the load for the allies, they say the United States would serve the Europeans better by withdrawing from the alliance and encouraging the Europeans to make their own security arrangements. Two of their themes that fall upon receptive American ears are: (1) unfair sharing of the burden of defense, and (2) the potential but untapped strength of an almost but not quite united Western Europe.[1]

But if this is the view from the Right, there is equal ardor for withdrawal from some pundits of the Left. Richard Barnet, for example, supports the termination of NATO on grounds that the Soviet threat is no longer valid and that Europe is capable of handling its own defense while the United States uses its good offices to continue its efforts toward demilitarizing the Continent. On the Left also appear European critics who see in NATO an American obstacle to peace in Europe, from the Greens of Germany to the radical wing of the British Labour party. Rand analyst Robert Levine has called the American opponents "withdrawers" and their European counterparts "removers."[2]

Most critics of the alliance, whatever their political orientation, share many of these views. David Calleo, in his case for "devolution," urges the reduction of the U.S. presence in NATO and its replacement by Europeans hitherto excessively dependent upon U.S. assistance. Calleo approaches the subject from an economic standpoint, pointing to the enormous cost that the United States has borne. What was bearable in the time of American preeminence is dangerous in time of relative decline. The idea of a decline, if not a fall, in American power was given wide circulation in Paul Kennedy's comparative studies of empires, ranging from sixteenth-century Spain to twentieth-century America. Each had its period in the sun, and each found its underpinnings distorted by economic strain. The "imperial overstretch" cited by Kennedy in each imperial power would apply to the American role in NATO.[3]

The arrival to power of Mikhail Gorbachev in the Soviet Union has helped to bolster arguments of critics. General Secretary Gorbachev seemed to herald a new foreign policy in which the Soviet Union would face inward, reduce its military establishment, and become a regular, if still powerful, member of the nation-states of the world without the revolutionary engine of Communist expansion to threaten its neighbors. Since it was Soviet aggressiveness that brought the Western European states together in alliance, a reversal of that behavior could make the alliance in 1989 unnecessary. According to these critics, it has fulfilled its purpose and should disband.

Although most of the voices responding to Gorbachev's invitation were from the Left, they found resonance throughout the West, notably among Germans and other West Europeans eager to change the status of the long Cold War. The air of relaxation in Europe matched the mood of those in the United States whose various grievances over burden sharing or lack of appreciation for the American presence in Europe impelled them to look to the Pacific as the major focus for American foreign relations in the 1990s.

The rise of Japan and the Asian nations reminds many Americans that the United States is a Pacific as well as an Atlantic power. Should the United States continue to pour its resources and its energies into Western Europe when increasingly its vital interests are involved in a Pacific connection—with Japan, Korea, and the ASEAN group? On two fronts the traditional American connections with the Far East are reawakening. First, with the increased trade with Japan and the other Asian powers on the Pacific rim; and second, with the steady westward movement of the American population from the East to the West Coast, from the Rust Belt to the Sun Belt. Asia was the focus of California, the most populous of the American states, not Europe. If this trend continues, Europe's position on the American horizon will inevitably be diminished.

The 1987 INF treaty between the United States and the Soviet Union gave credence to European concern that the United States was turning away from its allies. Like the abortive Reykjavík plans of 1986, the INF arrangements might be a Soviet-American trade-off at the expense of Europeans. Despite the demands that the NATO allies had made for a Western counteraction against the SS-20s, and despite the obvious success of the dual-track initiative of 1979 in effecting their removal—and moreover forcing the Soviets into serious negotiations for reductions in nuclear weapons—there was fear that disengagement for American forces from Europe would be the end product of de-escalation efforts. Inconsistent though this sentiment may be with the new confidence Europeans have in living alongside a restructured Soviet Union, it was nonetheless a factor in straining the Western alliance. After more than thirty-five years of an American military presence in Europe, many wondered if the removal of intermediate nuclear weapons would lead to the removal of American troops as well. If so, what effect would this action have on the security of the West?

As a result of Europe's reexamination of both the American ally and the Soviet foe, there is a new sense of European unity abroad. For half a generation, since the *Wirtschaftswunder* of the 1960s, Europe has had the potential of equalling both America and the Soviet Union in economic power. In 1992 the remnants of economic nationalism are expected to fall. And with them the idea of a United States of Europe could become a reality. Political and military integration could be built on the infrastructure of the Western European Union, enlarged to serve the European Community as a whole. Two of its members—the United Kingdom and France—are already nuclear powers. There is reason to anticipate the flowering of a genuine third force in Western Europe in the 1990s.

In light of the challenges of 1989, critics have a right to suspect that the alliance is on the threshold of dissolution. As one acute observer has written:

> The Atlantic Alliance, which has been the keystone of American foreign policy during three administrations, has begun to founder under the impact of Europe's new nationalism and the apparent decline of the Russian military threat. There is no longer any agreement on how NATO shall be organized, where it is going, or what its purposes are . . .
> This disarray within the alliance is more than simply a dispute among allies as to the proper means toward a commonly desired end. It is the ends themselves which are now in question. The problem facing the Atlantic Alliance today is not so much how it shall protect Europe from Russian invasion—an invasion no one now believes in—but what kind of political settlement will be made between Russia and the West in Europe. The collapse of Atlantic unity is merely the result of the trans-

formation of the old military impasse into a period of diplomatic fluidity where Europe's political future is at stake.[4]

The extended quotation above encapsulates most of the issues that would account for the "end of the alliance," the title of the book from which the quotation was taken. They include: Europe's new nationalism, decline of the Soviet threat, lack of agreement over the purpose of the alliance, and the consequent irrationality of stationing American troops in Europe. These are lively issues in 1989. But they were equally valid in 1964, when Ronald Steel published this book. In the foregoing paragraphs only the reference to "three administrations" instead of "eight" anchor this passage in time. In other words, all the generalizations made in 1964 about the impending termination of the alliance were as pertinent in the early 1960s as they are in the late 1980s.

Given these constants why did NATO survive its twenty-fifth anniversary and live on to commemorate its fortieth anniversary? One possible answer might lie in the force of bureaucratic inertia. By 1962 NATO had in place a large and politically powerful establishment, both civilian and military. Both headquarters were located in Paris and included influential soldiers and politicians from all the allied nations. The supreme allied commanders, Europe, were all men of distinction and status, with ranking that rivaled positions in the Joint Chiefs of Staff in Washington. Although the offices of the secretary-general and the permanent representative to NATO lacked Americans with comparable visibility, the American ambassadors were diplomats or politicians of superior intellectual ability, as in the cases of Thomas Finletter and Harlan Cleveland in the 1960s. The Europeans in NATO were drawn from the summits of their respective national political communities: Paul-Henri Spaak and Dirk Stikker—the secretaries-general between 1957 and 1964—had been premiers of Belgium and the Netherlands respectively.

Today there are approximately thirty-nine hundred people employed in the political headquarters in Brussels; another twenty-five hundred military personnel, along with seven thousand dependents, are located thirty miles away in SHAPE's headquarters at Casteau.[5] When local employees are included in the figures, the numbers mount to twelve thousand people. The numbers employed in Paris a generation ago were not substantially fewer. Could it be that the weight of this apparatus was too heavy to dissolve? Could NATO's survival be a product of a bureaucratic mass that has taken on a life of its own? Could NATO personnel comprise a formidable factor in keeping the organization alive?

Comparisons with other such organizations that outlived their usefulness and eventually dissolved do not give much credibility to this thesis. SEATO and CENTO, products of the Dulles chain of alliance organizations in the 1950s, disappeared in the late 1970s without many ripples. Their headquarters, however, were modest affairs, not comparable in prestige or numbers with NATO's. A better example may be the League of Nations, with an apparatus and branches more closely approximating NATO's. Despite its visibility, its impotence in the 1930s caused it to collapse in the wake of World War II, to be succeeded by the United Nations. Even though the successor organization incorporated some of the league's subunits into its own organization, the size of the league did nothing to prevent it from dwindling into irrelevancy and dissolution. One needs more than the self-preserving nature of a large bureaucracy to explain the survival of the organization and alliance in the 1960s. A more pertinent question would be to ask if and how the alliance addressed some of the pressing problems that seemed to be bringing it to the brink of disintegration a generation ago.

From the American side in the 1960s, a major issue was burden sharing, particularly in the form of the six U.S. divisions in Europe. These divisions had been the fruits of the great debate of 1951, when General Eisenhower used his influence to win over a restless Senate to accept the administration's decision to send four divisions to the support of the newly established SHAPE. The Truman administration succeeded, but not without dissenting voices over the limits of executive right to send troops without the explicit permission of the Congress.

In 1951 the defense of Europe demanded the American contribution, as plans were made to build up allied forces to provide a deterrence that had been absent in Korea the year before. Even when nuclear weaponry reduced the numbers of ground forces necessary to maintain the deterrent, the American forces remained in Europe, now more as a trip wire than a conventional force. The Eisenhower administration continued the policies of the Truman administration.

But with the amazing economic recovery in the West, questions arose over the ability of Europeans to provide a greater share of the economic burden of maintaining troops in Europe. These questions were made all the sharper because the older fears of invasion had lessened in the Khrushchev years. While such questions could be deflected by observing the continued threats from the East, given Soviet behavior in Berlin or in Cuba, another question was not so easily answered. In 1960 there was danger of excessive outflow of the American gold reserve, blamed—fairly or not—on the drain on the U.S. dollar. If that drain was caused in good measure by the enormous cost of maintaining the divisions abroad—250,000 to 300,000 troops, then why should not the Europeans pick up those costs?

This was a concern that the Kennedy administration had to cope with. It was a legacy of the Eisenhower administration, and one that the new secretary of defense, Robert S. McNamara, was more than willing to manage. There was a potential $3 billion drain that he intended to bring down to no more than $1 billion as quickly as he could. If the Eisenhower solution—bring home American dependents in Europe—aroused too much opposition, other answers would have to be found. McNamara had them, and they disturbed the European partners.

The Kennedy administration in 1961 was looking as much—or more—to Asia and Latin America as it was to Europe. The crises points were as much in Laos and Vietnam as in Berlin, and the Kennedy administration undertook a sweeping revision of both the strategic thinking and the strategic emphasis of the Eisenhower administration. In the course of its evaluations, the heavy expenses of maintaining forces in Europe came under review.

High on McNamara's list of priorities was an emphasis on the need for highly mobile task forces to engage in low-intensity warfare, to strike out through counterinsurgency at the kinds of forces threatening American interest in Southeast Asia. It is noteworthy that the budgets for fiscal years 1962 and 1963 placed a premium on aircraft capable of lifting troops to areas of conflict with dispatch and with limited costs. The dangers of conflict with the Soviet Union were to be encountered in areas where wars of national liberation were sponsored or supported by the Soviet Union, rather than in Europe where NATO and the Warsaw Pact were in a static confrontation.

The consequences for the European partners were quickly apparent. If U.S. troops could be airlifted in a crisis, why should the United States maintain such a large standing army in Europe? If the allies wanted U.S. forces to remain in place, they should be prepared to pay a larger share of their expenses. They could afford the costs after a decade of rising prosperity. Although it is unlikely that there was a Machiavellian design in the Defense Department's development of a new strike force with a fleet of aircraft and ships to undergird it, it was equally unlikely that once conceived and implemented, the designers of foreign military policy would not be reluctant to press their advantage.

All of these actions helped to account for German and Italian willingness—and even French acquiescence—to enlarge their contributions to NATO in 1961. An aide-mémoire of 17 February 1961, less than a month after the Kennedy administration was in office, prepared the way. While directed at all the allies, it pointedly was delivered to the West German delegation in the course of bilateral talks on the balance of payments. The document made clear, though, that the issue was not bilateral: "The deficit of the United States arises wholly from the common defense of the free world," it stated. "Without these freely assumed obligations the United States would now be running a heavy surplus in its commitments and action in balance of payments."[6] Hence it was reasonable to expect a better balance to the partnership that would ease the balance of payments problem.

While the Europeans could resist the logic of this American assumption—including the long-term reality of the gold drain—they could not resist the tide of events. The Berlin Wall crisis of the summer of 1961 undercut German objections. It led to a rapid buildup of U.S. troops in Europe that forced the German hand as the projected U.S. dollar deficit rose to almost $3 billion. America insisted and received compensation from the Federal Republic. Germany could hardly do otherwise, since the United States was sending forty thousand additional troops to bolster NATO's defenses in Germany.

To soften the blunt edges of its demands, the United States avoided direct payment for U.S. troops. Instead, it accepted the purchase of American goods and equipment to offset U.S. expenditures in Europe. Direct sale of U.S. equipment was probably the least objectionable way of achieving results without offending German dignity.

Similar negotiations followed with other NATO allies, and although the results were more modest, there was some easing of the problem. It took time, however, before the extent of European cooperation entered into the congressional psyche. As late as February 1963, at hearings on military procurement authorizations for fiscal year 1964, Senator Richard Russell, chairman of the Armed Services Committee, was still asserting that "the NATO allies had been riding free and that the $50 billion establishment that you preside over, over there, has been the shield not only for Great Britain but for France and Germany. They got years behind in furnishing their troops." McNamara was able to respond that "We have signed agreements with the West Germans under which they are buying $650 million of equipment from us. We have signed an agreement in the last 90 days with the Italians under which they are buying initially $125 million of equipment from us."[7]

Offset agreements did not settle the issue. Europeans were concerned as well over a new U.S. emphasis on East Asian affairs that stemmed from problems in Laos and Vietnam.

Many of the fissures in the alliance in the early 1960s grew out of the confluence of two elements of change: (1) the successful launching of the first earth satellite, *Sputnik,* in 1957; and (2) the dramatic economic recovery of most European powers, reflected in the signing of the Treaty of Rome in the same year. *Sputnik* aroused alarm in the United States over Soviet advances in missile technology, which in turn stimulated the development of America's ICBM. Yet *Sputnik* raised fears that the United States soon would be vulnerable for the first time to direct Soviet attacks. Would the United States come to the aid of a missile attack on Paris or Bonn if their own cities were at stake?

This question was answered negatively by France, particularly after General de Gaulle assumed the presidency in the Fifth Republic. France assumed that it was unnatural for any nation to place another's security ahead of its own, and it was equally unnatural to expect that the United States would remain indefinitely in Europe. When the United States rejected a reorganization of NATO that would have made France part of a triumvirate controlling the organization, de Gaulle's course of subversion and separation was set. As earnests of what would come to pass, the French fleet in the Mediterranean in 1959 and in the Atlantic in 1963 were removed from SHAPE and SACLANT authority.

It was obvious that de Gaulle's stand appealed to many Europeans. They might not necessarily agree to French leadership, but most Europeans could respond favorably to complaints about charges of American hegemony. Certainly the American pressures to assume more financial burdens bred irritation over the preeminent position of the United States. But the availability of intercontinental ballistic missiles coinciding with the conception of a more flexible nuclear response raised a variety of suspicions among

Europeans. A less rigid reliance on nuclear defense could mean that America's new vulnerability to nuclear weapons dictated the Kennedy administration's new emphasis on conventional forces. Part of the reason for this pressure rested on the need for forces to cope with outbreaks where nuclear weapons might be counterproductive. To ask, as Secretary of Defense McNamara did, at the North Atlantic Council meeting in Athens in May 1962 (and then more publicly at a commencement address at Ann Arbor, Michigan, a month later) that Europeans prepare defenses on the basis of more troops on the ground was unsettling.

While McNamara actually spoke of a variety of weapons and a flexible response to the problem at hand, Europeans heard the implication of raising the nuclear threshold and the prospects of a conventional war on the ground. The allies, with the obvious exception of West Germany, considered the Berlin Wall crisis to be an aberration, a problem primarily for the Warsaw bloc, and not a reason to abandon the successful deterrent system of the past decade. To Americans the Berlin crisis of 1961 reinforced views that NATO required conventional forces to meet any level of nonnuclear aggression.

The result of these divergent views was European resistance to both the building of conventional defenses and the principle of flexible response. Europeans were unimpressed with McNamara's claim that the West had exaggerated the extent of Soviet military power. The new team of systems analysts at the Department of Defense was convinced that the figure of 150 divisions was unrealistic. The size of a Soviet division was smaller than those of the West, and the equipment was inferior. There should be no reason why a modest conventional buildup of NATO forces should not be sufficient to hold off aggression from the Warsaw Pact bloc, at least long enough for other means of coping to come into play.[8]

The allies did not accept this judgment. What they saw was a rationalization for American willingness to subvert the security of the West, which had been constructed under a nuclear umbrella. European discontent centered on the illogic of conventional defense. It could invite conflict by raising the nuclear threshold to excessive heights. If the Soviets knew that American nuclear power would not be employed immediately, they might be tempted to employ tactics that could lead to protracted land warfare in Europe. No matter how vigorously the United States asserted that a flexible response would increase not decrease, the deterrent capacity of the West,

Europeans could not erase from their memories images of World Wars I and II. Nor could they ignore the prospect of a war that would destroy Europe but leave the superpowers intact. On the other hand, they were much less vocal about their unwillingness to bear the financial burdens that raising conventional armies would incur.

The allies had forums outside NATO where their discontent with American leadership could be expressed. Although the Western European Union was a sham, the European Economic Community developed from the Treaty of Rome in 1957 was a reality, even if its accomplishments were more in the future than in the present. It contained a potential for a third force between America and the Soviet Union, which would be independent of both. This was President de Gaulle's vision of the future, when Europeans would not be second-class citizens with their fate decided by superpower politics. If there were tactical and intermediate nuclear weapons in Europe, they were controlled by the United States not by Europe. The result was pressure for development of national *forces de frappe,* particularly in France.

It is noteworthy that Europeans were successful in resisting American pressure to raise their troop strengths. It was the United States that gave way. By the late 1960s, Secretary of Defense McNamara had accepted these constraints on conventional forces. In fact, he converted the 1966 withdrawal of France from the organization into an asset, or at least into a circumstance "in no way disabling" to the military posture of the alliance.[9]

The secretary of defense used Europe's reluctance to increase its forces to justify the thinning of American troops in Europe during the Vietnam War. He was convinced that the combination of the NATO forces in place and the reduction of a Soviet threat would still permit a flexible response to any Soviet challenge.

Just as Europeans had to make repeated financial concessions to keep American troops in Europe, so American leaders had to make serious efforts to appease Europe's increasing insistence on equality within the alliance, particularly with respect to the control of nuclear weapons. De Gaulle's challenge had to be met, Germany's unhappiness with its inferior status in NATO could not be left unheeded, and the smaller powers' sense of isolation from policy making required attention as well.

The major effort was a multilateral force, which began under SACEUR Norstad's auspices in the Eisenhower administration and terminated in disarray under Johnson in 1964. Norstad's plan was to make NATO a fourth nuclear power in a way that would appease German if not French demands for equality and would dissolve doubts about America's dedication to the defense of Europe. The concept won adherents, particularly among American supporters of European unification. The multilateral force (MLF) eventually took the form of twenty-five surface vessels carrying eight Polaris A-3 missiles, each with mixed manned crews and nuclear warheads under joint ownership and custody. Each participating nation could veto the use of nuclear weapons, although the United States would retain final control of the weapons.

The MLF won some enthusiasm among dedicated American supporters of European unification. Robert Bowie, former director of the State Department's Policy Planning Staff, urged the United States "to concede to a European or NATO force the same degree of ultimate autonomy as it has already accepted in assisting the British force."[10]

But it was always an illusion, never becoming reality. If the United States kept its veto intact, nuclear sharing was a charade. If it did not, there would be the prospect of fifteen fingers—or at least thirteen if France and Iceland were discounted—on the nuclear button. France was going its way with its *force de frappe;* Britain was smarting over the SKYBOLT debacle. This left Germany as the major enthusiast for the MLF, and Germany's enthusiasm had a dampening effect on the other allies. The multilateral force disappeared from the NATO communiqués by the end of 1964.

Like offset agreements, the MLF was an action on the part of Americans and Europeans to take into account the other side's concerns. If the MLF failed, at least it bought time for the alliance to sort out paths for survival. It represented a spirit of accommodation, even if the results were mixed or negative.

Admittedly, the MLF has gone down in NATO's history as a fiasco, while the offset agreements have been identified as an example of American blackmail. Neither served its intended purposes for very long. The American monopoly on the control of nuclear warheads led to the departure of France from the organization in 1966 and the demand for détente on the part of the other allies, as demonstrated in the Harmel initiative in 1967. And the need for further offset measures became more urgent as the Vietnam War diverted American troops and American attention from its NATO obligations. Pressures for more burden sharing increased by the end of the decade. Yet each concession in its way postponed the dissolution foreseen by pundits at the beginning of the decade. And each represented the continuing importance NATO represented for the allies. After all, in 1969 under the treaty terms Article 13 any member nation could have issued a "notice of denunciation" to leave the alliance. None of the members, not even France, followed this pattern.

The answers may be found in part in a transformation that occurred without fanfare in the mid-1960s. On the surface the organization was essentially unchanged; SACEUR and SACLANT and the secretary-general remained in place. But with France's departure there was a subtle increase in the influence of the smaller nations of the alliance. NATO's Defense Planning Committee, created in 1963, assumed greater authority, with consequent lessening of American influence over military affairs. Similarly, the Nuclear Planning Group, founded in 1967 after France's withdrawal from the organization, brought nuclear questions more closely into the purview of the secretary-general. If the nuclear warhead remained an American monopoly, nuclear planning became more oligopolistic after the secretary-general moved from Paris to Brussels.

An unintended and perhaps unexpected by-product of that move was a diminution of the powers of the SACEUR. The old Standing Group, composed of the three major NATO powers in Washington, was replaced by a military representative system with a wider NATO membership and with its center in Brussels. With the Standing Group dissolved, the smaller nations had a greater voice in military planning at the expense of the supreme allied commander, Europe. Even the locus of his headquarters, thirty miles away from Brussels, helped to reduce the stature and influence that the SACEUR had enjoyed in Paris. While none of these changes was advertised as American responses to complaints against its dominance over NATO, they helped to elevate the role of the junior partners in the organization.

Nonetheless, these alterations in the NATO structure may be labeled as cosmetic. America's commitment in 1969 remained as important as the American "pledge" of 1949. The centripetal force through much of this decade was the continuing fear of a powerful and still dangerous Soviet Union.

The Berlin Wall crisis of 1961, the Cuban missile crisis of 1962, and the Czech crisis of 1968 reminded Europeans of the reasons for the founding of NATO, even as they noted with ambivalence American reactions to those crises. Contradictions continued to abound. The strength of the Soviet superpower—and its willingness on selected occasions in the 1960s to display it—generated pressures to keep American forces in Europe, where they served as a guarantor of NATO's stability. At the same time there was a sense of a new era dawning in which the Soviets had moderated their ideological drive and were ready to coexist with the Western democracies. This manifested itself in the Harmel Report of 1967, calling for steps toward détente to accompany military preparedness, and a subsequent declaration—the "Reykjavík signal" on mutual and balanced force reductions at the Reykjavík meeting of the North Atlantic Council in 1968.[11]

The Reykjavík declaration was announced in June 1968, before Soviet intervention in Czechoslovakia. While the council at Brussels in the fall of that year determined that Soviet action "has seriously set back hopes of settling the outstanding problems which still divide the European continent," it also supported "continuing consultations with the Warsaw Pact bloc," preparing for a time when the atmosphere for fruitful discussions would be more favorable.[12] In this tense situation, even Europeans most optimistic about détente and most hostile to the American role in NATO would be reluctant to risk destabilizing NATO through altering the force structure, let alone through a major reduction in the American presence in Europe. NATO itself remained vital for both defense and détente.

Was NATO still a vital force in 1989? The parallels of the 1980s and the 1960s have considerable validity, but how compelling are they? No historical situation can be completely replicated. There are obvious differences over the twenty-year span, if only in emphasis. European unity in the 1960s was still undeveloped; the United Kingdom's effort to join the European Community had failed in 1963. De Gaulle, the dominant personality in Western Europe, was also a disruptive force. In 1989 the United Kingdom was a full member of a considerably enlarged European Community. Europe appeared closer to an integrated whole than it had ever been before. Given this evolution Europe could develop into a third force as readily as it could become a genuine second pillar of the Atlantic alliance. Is NATO needed any longer, as it obviously was two decades ago? Cannot Europe stand alone at last?

These questions take on a special relevancy in light of the new spirit animating the Soviet Union under Mikhail Gorbachev. His challenge to the Soviet past appears far more credible than

Khrushchev's. The latter may have demonized Stalin's image and opened the way to détente, but his own volatile personality stood in the way of full confidence in the West's relations with the Soviet Union. His aggressiveness in supporting "wars of national liberation" in the Third World and the risks he took in installing missiles in Cuba diminished expectations among the European allies. The Brezhnev succession did little to support a belief in a fundamental change in Soviet foreign relations, even though Brezhnev's conservative style encouraged hopes for détente.

Gorbachev, however, has made *glasnost* and *perestroika* concepts that inspire much more than simple relaxation of tensions. He has recognized fundamental flaws in communism as an economic system, and has moved to make the Soviet Union a partner rather than enemy of a peaceful world order. Wherever one looked in 1989— the United Nations, Afghanistan, southern Africa, the Middle East— and notably U.S.-U.S.S.R. relations—Gorbachev appeared to have changed the face of the Soviet Union. A new order had arrived. The projections of George Kennan about the future of communism forty years before appear to have been realized. Containment has worked. NATO in this case may be an anachronism, an alliance that has fulfilled its functions of protecting the West against Communist ambitions.

After forty years of confrontation, the alliance might be dismantled on the prospect of a new Soviet leader infused with what the North Atlantic assembly has accepted as "benign" intentions.[13] But undermining this acceptance are doubts of at least two varieties. One is over the question of the Soviet Union's new foreign policy objectives. With all the openness and reconstruction that has been exhibited, the Soviet Union remains a superpower whose military strength plays a role independent of its ideological bent. Gorbachev's objectives in many respects resemble those of his predecessors, namely, the removal of the United States from Europe. Gorbachev's posture could achieve this goal through the dissolution of the alliance. Are the members of NATO certain that destabilization would not result, leaving Europe exposed, as it has not been since the 1940s, to the influence of the strongest military power on the continent? Denuclearization of Europe increases the imbalance in conventional weapons between East and West.

There is, however, another consideration. What if Gorbachev fails to maintain control of the Soviet Union? The pull of conservative forces is strong, and resistance to his reforms could result in his departure, even without a failed policy such as marked Khruschev's removal. And if Soviet conservatives cannot stem the tide of change, what new tensions would the dissolution of the Soviet Empire generate? NATO remains an insurance against such a turn of events.

If uncertainty about Soviet goals and about the Soviet political system remains alive, even though less intense than in the 1960s, the condition of Western Europe as a political entity remains equally uncertain. European unity does not rest on the number of members in a community, nor even in the promises of an economic union in 1992. The major question centers on its willingness to compromise national sovereignty in favor of a united Europe. Despite periodic expressions of common purpose, in the Western European Union as well as in the European Community, centrifugal forces remain strong. Nationalism still survives. The community could come apart over economic issues alone. As long as there is no United States of Europe in place, the termination of the alliance risks not only a political and military imbalance with the Warsaw bloc but also new divisions within the West that could set back accomplishments of the past generation.

These cautionary notes are on one level of concern about the future of Europe. There is another level that is rarely aired. This involves a post-NATO Germany. Where will it fit into a united Europe, or a divided Europe? What role would it have in East-West relations? Unfettered by NATO ties, a unified Germany would stay inside the European Community to dominate the West and shape its foreign policy toward an Ostpolitik that neither its fellow members nor the Soviet bloc welcome? These considerations are alive, though unspoken. They bring to mind the assumption, going back to the 1950s, that a West Germany inside NATO was more acceptable to the Soviet Union than Germany armed and outside. Could conflict break out in Europe, not from the Soviets moving in on a weakened West after the departure of the United States, but from ambitions, real or imagined, or German irredentism?

Do any of these considerations affect the United States? If the anger over unfair burden sharing is fueled by an economic recession, or if the anti-American sentiment in Europe reaches a new volume, it would be understandable if a new administration should wish to leave the organization. Even if there are sufficient brakes against such a crisis, America in the 1990s—for all the reasons that surfaced in the 1980s, or in the 1960s—could lead NATO into dissolution. The Pacific emphasis, the troops issue, the relative decline of American power could all work toward a devolution into irrelevance, even if there is no violent crisis to mark its end. Yet, it is unlikely that any administration will take this path to dissolution.

Scenarios of this sort have never been a part of any administration's agenda, for the obvious reason that NATO figures as a fixture in the late twentieth century with as much force as isolationism did a century ago. Disengagement from Europe into a fortress America poses too many disruptive prospects for any political figure or political party to take seriously. It would mean, among other things, leaving Europe to a Soviet influence of an order that the Soviet Union itself would not have dreamed possible in the last two generations. Furthermore, a breakdown of Europe's will to survive as an entity could follow from the loss of American presence. As Colin Gray has put it, "The geopolitical realities of European security are such that the security-producing potential of NATO-Europe is far less than is the sum of its several columns of national assets."[4] America's vital interests would be endangered by a recrudescence of the nationalist passions of the past, not least of which would be the revival of a German problem. Third, does the technology of the twentieth century permit a withdrawal of the United States into its hemisphere in the fashion of the Monroe Doctrine? If it does not, in the world's interrelated, interlocked economies and politics of the 1990s, America's own security would be affected by a breakdown in an important part of the world.

Europeans recognize these possibilities even as they chafe against American controls, or against American bases, training exercises, or mistakes in statecraft. They show this by responding to charges of unequal burden sharing with evidence of their contributions. They urge the United States to look beyond superficial statistics. Colin Howgill of the British Embassy in Washington observed that the overall contribution to Atlantic security defensive capability should be identified not merely by the amount of money spent; toleration of noise pollution caused by thousands of low-level jet fighters flying in maneuvers over Europe's countryside was itself a sharing of the defense burden not to be measured in dollars and cents. A report from the nonpartisan Center on Budget and Policy Priorities in Washington made the same point by noting that "the European states are carrying a substantial share of the alliance's military burden."[5]

What is significant about these reports and Europe's efforts to rebut American criticism is not the number of governmental and private bodies and individuals criticizing Europe but the need Europe still feels to satisfy the United States about its activities. Equally significant, the repetitive American complaints always stop short of genuine action. There have been no formal withdrawals of troops, although division size has varied over the years, particularly in the Vietnam period. In 1987 when the question once again arose in Congress, the Senate passed an amendment to keep American forces intact in Europe.[16]

The most eloquent evidence of American response to the need for stability in Europe derives from the silence in the presidential campaigns themselves. In 1984 Europeans were aroused by Senator Nunn's variation on troop withdrawal in June of that year—phased withdrawal would follow from failure of Europeans to increase their share. But even then the resolution was watered down to a pious hope for change.

Just as Europe fears that American exasperation over military costs could lead to American withdrawal of forces, so the United States fears the exclusionary potential of a United States of Europe. A united Europe was a goal of the founding fathers of NATO, but if achieved it could damage America's economy. Even more that this, a genuinely united Europe could challenge the United States politically as well. Is this then a reason for cutting loose? The consensus among American leaders has always been that European unification was in the long-term interest of the United States, if only because a united Europe would block Soviet expansionism. There was little prospect for change in 1989, no matter how high the level of frustration over policies, political and economic, a united Europe might make.

Looking ahead to the 1990s, a bipartisan panel of former policy makers that included former secretaries of defense Republican Melvin Laird and Democrat Harold Brown, as well as former SACEURs Alexander Haig and Bernard Rogers, concluded that after forty years the original vision of the wise, skillful, and determined founders who understood mutual benefits that would result from a coupling of both sides of the Atlantic has been confirmed again and again. Changes such as greater efforts to reduce duplication through specialization, or greater increases in defense expenditures on the part of smaller members, or the "progressive takeover of Europe's defense requirements by Europeans should be gradual and progressive."[17] Whatever changes take place over the next generation should be made through multilateral, not unilateral, action.

same. Even if the more extravagant hopes of 1989 should come to pass and the Cold War between East and West should be permanently terminated, NATO will still have functions to perform. The alliance has always been more than a military organization, and West-West relations more often than not have figured more prominently than East-West confrontations. Removal of American troops could follow the reduction in arms and tension in Europe without necessarily ending the alliance. Even if the machinery of SHAPE were dismantled, wholly or partly, the transatlantic ties could keep the treaty if not the organization intact, not as an empty shell but as a bond of reassurance to both sides of the Atlantic. But until this happier climate among nations becomes a reality, there is no serious alternative to the relationships in the West that NATO has built over the past forty years.

Notes

Introduction

Portions of this chapter were drawn from a keynote address delivered at the Truman Library Conference on NATO, 20 September 1989.

The Formation of the Alliance, 1948–1949

1. H. R. Trevor-Roper, "The Lost Moments of History," *New York Review of Books*, 27 October 1988.
2. "Whatever their views, most cold-war historians have neglected an important topic: the military capability of the major powers. Most would agree that military strength largely determines how vigorously or extensively a nation may pursue foreign policy objectives, but few historians have paid serious attention to such capabilities in their studies.... As a result, scholars have made uncritical assumptions about military capability, particularly that of the United States." Harry R. Borowski, *A Hollow Threat: Strategic Air Power and Containment before Korea* (Westport, Conn.: Greenwood Press, 1982), 3.
3. Melvyn P. Leffler, "The American Conception of National Security and the Beginnings of the Cold War, 1945–1948," *American Historical Review* 89 (April 1984): 346–81.
4. Richard A. Best, Jr., *"Co-operation with Like-Minded Peoples": British Influences on American Security Policy, 1945–1949* (Westport, Conn.: Greenwood Press, 1986), 181.
5. Ibid., 185–86.
6. Oral history, by Richard D. McKinzie, 13, 18 November 1972, p.25, Harry S. Truman Library; André Beaufre, *NATO and Europe* (New York: Alfred A. Knopf, 1966), 27.
7. Borowski, *A Hollow Threat*, 116–17.
8. Ibid., 100–101.
9. David Alan Rosenberg, "American Atomic Strategy and the Hydrogen Bomb Decision," *Journal of American History* 66 (June 1979): 64, 68–69; Thomas H. Etzold and John Lewis Gaddis, eds., *Containment: Documents on American Policy and Strategy, 1945–1950* (New York: Columbia University Press, 1978), 318.
10. *The Journals of David E. Lilienthal*, vol. 2, *The Atomic Energy Years* (New York: Harper and Row, 1964), 464.

11. Robert H. Ferrell, ed., *The Eisenhower Diaries* (New York: Norton, 1981), 157.

12. David Alan Rosenberg, "U.S. Nuclear Stockpile 1945 to 1950," *Bulletin of the Atomic Scientists* (May 1982), 25–31; Steven L. Rearden, *History of the Office of the Secretary of Defense.* Vol. 1, *The Formative Years: 1947–1950* (Washington, D.C.: Office of Secretary of Defense, 1984), 439. Rosenberg offers no figures for mid-1949 but says there were at least 292 bombs by mid-1950 and approximately four hundred by 1 January 1951; Rearden has no figures beyond mid-1948. President Truman, incidentally, seems to have been fairly well versed on the size of the stockpile. Rosenberg in "American Atomic Strategy and the Hydrogen Bomb Decision," 66, relates that the president did not even know the stockpile's size until his first briefing by Lilienthal on 3 April 1947, when Truman appeared to be shocked by the figure Lilienthal gave him. *The Journals of David E. Lilienthal*, vol. 2, 165–66. According to Rosenberg, Lilienthal told the president there were seven complete weapons; more nuclear cores were available, but there was a shortage of polonium initiators. But someone was giving figures to the president, and in his later article on the stockpile Rosenberg presumes it was General Eisenhower, army chief of staff 1945–48—the Manhattan Project was under army control 1945–46. In this article Rosenberg cites a presidential comment from the diary of Eben A. Ayers, assistant White House press secretary, who attended the morning staff conferences, and whose diary is in the Truman Library. According to Ayers, on 14 October 1946 Truman said he "did not believe that there were over a half dozen" bombs in the stockpile. This figure would have been about right, considering that nine bombs were ready by 30 June and the two Bikini tests followed. Moreover, on 7–8 February 1947, also before Lilienthal briefed Truman, the president entertained his World War I first lieutenant in Battery D, 129th Field Artillery Regiment, Vic Housholder, who stayed overnight in the White House, and told him there were fourteen atomic bombs. The Rosenberg-Rearden figure for 30 June 1947, is thirteen, and because of the problem with polonium initiators Truman's figure must have been momentarily correct. Robert H. Ferrell, ed., "A Visit to the White House, 1947: The Diary of Vic H. Housholder," *Missouri Historical Review* 38 (1983–84), 329.

13. Borowski, *A Hollow Threat*, 82.

14. Ibid., 167.

15. President Truman and foreign ministers, meeting, 3 April 1949, Miscellaneous Historical Documents Collection, no. 626 Harry S. Truman Library, Independence, Missouri; Lawrence S. Kaplan, *The United States and NATO: The Formative Years* (Lexington: University Press of Kentucky, 1984), 6.

16. " . . . and the vast problem of subduing a sprawling empire stretching from Kamchatka to the Skaggerak with this weapon, to say nothing of the problem of using it against our occupied Western European allies. In any case, a Soviet attack today, while we could eventually defeat it, would involve an operation of incalculable magnitude in which, even if eventual victory is sure, the consequences to the U.S., and particularly to Western Europe, might well be disastrous."

17. Oral history by Dennison, 10 September 1971, Harry S. Truman Library, 22.

18. Interview in *New York Times Book Review*, 12 October 1969.

19. John Lewis Gaddis critiqued Leffler's article, and in reply the author stressed his conclusions. "Accordingly, I find Professor Gaddis's emphasis on the Soviet military threat in Eurasia very misleading. Soviet military capabilities did not constitute 'a threat of the first order,' because neither American officials nor European statesmen expected Soviet military aggression." Leffler, "The American Conception of National Security," 396. As for the manner in which American officials, military and civil, created their own problem: "Professor Gaddis wrote in *Strategies of Containment* that the Truman administration 'lost sight of the objective that strength was supposed to serve: ending the Cold War.' What Gaddis failed to recognize is that strength was not designed to end the Cold War; strength was designed to achieve the national security objectives I describe in my essay, regardless of the impact on the Cold War or on the Soviet Union. And the result of this may have been to discourage Soviet leaders from defining their opportunities in terms of a cooperative as well as a competitive relationship with the United States." Ibid., 398–99.

20. Ibid., 359–60; Truman's note of 5 March is in "Cabinet—meetings, 1946–50," President's Secretary's Files, box 154, Harry S. Truman Library; for the Truman testimony of 13 September 1948, see Robert H. Ferrell, *George C. Marshall* (New York: Cooper Square Publishers, 1966), 246–47; of 31 August 1949, Ayers diary of same date.

21. Alan Bullock, *Ernest Bevin: Foreign Secretary, 1945–1951* (New York: Norton, 1983), 614–82; Dean Acheson, *Sketches from Life of Men I have Known* (New York: Harper and Brothers, 1961), 1; diary of Eben A. Ayers, 10, 22, January, 21 March 1949; Hickerson oral history, by Richard D. McKinzie, Harry S. Truman Library, 53–54.

22. Sir John R. Colville, *The Personality of Sir Winston Churchill*, address at Westminster College, Fulton, Missouri, 24 March 1985, copy in Harry S. Truman Library.

23. Lewis W. Douglas to Lovett, 17 April 1948, *Foreign Relations of the United States: Government Printing Office, 1948* (Washington, D.C.: 1974) 3: 90. When the Soviets got the atomic bomb, Churchill said, war was a certainty.

24. Achilles oral history, 8–9, 12, 26; Kaplan, *The United States and NATO*, 58. As for the fish house punch, Achilles explained that the Metropolitan Club in Washington always held open house on Christmas Eve and New Year's Eve, and on the former they served free drinks and charged for lunch, and the latter charged for drinks and served free lunch. "Between the two they make a tidy profit."

25. Hickerson oral history, 56–57.

26. "Sphere of Influences: The United States and Europe, 1945–1949," in *The Long Peace: Inquires Into the History of the Cold War* (New York: Oxford University Press, 1987), 48–71.

27. Memorandum by Marshall of a conversation with the Swedish foreign minister, 14 October 1948, *Foreign Relations of the United States, 1948* 3: 264–66. Earlier the foreign minister of Norway, Halvard Manthey Lange, had reminded Marshall that Sweden was the only military factor in Scandinavia and could possibly develop trained ground forces of 600,000 men. Its navy was slightly weaker than the Soviet navy, and although its air force was small, it constituted the only air strength in the area. Sweden had a very large industrial potential. As against its potential he spoke of the vulnerability of Denmark and the short distance—

the narrow waters—separating Danes from Russians at Lübeck, the long borders, sparse population, and general military weakness of Norway. Marshall to Lovett, 30 September 1948, ibid., 256–57.

28. Theodore Achilles oral history, 132–33; Escott Reid, *Time of Fear and Hope: The Making of the North Atlantic Treaty, 1947–1949* (Toronto: McClelland and Stewart, 1977); John A. Munro and Alex I. Inglis, eds., *Mike: The Memoirs of the Right Honourable Lester B. Pearson, 1948–1957* (New York: Quadrangle Books, 1973).

29. Kaplan, *The United States and NATO*, 44.

30. Francis O. Wilcox oral history by Donald A. Ritchie, 1, 10 February, 21 March, 13 April, 13 June 1948, Senate Historical Office, copy in Harry S. Truman Library, 31.

31. "Senator Vandenberg, faced with a proposal to take a step into the strange and frightening postwar world, invariably began by resisting the proposal. He declared the end unattainable, the means harebrained, and the cost staggering, particularly some mysterious costs which he thought were bound to occur but which the proposer had not foreseen because of faulty preparation. This first phase, the phase of opposition, usually lasted through one meeting and sometimes longer." Acheson, *Sketches from Life of Men I have Known*, 126.

32. Theodore Achilles oral history, 20–21.

33. Bullock, *Ernest Bevin: Foreign Secretary*, 680; Kaplan, *The United States and NATO*, 93; Robin Edmonds, *Setting the Mould: The United States and Britain, 1945–1950* (New York: Norton, 1986), 182–84; Howard Jones, "*A New Kind of War*": *American's Global Strategy and the Truman Doctrine in Greece* (New York: Oxford University Press, 1989), 214ff.

34. For "Offtackle" see Thomas H. Etzold and John Lewis Gaddis, eds., *Containment: Documents on American Policy and Strategy, 1945–1950*, 324–34.

35. Steven L. Rearden, *The Formative Years*, 483; Kaplan, *The United States and NATO*, 143.

36. Rearden, *The Formative Years*, 481, 514. The definitive work on MDAP is Lawrence S. Kaplan, *Community of Interests: NATO and the Military Assistance Program, 1948–1951* (Washington, D.C.: Government Printing Office, 1980). Title II was Greece and Turkey, Title III was Iran, Korea, and the Philippines. Emphasis on NATO powers was instructive. As Truman said to the foreign ministers on the night before the signing of the treaty, "I intend to order the Joint Chiefs of Staff to keep aid to strategically peripheral areas to the minimum. Such aid is more for internal security and psychological purposes and to warn the U.S.S.R. to keep off than for anything else. We will have to get clearly across the basic principle that any future war is going to be global, as the boys in the Kremlin well know, and that if we are strong in the decisive theaters it will keep them from striking anywhere else." Miscellaneous Historical Documents Collection, no. 626.

37. *The Journals of David E. Lilienthal*, vol. 2, 632.

38. Truman to Murray, 19 January 1953, "Atomic Bomb," President's Secretary's Files, box 112. See also *The Journals of David E. Lilienthal*, vol. 2, 286 (28 January 1948), 342 (18 May), 388–92 (21 July), 474–75 (14 February 1949).

39. Borowski, *A Hollow Threat*, 153–54, 169, 191.

40. Rearden, *The Formative Years*, 486.

41. Beaufre, *NATO and Europe*, 28–29.

42. Miscellaneous Historical Documents Collection, box 626. The president said that "the decisive theater is Western Europe, the only power complex sufficiently strong, combined with the U.S., to decisively redress the world power balance and the only one which, if seized by the U.S.S.R., might render her almost impregnable."

43. "The American Origins of NATO: A Study in Domestic Inhibitions and Western European Constraints" (Ph.D. diss., University of Edinburgh, 1984), 38. Unfortunately for Foot's theory about American fascination with European integration, Lawrence Kaplan's *The United States and NATO* appeared the same year as Foot completed his studies at Edinburgh, and the book relates how talk about integration roused the old war horse of a United States of Europe, Count Richard Coudenhove-Kalergi, who came to the United States full of zeal but failed to sense the inner feeling about his project among senior officials of the Department of State. Counselor Bohlen sent the following note to Hickerson: "Coudenhove-Kalergi has been on my neck. I saw him when he was down here. You will note that he wants me to try to get him in to see the secretary. Could you let me have an estimate of his standing in Europe and whether his advocacy of European federation is taken sufficiently seriously abroad to justify recommendation that the secretary see him or is it more of a personal gambit?" Ibid., 57. In the event, the count saw Secretary Marshall for a few minutes and went away happy.

NATO and the Korean War: A Context

1. Lawrence S. Kaplan, *The United States and NATO: The Formative Years* (Lexington: University Press of Kentucky, 1984, 8–9. The author thanks the staff of the Harry S. Truman Presidential Library; David Langbart of the National Archives; Professors Lawrence Kaplan, Fred Harvey Harrington, Thomas McCormick, and William Appleman Williams for important materials and comments that informed this essay; and Nancy Skipper of Cornell's Olin Library for bibliographic help.

2. John Lewis Gaddis, "Was the Truman Doctrine a Real Turning Point?" *Foreign Affairs* 52 (Spring 1974): 386.

3. Senate Foreign Relations Committee, *Review of the World Situation; 1949–1950*, 81st Cong., 1st and 2d sess., Historical Series (Washington, D.C., 1974), 6, 12–13; Chancery to Washington, 4 June 1949, FO 371 AN1856, Public Record Office (PRO), Kew, England (hereafter cited as FO 371, with appropriate filing designations).

4. Diary, 26 August 1949, Eban A. Ayers Papers, box 17, Harry S. Truman Library.

5. Harrison to Foreign Office, Moscow, 23 June 1949, FO 371 N5696/1024/38, PRO; Nicholls to Harrison, 20 December 1949, FO 371 NS1023/1, PRO; "Review of the World Situation," 14 September 1949, NSC Meeting no. 45, 9/15/49, President's Secretary's File, National Security Council Meetings, box 206, Harry S. Truman Papers, Harry S. Truman Library, contains the CIA report; Michael J. Hogan outlines "the crisis of confidence that gripped the Western alliance in late 1949 and early 1950" in *The Marshall Plan: America, Britain and the Reconstruction of Western Europe, 1947–1952* (New York: Cambridge University

Press, 1987), 310–12; Samuel F. Wells, Jr., "Sounding the Tocsin: NSC-68 and the Soviet Threat," *International Security* 4 (Fall 1979): 117–18.

6. "Secretary's Off the Record Press Conference, August 26, 1949," Secretary of State Press Conferences, 1949–1953, Dean G. Acheson Papers, box 68, Harry S. Truman Library; McGeorge Bundy, ed., *The Pattern of Responsibility* (Boston: Houghton Mifflin, 1952), 68–69; "Meeting with the President on 1951 Budget Ceilings for National Defense and Foreign Aid," 1 July 1949, "Truman, President Harry S." file, Frederick J. Lawton Papers, box 6, Harry S. Truman Library; *Public Opinion Quarterly* 13 (Winter 1949–50): 725; Hogan, *The Marshall Plan*, 311–12, 340, 441–42.

7. Chancery to Foreign Office, 16 November 1949, FO 371 SN3600/1023/45, PRO; Chiefs of Staff Committee, 26 October 1949, COSC38/vol. 7, DEFE 4 (25), PRO.

8. "Brief for the Chief of the Imperial General Staff on Strategic Position of Ceylon," 28 September 1949, COSC38/vol. 7, DEFE 4 (25); Chiefs of Staff Committee, Joint Planning Staff, 21 November 1949, COSC/39/vol. 8, DEFE 4 (26), PRO.

9. "Press and Radio News Conference, Wednesday, Nov. 30, 1949," Secretary of State Press Conferences, 1949–1953, Acheson Papers, box 68; "Summary of Telegrams," 5 October 1949, Naval Aide Files, State Department Briefing folder, September–December 1949, Truman Papers; Chiefs of Staff Committee, "United Kingdom Contribution to the Defence of Western Europe," C.O.S. (49) 387, 12 November 1949, DEFE 5 (18), PRO; Chiefs of Staff Committee, Joint Planning Staff, "Japanese Peace Treaty–Defence Aspects. Report by the Joint Planning Staff, 20 December 1949," COSC 40/vol. 9, DEFE 4 (27), PRO; Richard Barnet, *The Alliance* (New York: Simon and Schuster, 1984), 55–56; "Conversations, with the President," 17 November 1949, Memoranda of Conversations, 1949, Acheson Papers, box 64; Manfred Jonas, *The United States and Germany: A Diplomatic History* (Ithaca, N.Y.: Cornell University Press, 1984), 289.

10. "Memorandum of Conversation, Dec. 1, 1949," Memoranda of Conversations, 1949, Acheson Papers, box 64; Sir O. Franks to Sir Wm. Strang, secret and personal, 27 November 1949, FO 371 AU1053/1, PRO.

11. "Study Group Reports," 1 November 1949, Group: Economic Policy, 1949–1950, Council on Foreign Relations, New York; Senate Foreign Relations Committee, *Review of the World Situation, 1949–1950*, Kennan draft memorandum to the secretary of state, 17 February 1950, U.S. Department of State, *Papers Relating to the Foreign Relations of the United States, 1950* (Washington, D.C.: Government Printing Office, 1977), 1: 165 (hereafter *FRUS, 1950*).

12. "Memorandum of Conversation, Oct. 13, 1949," Memoranda of Conversations, 1949, Acheson Papers, box 64; Dean Acheson, Oral History Interview, 16 February 1955, Harry S. Truman Post-Presidential Papers, Harry S. Truman Library; "A Report to the National Security Council by the Executive Secretary (Lay)" Enclosure 2 [NSC-68], *FRUS, 1950* 1: 250–51, 258–59.

13. An important analysis of the document's origins, including Kennan's role, is in Wells, "Sounding the Tocsin," 120–28.

14. *FRUS, 1950* 1: 260–61, 265.

15. Senate Foreign Relations Committee, *Review of the World Situation, 1949–1950*, 108; "F.O. Minute: Minutes of Russia Committee Meeting held on 9th January 1950," FO 371, NS1053/1/e, PRO.

16. Sir O. Franks to Foreign Office, 14 February 1950, FO 371, AU 1027/1, PRO.

17. Barrett to Acheson, 6 April 1950, *FRUS, 1950* 1: 225–26; Taft to Bruce Barton, 18 September 1949, "1949 A–B" correspondence, Robert Taft Papers, box 36, Library of Congress, Washington, D.C.; handwritten memorandum by Taft, undated but probably January 1950, "China-Formosa, 1950" file, Taft Papers, box 506; a good brief analysis of the internal criticism (including Truman's) is in Wells, "Sounding the Tocsin," 135–38.

18. Hogan, *Marshall Plan*, 311–16, 443–45; Lloyd C. Gardner, *Approaching Vietnam: From World War II through Dienbienphu, 1941–1954* (New York: Norton, 1988), 84–87; George McT. Kahin, *Intervention: How America Became Involved in Vietnam* (New York: Alfred A. Knopf, 1986), 32–38.

19. Donald C. McKay, *The United States and France* (Cambridge, Mass.: Harvard University Press, 1951), 242; important background for the decision is in William S. Borden, *The Pacific Alliance: United States Foreign Economic Policy and Japanese Trade Recovery, 1947–1955* (Madison: University of Wisconsin Press, 1984), 44–51, 122–24; Michael Schaller, "Securing the Great Crescent; Occupied Japan and the Origins of Containment in Southeast Asia," *Journal of American History* 69 (September 1982): 392–414; Michael M. Harrison, *The Reluctant Ally: France and Atlantic Security* (Baltimore: Johns Hopkins University Press, 1981), 14–15.

20. Senate Foreign Relations Committee, *Review of the World Situation, 1949–1950*, 267–69; "Record of a Meeting at No. 1 Carlton Gardens on the 10th May, 1950," PREM 8, PRO.

21. "Notes on a Conversation After Lunch at 1 Carlton Gardens on May 9th 1950," FO 371 AU1027/14G, PRO; Permanent Undersecretary's Committee, "A Third World Power or Western Consolidation?" 9 May 1949, PREM 8, PRO; F.O. Minute, 6 May 1950, FO 371, AU10512/2, PRO; Senate Foreign Relations Committee, *Review of the World Situation, 1949–1950*, 297.

22. "Study Group Reports," 28 March 1950, Group: Germany, 1949–1950, Council on Foreign Relations, New York; Ibid., 1 March 1950.

23. "Record of a Meeting at No. 1 Carlton Gardens on the 10th May, 1950," PREM 8, PRO; Alan Bullock, *Ernest Bevin, Foreign Secretary, 1945–1951* (New York: Norton, 1983), 768–70.

24. Laurence W. Martin, "The American Decision to Re-arm Germany," in *American Civil-Military Decisions*, ed. Harold Stein (Birmingham: University of Alabama Press, 1963), 649–51; Bullock, *Bevin*, 763–67.

25. Acheson to Harold Stein, 23 August 1957, "Walter Millis–Case Writer" file, Harold Stein Papers, Harry S. Truman Library; Glenn D. Paige, *The Korean Decision, June 24–30, 1950* (New York: Free Press, 1968), 147, 177; U.S. Department of State, *Monthly Survey of American Opinion* (August 1950), 1–3; Gaddis Smith, "A History Teacher's Reflections on the Vietnam War," *Ventures* 8 (Spring 1968), 60.

26. Steven Rearden, *Evolution of American Strategic Doctrine: Paul H. Nitze and the Soviet Challenge* (Boulder, Colo.: Westview Press, 1986), 30; Arthur Krock, *Memoirs* (New York: Funk and Wagnalls, 1968), 260; Sir O. Franks to Sir Wm. Strang, 12 July 1950, FO 371 AU1Q53/7, PRO; Martin, "The American Decision to Re-arm Germany," 652.

27. Senate Foreign Relations Committee, *Review of the World Situation, 1949–1950*, 329–30; *New York Herald Tribune*, 12 July 1950; *Department of State Bulletin* 23 (30 October 1950), 704.

28. Princeton Seminar, 10–11 October 1953, Acheson Papers.

29. FO Minute by Sir Wm. Strang, 21 July 1950, FO 371 FK1022/243, PRO.

30. Aide-Mémoire, received by Allen Dulles from intermediary from Adenauer; sent to J. F. Dulles and forwarded to Henry Byroade on 11 September 1950, John Foster Dulles Papers, Princeton University, Princeton, N.J.; Bevin to Attlee, 6 December 1950, PREM 8, PRO; "C. P. (50), 223, 6 October 1950, Cabinet: New York Meetings Memorandum by the Secretary of State for Foreign Affairs," PREM 8, PRO.

31. Anthony Eden, *Full Circle* (London: Cassell, 1960), 34; Sir P. Dixon for Bevin, brief, undated but probably 25 November 1950, PREM 8, PRO; *Department of State Bulletin* 23 (27 November 1950), 846–47.

32. "Copy of a private report from James Reston, December 11, 1950," Arthur Krock Papers, Black Book no. 2, Princeton University; Rosemary Foot, *The Wrong War: American Policy and the Dimensions of the Korean Conflict, 1950–1953* (Ithaca, N.Y.: Cornell University Press, 1985), 105–23.

33. Colonel G. A. ("Abe") Lincoln to Joseph Alsop, 1 December 1950, Joseph and Stewart Alsop Papers, General Correspondence, box 6, Library of Congress, Washington, D.C.

34. Bevin to Attlee, 6 December 1950, PREM 8, PRO; "Tripartite Meeting," 19 December 1950, PREM 8, PRO; Dean Acheson, *Present at the Creation: My Years at the State Department* (New York: Norton, 1969), 629–32.

35. Wells, "Sounding the Tocsin," 158.

The American Commitment to Germany, 1949–1955

1. U.S. Department of State, *Foreign Relations of the United States, 1949* (Washington, D.C.: Government Printing Office, 1974) 3: 352–56 (hereafter *FRUS*, with year and volume information). Details on drafting in *FRUS, 1950* (Washington, D.C.: Government Printing Office, 1977) 3: 1; and Kenneth W. Condit, *The History of the Joint Chiefs of Staff: The Joint Chiefs of Staff and National Policy*, vol. 2, *1947–1949* (Wilmington, Del.: Michael Glazier, 1979), 399–400.

2. Quoted in Gaddis Smith, *Dean Acheson* (New York: Cooper Square Publishers, 1972), 77.

3. *FRUS, 1949* (Washington, D.C.: Government Printing Office, 1975) 4: 354.

4. Ibid., 354–56.

5. U.S. Department of Defense, *Semiannual Report of the Secretary of Defense . . . January 1 to June 30, 1955* (Washington, D.C.: Government Printing Office, 1955), 54–55. On the first stages of this aid see Lawrence S. Kaplan, *A Community of Interests: NATO and the Military Assistance Program, 1948–1951* (Washington, D.C.: Office of the Secretary of Defense, 1980).

6. "Challenge and Response," *Time*, 26 December 1955, 15.

7. John Coppock, "NATO Improves its Aircraft Training," *Aviation Week*, 14 March 1955, 92–93.

8. The essence of MC-48 was never a secret. See *Department of State Bulletin* 33 (3 January 1955): 10; German press reports summarized in Gordon A.

Craig, "NATO and the New German Army," in *Military Policy and National Security*, ed. William W. Kaufmann (Princeton, N.J.: Princeton University Press, 1956), 220–22 and Klaus Knorr, ed., *NATO and American Security* (Princeton, N.J.: Princeton University Press, 1959), 13–29. Published U.S. documents concerning Western European security in the mid-1950s contain many references to MC-48 but not the document itself. NATO headquarters keeps it under lock and key. See *FRUS, 1952–1954* (Washington, D.C.: Government Printing Office, 1983) 5:536, n. 3. For not publishing later versions, the editors' explanation is that no copies were found in State Department files. See *FRUS, 1955–1957* (Washington, D.C.: Government Printing Office, 1986) 4:35. Further information can be gleaned from Robert J. Watson, *The Joint Chiefs of Staff and National Policy*, vol. 5, *1953–1954* (Washington, D.C.: Historical Division, Joint Chiefs of Staff, 1986), 316–21. The best reconstruction of the text, based largely on British chiefs of staff committee records, will be found in a doctoral dissertation by Robert A. Wampler near completion at Harvard University.

9. Science Advisory Committee, Office of Defense Mobilization, Technological Capabilities Panel, "Report to the President," 14–24 February 1955, White House Office, Office of the Staff Secretary, Subject series, box 16, Dwight D. Eisenhower Library, Abilene, Kansas.

10. Arthur M. Schlesinger, *The Age of Roosevelt*, vol. 1, *The Crisis of the Old Order, 1919–1933* (Boston: Houghton Mifflin, 1957), 57.

11. See Steven Skowronek, *Building a New American State: The Expansion of National Administrative Capacities, 1877–1920* (New York: Cambridge University Press, 1982); Barry D. Karl, *The Uneasy State: The United States from 1915 to 1945* (Chicago: University of Chicago Press, 1983); and Louis Galambos, ed., *The New American State: Bureaucracies and Policies since World War II* (Baltimore: Johns Hopkins University Press, 1987).

12. The most thoughtful study of American "officials" is Hugh Heclo, *A Government of Strangers: Executive Politics in Washington* (Washington, D.C.: Brookings Institution, 1977). The alternative term "political executive" is used in Joel D. Aberbach, Robert D. Putnam, and Bert A. Rockman, *Bureaucrats and Politicians in Western Democracies* (Cambridge, Mass.: Harvard University Press, 1981). I do not borrow that term because it does not distinguish between men and women who come to office because they take part in electoral politics and those who come to office because of status, expertise, or other such attributes. For similar reasons, I do not use the term "super bureaucrat" coined by Canadian political scientists: Colin Campbell and George J. Szablowski, *The Super-Bureaucrats: Structure and Behavior in Central Agencies* (Toronto: Macmillan of Canada, 1979). My argument here is developed at greater length in an essay entitled "Cold War and Defence" due to be published in a colloquium volume to be issued by the Royal Military Academy of Canada.

13. See Charles E. Neu, "The Rise of the National Security Bureaucracy," in *The New American State*, 85–108; Richard E. Neustadt, *Presidential Power: The Politics of Leadership from FDR to Carter* (New York: John Wiley, 1980); Hugh Heclo and Lester Salomon, eds., *The Illusion of Presidential Government* (Boulder, Colo.: Westview Press, 1981); and essays in John E. Chubb and Paul E. Peterson, eds., *The New Direction in American Politics* (Washington, D.C.: Brookings Institution, 1985), especially those by the editors, Steven S. Smith and Terry M. Moe.

14. See John Lewis Gaddis, *The United States and the Origins of the Cold War, 1941–1947* (New York: Columbia University Press, 1972), 337–46, and, for Fulbright, his 17 May 1946 speech for the American Academy of Arts and Letters in New York, excerpted in Karl E. Meyer, ed., *Fulbright of Arkansas: The Public Positions of a Private Thinker* (Washington, D.C.: R. B. Luce, 1963), 51–52. Lloyd C. Gardner, "Lost Empires," *Diplomatic History* 13 (Winter 1989): 5, argues that this concern was so strong as to be the equivalent of hysterical fixation.

15. For illustrations of the earlier porousness of the American political system, see William D'Arcy, *The Fenian Movement in the United States, 1858–1886* (Washington, D.C.: N.p., 1947); Alfred Vagts, *Deutschland und die Vereinigten Staaten in der Weltpolitik* [Germany and the United States in World Politics], 2 vols. (New York: N.p., 1935), vol. 1, chaps. 1–4, 8–9; and Joseph P. O'Grady, ed., *The Immigrants' Influence on Wilson's Peace Policies* (Lexington: University of Kentucky Press, 1967).

16. See Paul Y. Hammond, "Super Carriers and B-36 Bombers," in *American Civil-Military Decisions: A Book of Case Studies*, ed. Harold Stein (Birmingham: University of Alabama Press, 1963), 465–567; and Vincent C. Davis, *The Admirals Lobby* (Chapel Hill: University of North Carolina Press, 1967).

17. See Edward A. Kolodziej, *The Uncommon Defense and Congress, 1945–1963* (Columbus: Ohio State University Press, 1966); Vincent C. Davis, *Postwar Defense Policy and the U.S. Navy, 1943–1946* (Chapel Hill: University of North Carolina Press, 1966); Paolo E. Coletta, *The United States Navy and Defense Unification, 1947–1953* (Newark: University of Delaware Press, 1981); and Steven L. Rearden, *History of the Office of the Secretary of Defense*, vol. 1, *The Formative Years, 1947–1950* (Washington, D.C.: Office of the Secretary of Defense, 1984).

18. The best studies of service rivalries are still Samuel P. Huntington, *The Common Defense: Strategic Programs in National Politics* (New York: Columbia University Press, 1961); Warner R. Schilling, Paul Y. Hammond, and Glenn H. Snyder, *Strategy, Politics, and Defense Budgets* (New York: Columbia University Press, 1962); Hammond, "Super Carriers and B-36 Bombers"; and Kolodziej, *The Uncommon Defense and Congress*. Evidence of discussion of European strategy paralleling discussion of service budgets can be found in Doris M. Condit, *History of the Joint Chiefs of Staff*; and Alfred D. Chandler et al., eds., *The Papers of Dwight D. Eisenhower*, 11 vols. to date (Baltimore: Johns Hopkins University Press, 1970–), vols. 10, 11. Original records abound in Records of the Joint Chiefs of Staff, pt. 2, 1946–1953 (Microfilm Project of University Publications of America, 1981), hereafter cited as JCS Records.

19. There is an extensive literature on Nitze's work in this period. Particularly noteworthy are the Hammond essay in the Schilling, Hammond, and Snyder book cited above; Samuel F. Wells, Jr., "Sounding the Tocsin: NSC-68 and the Soviet Threat," *International Security* 4 (Fall 1979): 116–58; comments on Wells by John Lewis Gaddis, "NSC-68 and the Problem of Ends and Means," and Paul Nitze, "The Development of NSC-68," ibid. (Spring 1980): 164–70 and 170–76; and Steven L. Rearden, *The Evolution of American Strategic Doctrine: Paul H. Nitze and the Soviet Challenge* (Boulder, Colo.: Westview Press, 1986). What follows here draws upon these writings, documents in *FRUS, 1950* 1; Strobe Talbott's penetrating biographical sketch, *Master of the Game* (New York: Alfred A. Knopf, 1988); and Paul H. Nitze, *From Hiroshima to Glasnost: At the Center of*

Decision, a Memoir (New York: Grove Weidenfeld, 1989). Needless to say, however, I alone am to blame for the interpretation.

20. Memo by Nitze, 31 January 1949, *FRUS, 1949* 4: 54–59.

21. Hammond, "Origins of NSC-68," 294–304; Walter Isaacson and Evan Thomas, *The Wise Men: Six Friends and the World They Made: Acheson, Bohlen, Harriman, Kennan, Lovett, McCloy* (New York: Simon and Schuster, 1986), 500–503.

22. Wells, "Sounding the Tocsin," 139, argues that the increase would probably not have gone higher than $3 billion a year, absent the Korean War; Nitze, in his rejoinder to Wells, "The Development of NSC-68," 172–74, suggests that the increase might have reached $40 billion a year.

23. *FRUS, 1950* 1: 234 (emphasis in the original).

24. Press conference of 4 May 1950, *Public Papers of Harry S. Truman, 1950* (Washington, D.C.: Government Printing Office, 1965), 284–88.

25. William Whitney Stueck, Jr., *The Road to Confrontation: American Policy toward China and Korea, 1947–1950* (Chapel Hill: University of North Carolina Press, 1981), 130–31, 216–18; Robert Griffith, *The Politics of Fear, Joseph R. McCarthy and the Senate*, 2d ed. (Amherst: University of Massachusetts Press, 1987), 122–31.

26. Athan Theoharis, *Seeds of Repression: Harry S. Truman and the Origins of McCarthyism* (Chicago: Quadrangle Books, 1971); Richard M. Freeland, *The Truman Doctrine and the Origins of McCarthyism: Foreign Policy, Domestic Politics, and Internal Security, 1946–1948* (New York: Alfred A. Knopf, 1972); Edward A. Shils, *The Torment of Secrecy: The Background and Consequences of American Security Policies* (Glencoe, Ill.: Free Press, 1956), 77–104; Richard Hofstadter, *The Paranoid Style in American Politics* (New York: Alfred A. Knopf, 1967); Paul Boyer, *By the Bomb's Early Light: American Thought and Culture at the Dawn of the Atomic Age* (New York: Pantheon, 1985).

27. Kolodziej, *The Uncommon Defense and Congress*, 137–39.

28. The best summation of the budget story is in Doris M. Condit, *History of the Office of the Secretary of Defense*, vol. 2, *The Test of War, 1950–1953* (Washington, D.C.: Office of the Secretary of Defense, 1988).

29. Condit, *Test of War*, 233–42.

30. The authoritative survey is Lawrence S. Kaplan, *NATO and the United States: The Enduring Alliance* (Boston: Twayne, 1988).

31. JIC 435/12, "Soviet Intentions and Capabilities, 1948, 1952/57," 30 November 1948, JCS Records: Soviet Union, reel 3; Thomas W. Wolfe, *Soviet Power and Europe, 1945–1970* (Baltimore: Johns Hopkins University Press, 1970), 46; "Peace and the High Cost Thereof," *Newsweek*, 12 June 1950, 20; "How Strong is Russia?" *Time*, 27 November 1950, 22–25. Matthew Evangelista, "Stalin's Postwar Army Reappraised," *International Security* 7 (Winter 1982–83): 110–38, questions the validity of contemporaneous estimates of Soviet strength. V. N. Donchenko, "Demobilizatsiya Sovetskoi armii i reshenie problemy kadrov v pervye poselevoennye gody" [Demobilization of the Soviet army and decision on questions of cadres during the first postwar year], *Istoriya SSSR* 3 (1970): 97–98, is, so far as I know, the only discussion of the question by a Soviet historian. Though Donchenko deals in numbers of troops rather than numbers of divisions, his figures tend to support the American 1950–54 intelligence estimates.

32. Alexander Boyd, *The Soviet Air Force since 1918* (London: Macdonald and Jane's, 1977), 215–16; William T. Lee and Richard F. Staar, *Soviet Military Policy*

since World War II (Stanford: Hoover Institution, 1986), 12. There is considerable Soviet literature on the TU-4. See particularly L. L. Kerber, *TU: chelovek i samolët* [TU (pelov): Man and plane] (Moscow: Sov. Rossiya, 1973).

33. Boris I. Nicolaevsky, *Power and the Soviet Elite* (New York: Praeger, 1965) gives a good indication of what passed through the emigré rumor mill. Karel Kaplan, *Dans les archives du comité central: Trente ans de secrets du bloc soviétique* [In the archives of the Central Committee: thirty years of Soviet bloc secrets] (Paris: A. Michel, 1978), 164–66; and Bela Kiraly, "The Aborted Soviet Military Plans against Tito's Yugoslavia," in *War and Society in East Central Europe*, vol. 10, *At the Brink of War and Peace: The Tito-Stalin Split in a Historic Perspective*, ed. Wayne S. Vucinich (New York: Brooklyn College Press, 1982), 273–88, provide possible evidence that these rumors were not unfounded. See Vojtech Mastny, "Stalin and the Militarization of the Cold War," *International Security* 9 (Winter 1984–85): 109–29.

34. On Adenauer, the work now superseding all others is Hans-Peter Schwarz, *Adenauer: der Aufstieg, 1876–1952* [Adenauer: the Rise, 1876–1952] (Stuttgart: Deutsche Verlags-Anstalt, 1986), the first volume of a comprehensive biography. Still valuable, especially for events not yet covered by Schwarz, are Gerhard Wettig, *Entmilitarisierung und Wiederbewaffnung in Deutschland, 1943–1955* [Demilitarization and Rearmament in Germany, 1943–1955] (Munich: Oldenbourg, 1967), Arnulf Baring, *Aussenpolitik in Adenauers Kanzlerdemokratie* [Foreign Policy in Adenauer's Chancellor-Democracy] (Munich: Oldenbourg, 1969); and Hans Buchheim et al., "Aspekte der deutschen Wiederbewaffnung bis 1955" [Aspects of German rearmament before 1955], *Militärgeschichte seit 1945* 1 (Boppard: Boldt, published for the Militärgeschichtliches Forschungsamt, 1975). The first essay, by Gerhard Wettig, discusses the question of why the Soviets decided so early to arm the East Germans. On McCloy and the Germans, the outstanding work is Thomas A. Schwartz, "From Occupation to Alliance: John J. McCloy and the Allied High Commission in the Federal Republic of Germany, 1949–1952" (Ph.D. diss., Harvard University, 1985).

35. Konrad Adenauer, *Memoirs*, vol. 1, *1945–53* (Chicago: Henry Regnery, 1965), 246.

36. Theodore H. White, *In the Search of History: A Personal Adventure* (New York: Harper and Row, 1978), 261, 337–40. See his *Fire in the Ashes: Europe at Mid-Century* (New York: William Sloane, 1953).

37. Examples abound in volumes of *FRUS* for 1949 and 1950 concerning Western Europe.

38. McCloy to Acheson, 4 August 1950, *FRUS, 1950* (Washington, D.C.: Government Printing Office, 1980) 4: 704.

39. Bruce to Acheson, 1 September 1950, *FRUS, 1950* 3: 1384.

40. See, for example, JCS 2073/58, Joint Strategic Plans Group, "Availability of Military Forces for Short-Term Planning, NATO Regions," 18 May 1950, JCS Records: Europe and NATO, reel 5.

41. See Laurence W. Martin, "The American Decision to Rearm Germany," in *American Civil-Military Decisions*, 643–66; Robert McGeehan, *The German Rearmament Question: American Diplomacy and European Defense after World War II* (Urbana: University of Illinois Press, 1971); Christian Greiner, "The Defence of Western Europe and the Rearmament of West Germany, 1947–1950," and Norbert Wiggershaus, "The Decision for a West German Defence Contribution,"

in *Western Security: The Formative Years*, ed. Olav Riste (New York: Columbia University Press, 1985), 150–80 and 198–214, respectively; and the various works cited in note 34 above.

42. Most earlier work on the EDC is superseded by the essays in Klaus A. Maier et al., "Die europäische Verteidigungsgemeinschaft" [The European defense community], *Militärgeschichte seit 1945* 5 (1985). For the American side, the best study is Jennifer Laurendeau, "Webs of Influence: Policy Development and Decision Making during the Presidential Transition, 1952 and 1960" (Ph.D. diss., Harvard University, 1986), chap. 3.

43. McCloy to Acheson, 11 October 1950, *FRUS, 1950* 4: 369–71; Acheson to McCloy, 19 October 1950, ibid., 394–95; Douglas to Acheson, 27 October 1950, ibid., 412–15; Spofford to Acheson, 16 November 1950, ibid., 457–60; Acheson to Spofford, 18 November 1950, ibid., 471–72.

44. Condit, *Test of War*, 333–34; memo summarizing Acheson-Lovett telephone conversations, 15 December 1950, *FRUS, 1950* 4: 578–80.

45. See David R. Kepley, "The Senate and the Great Debate of 1951," *Prologue* 14 (Winter 1982): 213–26.

46. See Geoffrey Warner, "The British Labour Government and the Atlantic Alliance, 1949–1951," in *Western Security*, 247–65; Ritchie Ovendale, *English-Speaking Alliance: Britain, the United States, the Dominions and the Cold War, 1945–1951* (London: G. Allen and Unwin, 1985), 68–72, 281–82; and Robin Edmonds, *Setting the Mould: The United States and Britain, 1945–1950* (Oxford: Oxford University Press, 1986), 229–30.

47. Eisenhower to Gruenther, 27 October 1953, quoted in Stephen E. Ambrose, *Eisenhower, the President* (New York: Simon and Schuster, 1984), 143.

48. See, for example, JCS 1800/147, Joint Strategic Plans Committee, "Guidance for Programs and Budgets through FY 1953," 28 May 1951, JCS Records: Strategic Issues, Section 2—Postwar Military Requirements, reel 4; JCS 1800/179, Memorandum by the Chief of Staff of the Army, "Military Forces Required for National Security," 10 December 1951, ibid., reel 5; and JCS 1800/185, JCS, "Budget for Fiscal year 1954," 11 March 1952, ibid. For the British there is a great deal of evidence to this effect, derived from chiefs of staff committee records, in the Wampler dissertation cited in note 8 above.

49. George W. Perkins to J. Graham Parsons, 28 August 1951, 740.5/8–2851, General Records of the Department of State, Record Group 59, National Archives, Washington, D.C. This is one of a number of recently declassified documents included in a compilation prepared by Robert A. Wampler and David A. Rosenberg for the multinational Nuclear History Program.

50. Acheson to Schuman, 4 February 1952, *FRUS, 1952–1954* 5: 23; Acheson to Truman, 24 February 1952, ibid., 174.

51. Condit, *The Test of War*, 279.

52. Evelyn Shuckburgh, *Descent to Suez: Foreign Office Diaries, 1951–1956* (New York: Norton, 1986), 35; diary of Lord Moran, 7 January 1952, quoted in Martin Gilbert, *Winston S. Churchill*, vol. 5, *Never Despair, 1945–1965* (Boston: Houghton Mifflin, 1988), 678.

53. See Phil Williams, *US Troops in Europe* (London: Routledge and Kegan Paul, 1984) and *The Senate and US Troops in Europe* (New York: St. Martin's Press, 1985).

54. Edward Fursdon, *The European Defence Community: A History* (New York: St. Martin's Press, 1980), 1–49, summarizes the long background.

55. See Jean Monnet, *Memoirs* (Garden City, N.Y.: Doubleday, 1978) and Serge and Merry Bromberger, *Jean Monnet and the United States of Europe* (New York: Coward McCann, 1969).

56. Georgette Elgey, *La république des illusions, 1945–1951, ou la vie secrète de la IVe République* [The republic of illusions, or the secret life of the Fourth Republic] (Paris: Fayard, 1965), 431.

57. See William Diebold, Jr., *The Schuman Plan, A Study in Economic Cooperation 1950–1959* (New York: Praeger, 1959), chaps. 1–4; and Louis Lister, *Europe's Coal and Steel Community: An Experiment in Economic Union* (New York: Twentieth Century Fund, 1960), 3–18.

58. See, for example, Acheson to Bruce, 28 June 1951, *FRUS, 1951* (Washington, D.C.: Government Printing Office, 1981) 3: 801–5.

59. A Gallup poll of January 1951 showed Eisenhower the man Americans most admired: George H. Gallup, *The Gallup Poll: Public Opinion, 1935–1971*, 3 vols. (New York: Random House, 1972), 2: 963. Eisenhower consistently led all those mentioned as possible Republican candidates for the presidency: ibid., 926–27, 939–40, 953. He also led all those mentioned as possible Democratic candidates—indeed, by a margin of more than two to one: ibid., 977, 990. Truman's favorable rating was meanwhile falling from 43 percent in September 1950 to 22 percent in December 1951: ibid., 939, 958, 970, 989, 995, 1007, 1020, 1032.

60. Philip M. Williams, *Crisis and Compromise: Politics in the Fourth Republic* (New York: Anchor Books, 1966), app. 5.

61. Jules Moch, *Histoire de réarmement allemand* [History of German rearmament] (Paris: Robert Laffont, 1965), 268.

62. See Fursdon, *European Defence Community*, 303–39.

63. This argument is developed at greater length in essays by Josef Joffe, "Squaring Many Circles: West German Security Policy between Deterrence, Détente and the Alliance," and Ernest R. May, "American Forces in the Federal Republic: Past, Current and Future," in *The Federal Republic of Germany and the United States: Changing Political, Social, and Economic Relations*, ed. James A. Cooney et al. (Boulder, Colo.: Westview Press, 1984), 174–203 and 153–73, respectively.

64. Dulles statement to the North Atlantic Council, 14 December 1953, *FRUS, 1952–1954* 5: 463.

65. Press conference, 16 December 1953, *Public Papers of Dwight D. Eisenhower, 1953* (Washington, D.C.: Government Printing Office, 1960), 842.

66. See, for example, Townsend Hoopes, *The Devil and John Foster Dulles* (Boston: Little, Brown, 1973), 189–90.

67. *Aircraft of the Pima Air Museum* (Tucson, Ariz.: Pima Air Museum, 1987).

68. See John Baylis, *British Defence Policy in a Changing World* (London: Croom Helm, 1977), 101–03, 185; the phrase-maker was "Nye" Bevan.

69. An excellent official history is Richard G. Hewlett and Francis Duncan, *History of the United States Atomic Energy Commission*, vol. 2, *Atomic Shield, 1947/ 1952* (University Park: Pennsylvania State University Press, 1969), The inter-

related decisions are brilliantly analyzed in McGeorge Bundy, *Danger and Survival: Choices about the Bomb in the First Fifty Years* (New York: Random House, 1988), chap. 5. Another important work on the subject, written by Steven Rearden and Samuel R. Williamson, Jr., is currently being circulated in draft within the multinational Nuclear History Program.

70. See Chuck Hansen, *U.S. Nuclear Weapons, The Secret History* (Arlington, Tex.: Orion Books, 1988), 31–42, 171–76, 209–24; A. J. Bacevich, *The Pentomic Era: The U.S. Army between Korea and Vietnam* (Washington, D.C.: National Defense University Press, 1986), 71–102; and John J. Midgeley, Jr., *Deadly Illusions: Army Policy for the Nuclear Battlefield* (Boulder, Colo.: Westview Press, 1986), 1–86. Unofficial but plausible estimates concerning nuclear weapons characteristics and production appear in Thomas B. Cochran et al., *Nuclear Weapons Databook,* vol. 1, *U.S. Nuclear Forces and Capabilities* (Cambridge, Mass.: Ballinger, 1984) and vol. 2, *U.S. Nuclear Warhead Production* (Cambridge, Mass.: Ballinger, 1987). In 1959 President Eisenhower grumbled that "when we come to supplying small yield weapons for the Infantry and the Marines we are getting into the area of marginal utility." Memorandum of Conference with the President, 12 February 1959, White House Office, Office of the Special Assistant for National Security Affairs: NSC Series, Briefing Notes Subseries (WHO-SANSA), box 37, Eisenhower Library.

71. See note 8 above.

72. There is eloquent testimony to this effect in two long unsigned memoranda for Lewis Strauss, then chairman of the Atomic Energy Commission, 14–15 February 1957, the author of which identifies himself as a former nuclear operations planner on the SACEUR staff: WHO-SANSA, box 17, Eisenhower Library.

73. See the Bacevich and Midgeley studies cited in note 70 above.

74. See Michael D. Hobkirk's suggestive *The Politics of Defence Budgeting: A Study of Organisation and Resource Allocation in the United Kingdom and the United States* (Washington, D.C.: National Defence University Press, 1983).

75. See David N. Schwartz, *NATO's Nuclear Dilemmas* (Washington, D.C.: Brookings Institution, 1983), chaps. 3, 4.

76. I base this assertion partly on the works on Britain cited in note 46 above but mostly on evidence in the forthcoming Wampler dissertation cited in note 8.

77. See appendix 3, "The Interchangeable Ministers," in Williams, *Crisis and Compromise.*

78. His *Memoirs* provide plenty of examples but no explanation. See vol. 1, 202–4, 244–45, 267–69, 305–7, 315.

79. Geir Lundestad, "Empire by Invitation? The United States and Western Europe, 1945–1952," *Journal of Peace Research* 23 (1986) : 263–77.

80. The standard surveys are Roger Morgan, *The United States and West Germany, 1945–1973: A Study in Alliance Politics* (London: Oxford University Press, 1974) and Manfred Jonas, *The United States and Germany, A Diplomatic History* (Ithaca: Cornell University Press, 1984). While both are good, both miss this essential difference in perspective. It is better captured in Gregory F. Treverton, *The Dollar Drain and American Forces in Germany: Managing the Political Economics of Alliance* (Athens: Ohio University Press, 1978).

Charles de Gaulle and the French Withdrawal from NATO's Integrated Command

1. Christian Pineau quoted in Maurice Vaïsse, "Aux origines du mémorandum de septembre 1958," *Relations internationales* 58 (Summer 1989): 254.
2. Interview with General Andrew J. Goodpaster, U.S. Army (Ret.), 5 April 1989, Washington, D.C.
3. Général Jean Delmas, "A la recherche des signes de la puissance: l'Armée entre l'Algerie et la bombe A," *Relations internationales* 57 (Spring 1989), 79–87; Vaïsse, "Mémorandum de septembre 1958," 260–68; Michael H. Harrison and Mark G. McDonough, *Negotiations on the French Withdrawal from NATO* (Washington, D.C.: Johns Hopkins Foreign Policy Institute, 1987), 8–21.
4. Charles de Gaulle, *Discours et Messages: Avec le Renouveau* (May 1958–July 1962; reprint, Paris: Plon, 1970): 126–27.
5. Comment of Gabriel Robin at a conference on "American Historians and the Atlantic Alliance," 15 May 1989, Brussels; at a later conference of the Nuclear History Program at Wye Plantation in Queenstown, Maryland, 7 July 1989, Frederic Bozo of the Institut français des relations internationales and Amiral Marcel Duval, who in 1959 was commander of French naval forces in the Mediterranean, agreed with Robin's interpretation of the significance of the speech at the École militaire.
6. Goodpaster interview, 5 April 1989; Eisenhower's news conference, 3 February 1960, *Public Papers of the Presidents of the U.S.: Dwight D. Eisenhower, 1960–1961* (Washington, D.C.: Government Printing Office, 1961), 152.
7. For a discussion of the debate on nuclear assistance to France in 1959–1960, see John Newhouse, *De Gaulle and the Anglo-Saxons* (London: Deutsch, 1970), 111–19; and Richard H. Ullman, "The Covert French Connection," *Foreign Policy* 75 (Summer 1989): 5–7.
8. Robert S. McNamara, "Defense Arrangements of the North Atlantic Community," *Department of State Bulletin* 47 (9 July 1962): 67–68; McGeorge Bundy, *Danger and Survival: Choices About the Bomb in the First Fifty Years* (New York: Random House, 1988), 472–87, contains a well-argued analysis of Eisenhower and Kennedy policies toward the French nuclear force. A very sound treatment of French responses to the evolving strategy of flexible response can be found in Jane E. Stromseth, *The Origins of Flexible Response: NATO's Debate over Strategy in the 1960s* (New York: St. Martin's Press, 1988), 96–120.
9. De Gaulle, *Discours et Messages: Avec le Renouveau*, 403.
10. Ibid., 412–13.
11. Michael M. Harrison, *The Reluctant Ally: France and Atlantic Security* (Baltimore: Johns Hopkins University Press, 1981), 116–24.
12. Quoted in ibid., 106.
13. Charles de Gaulle, *Major Addresses, Statements and Press Conferences of General Charles de Gaulle: May 19, 1958–January 31, 1964* (New York: French Press Office, 1965), 208–22.
14. Comment of Gabriel Robin, 15 May 1989.
15. U.S. Department of State, *American Foreign Policy: Current Documents, 1966* (Washington, D.C.: Government Printing Office, 1969), 316–50.
16. Comment of Gabriel Robin, 15 May 1989; interview with Ambassadeur

de France François de Rose, 19 May 1989, Paris; interview with Jean Laloy, member of l'Institut de France, 17 May 1989, Paris.

17. Interview with Robert R. Bowie, 15 March 1989, Washington, D.C.; interview with Edgar J. Beigel, 29 March 1989, Washington, D.C.

18. Goodpaster interview, 5 April 1989.

19. Bowie interview, 15 March 1989.

20. Newhouse, *De Gaulle and the Anglo-Saxons*, 250–53, 267–68; W. W. Rostow, *The Diffusion of Power: An Essay in Recent History* (New York: Macmillan, 1972), 391–94.

21. Newhouse, *De Gaulle and the Anglo-Saxons*, 351–52.

"Nixingerism," NATO, and Détente

1. Robert S. Litwak, *Détente and the Nixon Doctrine: American Foreign Policy and the Pursuit of Stability, 1969–1976* (Cambridge: Cambridge University Press, 1984), 48. Kissinger coined this phrase "special relationship" in 1972 at the end of his successful pursuit to become Nixon's closest foreign policy adviser. See "Kissinger: An Interview with Oriana Fallaci," *The New Republic*, 16 December 1972, 20–21.

2. For details of what became a very "unhealthy" relationship between Nixon and Kissinger, see Joan Hoff-Wilson, *Nixon Without Watergate: A Presidency Reconsidered* (New York: Basic Books, 1990), chap. 6.

3. With Nixon's approval, Kissinger quickly transformed the National Security Council system into a personal foreign-policy secretariat. By subordinating the Senior Interdepartmental Group, formerly chaired by a representative of the State Department, to the Review Group, which he chaired, Kissinger effectively undercut the State Department's influence over policy making. Ultimately he chaired six special committees operating out of the NSC. Moreover, he created interdepartmental committees that prepared policy studies, which were submitted directly to his Review Group before they were presented to the NSC or to the president. He also tried to provide a "conceptual framework" for American diplomacy by establishing a series of National Security Study Memoranda (NSSMs). These were drafted by the NSC staff and signed by Kissinger on behalf of Nixon. They directed various agencies and groups within the government to prepare detailed policy options, not policy recommendations, which were then passed on by Kissinger to the NSC and argued out in front of the president.

The NSSM system was designed to prevent respondents, the State Department, and other executive departments from becoming advocates. By relegating them to analysts, the new NSC system supposedly put the bureaucrats in their "proper places." Even this elaborate restructuring did not completely satisfy the desire of the president and his secretary of state to control the process of foreign policy formulation. Most covert foreign policies of the Nixon administration, for example, bypassed the NSC. This says something quite significant about policy making under Nixon and the legacy he left in foreign affairs. When a decision could be carried that did not rely upon the civilian or military bureaucracy for implementation, the NSC was ignored whether the action was covert or not. It was utilized, however, whenever the covert or overt policy required bureaucratic support.

Using this guideline, it can be determined when the NSC system was employed as a debating forum for presenting options to the president and when it was not. The NSC did not debate the concept of Vietnamization, the Nixon Doctrine, the secret Kissinger negotiations with North Vietnam, the international aspects of Nixon's New Economic Policy (NEP) announced in August 1970, the various attempts by the CIA to undermine the elected Marxist government of Salvador Allende Gossens, or the planning of Nixon's historic trip to China to redirect U.S. Asian policy vis-à-vis the Soviet Union. All of these policies or actions were presented to the NSC, if at all, as fait accompli. However, the NSC did debate and approve of the secret bombing of Cambodia and the mild response of the United States to the EC-121 incident in the first year of the Nixon administration. Later it played a role in such policy decisions as the attempt to keep Taiwan in the United Nations with a "two China" policy, the decision to conduct incursions into Cambodia and Laos, the détente agreements with the Soviet Union, and Middle Eastern diplomacy before the 1973 Yom Kippur War. The key to understanding this varied track record of the NSC rests in the amount of bureaucratic support at home and abroad necessary to carry out respective policies.

4. Litwak, *Détente and the Nixon Doctrine*, 58. For more details see Hoff-Wilson, *Nixon Without Watergate: A Presidency Revisited*, chap. 6.

5. Even Nixon's early dealings with NATO were characterized by covert actions, as on 4 February 1969, when he told Kissinger that he wanted "to go forward with a heads of government meeting" during the NATO twentieth-anniversary gathering in April, but that this plan should be "very closely held until we complete our European trip. I will discuss this matter of other NATO heads of government and then make the announcement on my return from the trip." See Nixon to Kissinger, box 228, Haldeman Files, White House Special Files (hereafter WHSF), Nixon Presidential Materials Project (hereafter NPMP), National Archives and Records Administration (hereafter NARA), Alexandria, Virginia.

6. Raymond L. Garthoff, *Détente and Confrontation: American-Soviet Relations from Nixon to Reagan* (Washington, D.C.: Brookings Institution, 1985), 25, 32, 48; Richard W. Stevenson, *The Rise and Fall of Détente: Relaxations of Tension in U.S.-Soviet Relations, 1953–1984* (Urbana: University of Illinois Press, 1985), 11.

7. Richard M. Nixon, *The Memoirs of Richard Nixon* (New York: Grosset and Dunlap, 1978), 415; Garthoff, *Détente and Confrontation*, 29, 53, 57; Nixon to Kissinger, 16 June 1969, box 1, President's Personal Files (hereafter PPF), WHSF, Nixon Presidential Materials Project, NARA; Stevenson, *Rise and Fall of Détente*, 185.

8. For example, the Soviet Union never viewed détente as a static condition or status quo concept in the way the United States did. For the U.S.S.R., those perceptual factors promoting détente by the beginning of the 1970s were: the idea that history was on their side, improving Sino-American relations, U.S. unilateral troop withdrawals from Vietnam, Nixon's acceptance of strategic parity, certain economic considerations, and the personal relationship between Nixon and Brezhnev. By 1975, many of these perceptions had changed because of stalled CSCE and MBFR talks, congressional obstacles to Soviet-American trade, and the double standard code of conduct that the United States applied to its

own interference into the affairs of Third World countries compared to that accorded the U.S.S.R. And, of course, Nixon was no longer on the international (or domestic) scene.

9. Garthoff, *Détente and Confrontation*, 33–36, 47; U.S. Congress, Senate Committee on Foreign Relations, *Hearings on Détente*, 93d Cong., 2d sess., August-September 1974, pp. 239, 301 (quoting Dean Rusk and Kissinger); Stevenson, *Rise and Fall of Détente*, 6–11, 179–82, 188; Franz Schurmann, *The Foreign Politics of Richard Nixon* (Berkeley, Calif.: Institute of International Studies, 1987), 80–81, 88. For a strictly economic interpretation of détente, see Marshall I. Goldman, *Détente and Dollars: Doing Business with the Soviets* (New York: Basic Books, 1975); and Keith L. Nelson, "Nixon, Brezhnev, and Détente," unpublished paper delivered at the 1985 Pacific Coast Branch of the American Historical Association. For the argument that détente simply reflected a continuation of George Kennan's ideas about containment, see John Gaddis, *Strategies of Containment: A Critical Appraisal of Postwar American National Security Policy* (New York: Oxford University Press, 1982), 283.

10. Schurmann, *Foreign Politics of Richard Nixon*, 47–64, 84–90, 372–82. Schurmann makes a much more convincing case for Nixon's grand design than C. Warren Nutter does in *Kissinger's Grand Design* (Washington, D.C.: American Enterprise Institute for Public Policy Research, 1975).

11. Nixon to NATO General Secretary Brosio, 11 January 1969, Nixon NATO Proclamation, 28 March 1969, Kissinger to Congressman Paul Findley, 16 April 1969, box 10, Executive Files (hereafter EX), International Organizations 50 (hereafter IT 50), WHSF, NPMP, Alexandria, Va., NARA.

12. Nixon Address at the Commemorative Session of the North Atlantic Council, 10 April 1969, *Nixon Public Papers, 1969* (hereafter *NPP, year*), (Washington, D.C.: Government Printing Office, 1971), 145.

13. Nixon to Secretary of State, et al., 14 April 1969, box 1, PPF, WHSF, NPMP, NARA. This memorandum was not sent. The three recommendations he made in his April 10 address were: (1) "that deputy foreign ministers meet periodically for a high-level review of major, long-range problems before the Alliance"; (2) the "creation of a special political planning group . . . to address itself specifically and continually to the longer-range problems"; and (3) the "establishment of a committee on the challenges of modern society . . . to explore ways in which the experience and resources of the Western nations could most effectively be marshaled toward improving the quality of life of our peoples." See *NPP, 1969*, pp. 274–75.

14. See Garthoff, *Détente and Confrontation*, 24–29, for a discussion of when Nixon and Kissinger began to use the word *détente* as a general description of their overall foreign policies. Despite this delay of a little over a year, Nixon, at least, was using the term on a regular basis in private and in a less comprehensive fashion in public from the very beginning of his administration.

15. Robert Gilpin, *The Political Economy of International Relations* (Princeton, N.J.: Princeton University Press, 1987), 140, 149, 164–65; and Schurmann, *Foreign Politics of Nixon*, 368–74. While there is no dispute over the unilateral aspects of the NEP, there is still considerable debate over how international these economic moves on the part of the United States ultimately were.

16. Kissinger, "The Future of NATO," *The Washington Quarterly: A Review of Strategic and International Issues* 2 (Autumn 1979): 9; "The Future of the

Alliance: Report of the Council," in *NATO Final Communiqués, 1949–1970* (Brussels: NATO, 1971), 188–92. It should be remembered that some of the foreign policy documents in the Nixon presidential papers remain classified, so it is conceivable that some of them will reveal a greater reliance by the former president on the Harmel Report than now appears evident. For a description of changing relations between West and East Europe led by de Gaulle and various German chancellors in the last half of the 1960s, see Josef Korbel, *Détente in Europe: Real or Imaginary?* (Princeton, N.J.: Princeton University Press, 1972); Garthoff, *Détente and Confrontation*, 8–10, 106–26. Nixon's admiration for de Gaulle is documented in Schurmann, *Foreign Politics of Nixon*, 51–55. Schurmann also stresses the similarities between Nixon and de Gaulle in this book. Richard M. Nixon, *Leaders: Profiles and Reminiscences of Men Who Have Shaped the Modern World* (New York: Warner Books, 1982), 40–80.

17. February–March 1969, RN Notes—European trip, n.d., President's Speech File, PPF, WHSF, NPMP, NARA.

18. Ibid.

19. Nixon to Haldeman, Ehrlichman, and Kissinger, 2 March 1970 (emphasis added), box 229, Presidential Memoranda, Haldeman Files, Papers of Harry R. Haldeman, WHSF, NPMP, NARA.

20. Seymour Hersh, *The Price of Power: Kissinger in the White House* (New York: Summit Books, 1983), 148–49; *U.S. News and World Report*, 17 February 1969, pp. 46–47.

21. Garthoff, *Détente and Confrontation*, 25–36.

22. Nixon, *Memoirs*, 415–18.

23. Hersh, *The Price of Power*, 157–67; Gerald C. Smith, *Doubletalk: The Story of the First Strategic Arms Limitation* (Garden City, N.Y.: Doubleday, 1980), 60–64, 90. Also see note 46 below. In addition to telling Semenov that the ABM could not work, Smith praised his Soviet Colleague for having a better understanding of the necessity to reduce nuclear weapons than those trying to direct arms control from the White House.

24. In his 1957 book, *Nuclear Weapons and Foreign Policy*, Kissinger indicated that nuclear weapons were strategically useful not because they would be used, but because they deterred; in 1961, in *The Necessity for Choice*, he actually argued that some small nuclear weapons could play a tactical role under certain combat conditions.

25. Nixon, *Memoirs*, 418.

26. Alexander Butterfield to Nixon, 11 June 1969, Butterfield telephone calls, August 1969; Bryce Harlow to Nixon, box 2, 1 July 1969, President's Handwriting, box 30, 8, 13, 24 April, 11 May 1969, box 30, ANS, POF; Nixon to Herbert Klein, 13 March 1969, Nixon to Ehrlichman, 10 April 1969, box 1, PPF, WHSF, NPMP, NARA. Also see Kissinger, *White House Years*, 204–12; Schurmann, *Foreign Politics of Nixon*, 114–18.

27. Author's interview with Nixon, 26 January 1983; Nixon to Robert Litwak, 29 June 1984 (document in author's possession). Documents relating to Nixon's Midway meeting can be found in box 64, General Foreign Affairs 6–2, NPMP, NARA.

28. Litwak, *Détente and the Nixon Doctrine*, 136; Stevenson, *Rise and Fall of Détente*, 184.

29. Schurmann, *Foreign Politics of Nixon*, 118.

30. Ibid., 204; Cabinet meeting, 20 May 1971, box 43, Haldeman Notes, WHSF, NPMP, NARA.

31. This meant, of course, that from the beginning of the Nixon administration, entire areas of the world such as southern Asia, the Middle East, Africa, and Latin America—areas commonly referred to as the Third World—occupied a secondary place in the president's (and his national security adviser's) political approach to foreign policy. In particular, Nixon and Kissinger largely ignored economic foreign policy considerations in dealing with the Third World, preferring, instead, to "link" events in such countries to power relations between the major nations. "Linkage," therefore, accounts for many of the seemingly erratic aspects of U.S. foreign policy in Third World areas that fell outside of the parameters of pentagonal strategy. Nixon was more interested in maintaining American spheres of influence in the Third World than in the economic needs of these developing nations. Thus, the United States promoted the overthrow of Allende in Chile; restrained Egyptian and Syrian aggression in the Middle East while ignoring the potential instability of the Shah's regime in Iran and indirectly encouraging the rise in OPEC oil prices; continued to oppose Castro in Cuba; and supported Pakistan against India. The grand design may have been "grand" by superpower standards, but it remained ineffectually grandiose with respect to the Third World.

32. Garthoff, *Détente and Confrontation*, 31.

33. Ibid., 115.

34. Ken Belieu to Nixon, 17 May 1971, Clark MacGregor to Nixon, 18 May, 29 June 1971, Nixon to Harry Truman, 21 May 1971, Truman to Nixon, 7 June 1971, box 10, EX, IT 50; Dean Rusk to Kissinger, 21 May 1971, box 11, GEN IT 50, Mathias to Kissinger, 20 May 1971, Kissinger to Mathias, n.d., box 15, Confidential Files FG 6-11-1, Subject files. All in WHSF, NPMP, NARA.

35. Garthoff, *Détente and Confrontation*, 110–15; Kissinger, *White House Years*, 402.

36. Garthoff, *Détente and Confrontation*, 115; Kissinger, *White House Years*, 399; see footnote 32: MacGregor to Nixon, 17, 18 May 1971.

37. Garthoff, *Détente and Confrontation*, 115; Kissinger, *White House Years*, 949; MacGregor to Nixon, 17 May 1971.

38. With his usual propensity to exaggerate achievement and to turn coincidence into calculated success, Kissinger claimed that "the debate over the Mansfield amendment was a benchmark in the American domestic debate over foreign policy, though none of the participants understood this at the time. Until then the Administration had been on the defensive on the whole range of its policies.... With the SALT announcement on May 20 we seized the initiative. It was followed by my secret trip to Peking, the announcement of the Moscow summit, and a nearly uninterrupted series of unexpected moves that captured the 'peace issues' and kept our opponents off balance." See *White House Years*, 949.

39. J. F. Lehman to Kissinger, 6 March 1973, box 11, EX IT 50, handwritten Nixon note to Kissinger on 15 March 1973 news summary, box 49, ANS, POF—all in WHSP, NPMP, NARA; Henry Kissinger, *Years of Upheaval* (Boston: Little, Brown, 1982), 700, 707–22.

40. OMB legislative Referral Memorandum to DOD and NSC, 27 June 1973 (re: H. Con Res. 146, 168, 198), W. Marshall Wright to Thomas E. Morgan, n.d.

(attached to OMB memo), Kissinger to Nixon, 13 May 1974, box 11, EX IT 50, WHSF, NPMP, NARA.

41. Remarks on Arrival at Brussels, 25 June 1974, *NPP, 1974,* p. 547; Lester A. Sobel, ed., *Kissinger and Détente* (New York: Facts on File, Inc., 1975), 165.

42. Gaddis, *Strategies of Containment,* 280–81.

43. Hersh, *The Price of Power,* 350–82, 489–502.

44. For a discussion of the illegalities (comparable to those involved in the Iran-Contra affair) of the attempt under Reagan to reinterpret the ABM Treaty in order to find loopholes for development and deployment of the SDI, see Raymond L. Garthoff, *Policy versus the Law: The Reinterpretation of the ABM Treaty* (Washington, D.C.: The Brookings Institution, 1987).

45. Raymond L. Garthoff, *Perspectives on the Strategic Balance: A Staff Paper* (Washington, D.C.: The Brookings Institution, 1983), 6–8, 15.

46. Gordon R. Weihmiller, *U.S.-Soviet Summits: An Account of East-West Diplomacy at the Top, 1955–1985* (Lanham, Md.: University Press of America, 1986), 54–65. For details about Nixon's and Kissinger's confusion over whether the SLBMs had been included or excluded in certain drafts of the interim agreement because they bypassed knowledgeable bureaucrats and experts on this and other subjects, and for their generally unprofessional treatment of the SALT delegation, see Garthoff, *Détente and Confrontation,*155–88; Smith, *Doubletalk,* pp. 371–440; and Hersh, *The Price of Power,* 529–60.

47. Hersh, *The Price of Power,* 531–34; *New York Times,* Business Section, 23 June 1974.

48. Stevenson, *Rise and Fall of Détente,* 170–71; Garthoff, *Détente and Confrontation,* 453–63.

49. Joan Hoff-Wilson, *Ideology and Economics: U.S. Relations with the Soviet Union* (Lexington: University Press of Kentucky, 1971).

50. Buchen to Eva L. Ritt, 27 January 1976, Philip Buchen Papers, box 20, and Jackson to Kissinger, 22 August 1975, John Marsh Files, box 31, Gerald R. Ford Presidential Library, Ann Arbor, Mich. See also "Ford Aides Play Down Helsinki," *Christian Science Monitor,* 29 July 1975; and Helsinki folder, box 19, Buchen Papers, Ford Library.

51. U.S. Senate, Committee on Armed Services, *Hearing on FY 1976 Authorization for Military Procurement,* part 1, 94th Cong., 1st sess., 1975, 9–10. See also Coral Bell, *The Diplomacy of Détente: The Kissinger Era* (London: Martin Robertson, 1977), 218–22; Schurmann, *Foreign Policies of Nixon;* and Garthoff, *Détente and Confrontation,* 438–53.

52. Stevenson, *Rise and Fall of Détente,* pp. 173–77; Garthoff, *Détente and Confrontation,* pp. 440–42; Stephen E. Ambrose, *Nixon,* Vol. 2: *The Triumph of a Politician, 1962–1972* (New York: Simon and Schuster, 1989), p. 655; Kissinger folder, Ford Press Conference, 3 November 1975, box 5, David Gergen Files; "US-USSR Relations" (confidential State Department Briefing Paper), WHCF, Subject File 58–USSR, box 53, n.d. September 1976 (declassified for author 28 June 1989).

53. "Why Kissinger Woos Grass-roots Support," and "Kissinger Goes to People to Strengthen his Hand," *Christian Science Monitor,* 25 June 1975, p. 1, and 17 July 1975, p. 4.

The SS-20 Challenge and Opportunity

1. Cyrus Vance, *Hard Choices: Critical Years in America's Foreign Policy* (New York: Simon and Schuster, 1983), 441–62.
2. Gaddis Smith, *Morality, Reason, and Power: American Diplomacy in the Carter Years* (New York: Hill and Wang, 1986).
3. Excellent discussions of SALT II diplomacy are in Strobe Talbott, *Endgame: The Inside Story of SALT II* (New York: Harper and Row, 1986) and Raymond L. Garthoff, *Détente and Confrontation: American-Soviet Relations from Nixon to Reagan* (Washington: Brookings Institution, 1985).
4. Vance, *Hard Choices*, 57.
5. Jimmy Carter, *Keeping Faith* (New York: Bantam Books, 1982), 80–83.
6. Talbott, *Endgame*, 134–35.
7. *Survival* 20, no. 1 (January-February 1978), 2–10.
8. See the impressive four-part article by Jeffrey Smith, "Missile Deployments Roil Europe," *Science* 223 (27 January 1984) and subsequent issues.
9. Talbott, *Endgame*, 210–11.
10. Milton Leitenberg, "The Neutron Bomb—Enhanced Radiation Weapons," *Journal of Strategic Studies* 5 (September 1982), 341–69.
11. 6 June 1977.
12. Zbigniew Brzezinski, *Power and Principle: Memoirs of the National Security Adviser, 1977–1981* (New York: Farrar, Straus, Giroux, 1983), 301–6.
13. Vance, *Hard Choices*, 69.
14. Brzezinski, *Power and Principle*, 304.
15. Vance, *Hard Choices*, 94.
16. Garthoff, *Détente and Confrontation*, 853.
17. Jeffrey Smith, "Missile Deployments," 375.
18. U.S. Department of State, *American Foreign Policy Basic Documents, 1977–1980* (Washington, D.C.: Government Printing Office, 1983), doc. 199.
19. Brzezinski, *Power and Principle*, 309.
20. Ibid., 310.
21. Strobe Talbott, *Deadly Gambits* (New York: Harper and Row, 1984) and *Master of the Game: Paul Nitze and the Nuclear Peace* (New York: Knopf, 1988).
22. Colin S. Gray and Keith Payne, "Victory is Possible," *Foreign Policy* 39 (Summer 1980), 14–27.
23. Douglas C. Waller, *Congress and the Nuclear Freeze* (Amherst: University of Massachusetts Press, 1987).
24. McGeorge Bundy, George F. Kennan, Robert S. McNamara, and Gerard Smith, "Nuclear Weapons and the Atlantic Alliance," *Foreign Affairs* 60 (Spring 1982), 753–68.
25. The burgeoning antinuclear activity of those years can be followed in the pages of *The Bulletin of the Atomic Scientists* and at a more populist level, *Nuclear Times*. For a scholarly examination of the long hibernation of a popular antinuclear movement, until the advent of Reagan, see Paul Boyer, "From Activism to Apathy: The American People and Nuclear Weapons, 1963–1980," *Journal of American History* 70 (March 1984), 821–44.
26. Henry Brandon, *Special Relationships* (New York: Macmillan, 1988), 402.

The INF Treaty and the Future of NATO

A different version of this essay was published by the Woodrow Wilson International Center for Scholars as " 'The End of the Alliance': Lessons of the 1960s," in the series "Beyond the Cold War," *Current Issues in European Security*, September 1990.

1. Note for example Irving Kristol, "Does NATO Still Exist?" in Kenneth A. Myers, *NATO: The Next Thirty Years* (Boulder, Colo.: Westview Press, 1980), 361–71; Melvyn Krauss, *How NATO Weakens the West* (New York: Simon and Schuster, 1986).
2. Richard J. Barnet, "Reflections: The Four Pillars," *New Yorker* (9 March 1988), 80–83; Robert A. Levine, *NATO: The Subjective Alliance: The Debate Over the Future* (Santa Monica, Calif.: RAND, 1987), 215–20.
3. Paul Kennedy, *The Rise and Fall of the Great Powers* (New York: Random House, 1987), 515, 518–19; David Calleo, *Beyond American Hegemony: The Future of the Western Alliance* (New York: Basic Books, 1987), 215–20.
4. Ronald Steel, *The End of the Alliance: American and the Future of Europe* (New York: Viking Press, 1964), 15–16.
5. SHAPE pamphlet—"Supreme Headquarters Allied Powers Europe (SHAPE) at a Glance," 1987.
6. Aide-Mémoire, 17 February 1961, in the *New York Times*, 21 February 1961.
7. Military Procurement Authorization 1964, *Hearings* before the U.S. Senate Committee on Armed Services, 21 February 1963, 88th Cong., 1st sess., 342–43.
8. Alain C. Enthoven and K. Wayne Smith, *How Much Is Enough? Shaping the Defense Program, 1961–1969* (New York: Harper and Row, 1971), 147ff.
9. McNamara testimony, "The Atlantic Alliance," *Hearings* before the U.S. Senate Subcommittee on National Security and International Operations of the Committee on Government Operations, 21 June 1966, 89th Cong., 2d sess., pt. 6, 187.
10. Robert Bowie, "Tensions Within the Alliance," *Foreign Affairs* 42 (October 1963): 68.
11. The Future Task of the Alliance (Harmel Report), 13–14 December 1967, Brussels, North Atlantic Council, *Final Communiqués*, 198–202; ibid., 24–28 June 1968, Reykjavík, North Atlantic Council, *Final Communiqués*, 216.
12. Ibid., 15–16 November 1968, Brussels, 214.
13. "NATO in the 1990s: Special Report of the North Atlantic Assembly, 1988," 26.
14. Colin S. Gray, "NATO: Time to Call It a Day?," *The National Interest* (Winter 1987-1988): 24.
15. Quoted in Bernard E. Trainor, "Sharing the Defense Burden: Allies Are Listening," *New York Times*, 6 September 1988.
16. *Congressional Record*, 100th Cong., 1st sess., 8 May 1987, 3329–31. The amendment to a military authorization bill in support of maintaining U.S. troops in Europe was sponsored by Bill Richardson, and was accepted by voice vote.
17. "The Future of NATO," Policy Consensus Reports, The Johns Hopkins Foreign Policy Institute, August 1988.

Bibliography

Alting von Geusau, Frans A. M., ed. *NATO and Security in the Seventies.* Publications of the John F. Kennedy Institute Center for International Studies, no. 5. Lexington, Mass.: D. C. Heath, 1971.
Barnet, Richard J. *The Giants: Russia and America.* New York: Simon and Schuster, 1977.
Bell, Coral. *The Diplomacy of Détente: The Kissinger Era.* London: Martin Robertson, 1977.
Borowski, Harry R. *A Hollow Threat: Strategic Air Power and Containment before Korea.* Westport, Conn.: Greenwood Press, 1982.
Boutwell, Jeffrey D., ed. *The Nuclear Confrontation in Europe.* Dover, Mass.: Auburn House, 1986.
Brown, Seyom. *The Crises of Power: An Interpretation of United States Foreign Policy During the Kissinger Years.* New York: Columbia University Press, 1979.
Bullock, Alan. *Ernest Bevin: Foreign Secretary, 1945-1951.* New York: Norton, 1983.
Bundy, McGeorge. *Danger and Survival: Choices About the Bomb in the First Fifty Years.* New York: Random House, 1988.
Calleo, David. *Beyond American Hegemony: The Future of the Western Alliance.* New York: Basic Books, 1987.
Condit, Doris M. *History of the Office of the Secretary of Defense.* Vol. 2, *The Test of War, 1950-1953.* Washington, D.C.: U.S. Dept. of Defense, 1988.
Cook, Don. *Forging the Alliance: NATO 1945-1950.* London: Secker and Warburg, 1989.
Fedder, Edwin. *NATO and Détente.* St. Louis: Center for International Studies, University of Missouri, 1979.
———, ed. *NATO in the Seventies.* St. Louis: Center for International Studies, University of Missouri, 1970.
Foot, Rosemary. *The Wrong War: American Policy and the Dimensions of the Korean Conflict, 1950-1953.* Ithaca, N.Y.: Cornell University Press, 1985.

Fursdon, Edward. *The European Defence Community: A History.* New York: St. Martin's Press, 1980.
Gaddis, John Lewis. *Strategies of Containment: A Critical Appraisal of Postwar American National Security Policy.* New York: Oxford University Press, 1982.
Gardner, Lloyd, comp. *The Great Nixon Turn-around: America's New Foreign Policy in the Post-liberal Era (How a Cold Warrior Climbed Clean Out of His Skin).* New York: New Viewpoints, 1973.
Garthoff, Raymond L. *Perspectives on the Strategic Balance: A Staff Paper.* Washington, D.C.: Brookings Institution, 1983.
———. *Détente and Confrontation: American-Soviet Relations from Nixon to Reagan.* Washington, D.C.: Brookings Institution, 1985.
———. *Policy Versus the Law: The Reinterpretation of the ABM Treaty.* Washington, D.C.: Brookings Institution, 1987.
Harrison, Michael M. *The Reluctant Ally: France and Atlantic Security.* Baltimore: Johns Hopkins University Press, 1981.
Harrison, Michael M., and Mark G. McDonough. *Negotiations on the French Withdrawal from NATO.* Washington, D.C.: Johns Hopkins Foreign Policy Institute, 1987.
Hersh, Seymour M. *The Price of Power: Kissinger in the Nixon White House.* New York: Summit Books, 1983.
Hoff-Wilson, Joan. *Nixon Without Watergate.* New York: Basic Books, 1991.
———. "Richard M. Nixon: The Corporate Presidency." In *Leadership in the Modern Presidency,* edited by Fred I. Greenstein. Cambridge: Harvard University Press, 1988.
Hogan, Michael J. *The Marshall Plan: America, Britain and the Reconstruction of Western Europe, 1947–1952.* New York: Cambridge University Press, 1987.
Ireland, Timothy P. *Creating the Entangling Alliance: The Origins of the North Atlantic Treaty Organization.* Westport, Conn.: Greenwood Press, 1981.
Johnson, U. Alexis. *The Right Hand of Power: The Memoirs of an American Diplomat.* Englewood Cliffs, N.J.: Prentice Hall, 1984.
Jordan, Robert S. *The NATO International Staff/Secretariat, 1952–1957: A Study in International Administration.* New York: Oxford University Press, 1967.
———. *Political Leadership in NATO: A Study in Multilateral Diplomacy.* Boulder, Colo.: Westview Press, 1979.
———, ed. *General in International Politics: NATO's Supreme Allied Commander, Europe.* Lexington: University Press of Kentucky, 1987.
Kalb, Marvin, and Bernard Kalb. *Kissinger.* Boston: Little, Brown and Company, 1974.

Kaplan, Lawrence S. *NATO and the United States: The Enduring Alliance.* Boston: Twayne Publishers, 1988.
———. *The United States and NATO: The Formative Years.* Lexington: University Press of Kentucky, 1984.
Kaplan, Lawrence S. et al. *NATO after Forty Years.* Wilmington, Del.: Scholarly Resources, 1990.
Kissinger, Henry. *White House Years.* Boston: Little, Brown and Company, 1979.
Kissinger, Henry A. et al. "NATO the Next Thirty Years." *The Washington Quarterly: A Review of Strategic and International Issues* 2, no. 4 (Autumn 1979): 3–53.
Kolodziej, Edward A. *French International Policy Under De Gaulle and Pompidou: The Politics of Grandeur.* Ithaca: Cornell University Press, 1974.
———. *The Uncommon Defense and Congress, 1945–1963.* Columbus: Ohio State University Press, 1966.
Korbel, Josef. *Détente in Europe: Real or Imaginary?* Princeton, N.J.: Princeton University Press, 1972.
Krauss, Melvyn. *How NATO Weakens the West.* New York: Simon and Schuster, 1986.
Lacouture, Jean. *De Gaulle.* Vol. 3, *Le souverain, 1959–1970.* Paris: Editions du Seuil, 1986.
LaFeber, Walter. *The American Age: U.S. Foreign Policy since 1750.* New York: Norton, 1989.
Levine, Robert A. *NATO: The Subjective Alliance.* Santa Monica, Calif.: Rand, 1987.
Litwak, Robert S. *Détente and the Nixon Doctrine.* Cambridge: Cambridge University Press, 1984.
McGeehan, Robert. *The German Rearmament Question: American Diplomacy and European Defense after World War II.* Urbana: University of Illinois Press, 1971.
Maresca, John H. *To Helsinki: The Conference on Security and Cooperation in Europe, 1973–1975.* Raleigh, N.C.: Duke University Press, 1985.
Newhouse, John. *Cold Dawn: The Story of SALT.* New York: Holt, 1973.
———. *DeGaulle and the Anglo-Saxons.* London: Deutsch, 1970.
Nixon, Richard M. *Leaders: Profiles and Reminiscences of Men Who Have Shaped the Modern World.* New York: Warner Books, 1982.
North Atlantic Assembly Reports. *The State of the Alliance, 1986–1987.* Boulder, Colo.: Westview Press, 1987.
Nutter, G. Warren. *Kissinger's Grand Design.* Washington, D.C.: American Enterprise Institute for Public Policy Research, 1975.
Rearden, Steven L. *The Evolution of American Strategic Doctrine: Paul H. Nitze and the Soviet Challenge.* Boulder, Colo.: Westview Press, 1985.

———. *History of the Office of the Secretary of Defense*. Vol. 1, *The Formative Years*. Washington, D.C.: U.S. Dept. of Defense, 1984.

Reid, Escott. *Time of Fear and Hope: The Making of the North Atlantic Treaty, 1947–1949*. Toronto: McClelland and Stewart, 1977.

Riste, Olav, ed. *Western Security: The Formative Years, European and Atlantic Defence 1947–1953*. New York: Columbia University Press, 1985.

Schurmann, Franz. *The Foreign Politics of Richard Nixon: The Grand Design*. Berkeley, Calif.: Institute of International Studies, 1987.

Schwartz, David N. *NATO's Nuclear Dilemmas*. Washington, D.C.: Brookings Institution, 1983.

Secretary of State. *United States Foreign Policy, 1969–1970*. Washington, D.C.: Government Printing Office, 1970.

Sloan, Stanley R., ed. *NATO in the 1990s*. Washington: Pergamon-Brassey's, 1989.

Smith, Gaddis. *Dean Acheson*. New York: Cooper Square Publishers, 1972.

Smith, Gerard C. *Doubletalk: The Story of the First Strategic Arms Limitation Talks*. Garden City, N.Y.: Doubleday, 1980.

Sobel, Lester A. *Kissinger and Détente*. New York: Facts on File, 1975.

Steel, Ronald. *The End of the Alliance: America and the Future of Europe*. New York: Viking, 1962.

Stevenson, Richard W. *The Rise and Fall of Détente: Reflections of Tension in U.S.-Soviet Relations, 1953–1984*. Urbana: University of Illinois Press, 1985.

Stromseth, Jane E. *The Origins of Flexible Response: NATO's Debate over Strategy in the 1960s*. New York: St. Martin's Press, 1988.

Sulzberger, C. L. *The World and Richard Nixon*. New York: Prentice Hall, 1987.

Szulc, Tad. *The Illusion of Peace: Foreign Policy in the Nixon Years*. New York: Viking, 1978.

Ullman, Richard H. "The Covert French Connection." *Foreign Policy* 75 (Summer 1989): 3–33.

Vaïsse, Maurice. "Aux origines du mémorandum de septembre 1958." *Relations internationales* 58 (Summer 1989): 253–68.

Wasserman, Sherri. *The Neutron Bomb Controversy: A Study in Alliance Politics*. New York: Praeger, 1983.

Weihmiller, Gordon R. *U.S.-Soviet Summits: An Account of East-West Diplomacy at the Top, 1955–1985*. Lanham, Md.: University Press of America, 1986.

Williams, Phil. *The Senate and U.S. Troops in Europe*. New York: St. Martin's Press, 1985.

Willrich, Mason, and John B. Rhinelander, eds. *SALT: The Moscow Agreements and Beyond*. New York: Free Press, 1974.

Index

Acheson, Dean, 5, 20, 28, 58; and France, 42–43, 45, 66, 69, 71; and Germany, 37–38, 45, 48; and Great Britain, 27, 43–45; and military assistance, 41, 47, 68, 70, 77; and NATO, 19, 34–36, 42, 46, 49–52; and NSC-68, 39–41, 43, 44, 50; and Senate Foreign Relations Committee, 34, 40, 42; and Vietnam, 42–43
Achilles, Theodore, 14–15, 23, 25
Adenauer, Konrad, 37–38, 48, 63–65, 71–72, 77–79, 89
Afghanistan, 126, 127, 149
Algeria, 87; and Algerian War, 82, 83, 84, 87, 88, 90
Alliances: entangling, 1, 4, 23, 31. *See also* Isolationism
Anti-Ballistic Missile (ABM), 6, 96, 99, 101–4, 109–10, 113, 114, 174n. 23. *See also* Missiles
Anti-Ballistic Missile (ABM) Treaty, 6, 109, 176n. 44
Antinuclear movement: in Europe, 8, 129, 132; freeze movement, 130–33; in United States, 8, 128–32, 177n. 25
Arms control, 6, 7–9, 116–21, 125, 133
Arms race, 39, 41, 48, 133
Atlantic Alliance. *See* NATO
Atomic bomb. *See* Weapons, nuclear
Atomic Energy Commission, 28, 74–75
Attlee, Clement, 43

Berlin: blockade of, 21, 27, 30, 35; crisis preceding blockade, 5, 7, 16, 48, 84, 87–89; Wall, 141, 142, 144, 147
Bevin, Ernest, 43, 45; initiative in forming alliance, 4, 21–23, 25, 27. *See also* United States Foreign Relations: United States–British relations
Bohlen, Charles E., 24
Bombs. *See* Weapons, nuclear
Bonnet, Henri, 38
Borowski, Harry R., 13, 17, 18
Bowie, Robert, 91–92
Bradley, Omar, 45, 46, 67, 71–72
Brezhnev, Leonid, 107, 149
Brussels Pact, 13–15, 22, 23, 25. *See also* Western European Union
Brzezinski, Zbigniew, 123, 125–27

Canada, 22, 25, 81
Carter, James, 8, 113, 117; and armament reduction, 118–19, 123; election defeat of, 127–28; and NATO, 118, 123, 125, 127–28; and Reagan, 126–27; and Schmidt, 127; and Soviets, 119, 126; and Third World, 118. *See also* SS-20 Affair; Strategic Arms Limitation Talks (SALT); Weapons, nuclear
China, 33, 34, 37, 48, 49, 59, 104, 109. *See also* Nixon, Richard M.

183

Churchill, Winston, 22, 45, 70, 157n. 23
Clay, Lucius D., 14, 21
Cold War, 2, 11, 46, 79; and Soviets, 8, 20, 137, 153, 157n. 19; and United States government, 34, 54, 97, 103, 105, 109, 114
Communism, 112; in China, 33, 34; and containment of, 2, 3, 9, 149; in Czechoslovakia, 21, 30, 147; in France, 21, 63, 72; and Gorbachev, 137, 148–49; and Korean War, 46, 64; and NATO, 26, 32, 34, 35, 54. See also Cold War; Soviet Union
Conference on Security and Cooperation in Europe (CSCE), 112–13, 114
Connally, Tom, 3, 26, 28
Containment policy, 2, 3, 9, 97, 103, 109, 149
Council of Europe, 22
Cuban crisis, 5, 7, 141, 147
Czechoslovakia, 99, 106; Soviet intervention in (1968), 147–48; Soviet takeover of, 21, 30

Defense Committee paper number 6 (DC-6), 52–54, 56
de Gaulle, Charles, 5–6; and autonomy, 84–94, 145; and compromise, 90–94; and *force de frappe*, 85–89, 145; and Germany, 89; and Great Britain, 84, 89, 94; and nuclear weapons, 84–88; and return to power, 81–83; and Soviets, 84, 89, 93; and United States, 81–87; and withdrawal from NATO command, 84–93, 143. See also NATO
de Lattre de Tassigny, Jean, 15, 30
Détente, 6–7, 99–100, 102–15, 117; decline of, 114–15; definition of, 96–98, 101, 173n. 14; and Soviets, 40, 97, 172–73n. 8; and Vietnam War, 97, 109. See also Nixon, Richard M.
Disarmament. See Détente; Harmel Report
Dobrynin, Anatoly, 102–4, 107

Douglas, Lewis W., 14
Dual-Track Decision, 8, 135, 137; consequences of, 116–34; and NATO, 116–17, 122–26. See also Antinuclear movement; Arms control; Weapons, nuclear
Dulles, Foster, 71, 73, 77

Eisenhower, Dwight D., 6, 15, 67, 75, 121, 145, 169n. 70; and British, 78; on defense of Europe, 17, 68, 74, 140, 141; and EDC, 71–74; and French, 6, 71–74, 85–87, 90–92; popularity of, 72, 168n. 59; as SACEUR, 30, 49, 62, 66, 69, 77. See also Korean War; Troops, U.S.: in Europe
Enhanced Radiation Warhead (ERW), 122–23, 127
European Coal and Steel Community, 82
European Defense Community (EDC), 48, 65, 70–73, 83
European unity, 70–71, 138, 146, 148, 150, 152. See also Brussels Pact; Europe, united states of
Europe, united states of: antinuclear movement in, 8; economic revival in 5, 12, 35; and nationalism, 12; and regionalism, 7; and Soviets, 7, 9; status of defense, 5, 14, 35, 45; and United States, 5, 71, 136. See also European unity; Integration, European; Western European Union

Ferrell, Robert H., 3–4
Finland, 21, 24
Finletter, Thomas, 15, 139
Ford, Gerald, 112, 113, 114–15
Foreign policy, U.S. See United States Foreign Policy
Forrestal, James V., 16, 17, 20
France: and communism, 21, 63, 72; and EDC, 48, 65; and German rearmament, 37–38, 48, 64–65, 72, 83; and Germany, 34, 39, 72–73; and Great Britain, 30,

INDEX 185

65–66, 83; in Indochina, 64, 82; and Korean War, 64; and military aid, 47, 63; and NATO, 30, 37–38, 42, 47–49, 82; and Soviet Union, 6; and United States, 30, 63, 82–83; and withdrawal from NATO, 5–6, 146–47. *See also* de Gaulle, Charles
Franks, Oliver, 38

Germany: accession to NATO, 5, 72; and France, 34, 39, 72–73; and Great Britain, 37–38; and Korean War, 4–5, 64; and NATO, 3, 9, 34, 142, 145, 146, 150; rearmament of, 38–39, 44, 45, 63–65, 71–74; and Soviet Union, 8, 63; unification of, 9; and United States, 37–40, 44, 45, 49, 63–64, 76–80. *See also* Berlin: blockade of; West Germany
Goodpaster, Andrew, 86, 92
Gorbachev, Mikhail, 8, 110, 133, 134, 137, 148–50
"Grand Design." *See* "Nixingerism"
Great Britain: and France, 30, 65–66, 83; and German rearmament, 37–38; and NATO, 29, 34–36, 146; and troop commitment, 67–68; and United States, 22, 43, 67–68, 70
Greece, 21, 27, 33, 100
Gruenther, Alfred, 83

Harmel Report, 6, 99, 105–6, 146, 147
Helsinki Agreement of 1975, 7, 113, 114
Hickerson, John D., 22, 23
Hoff-Wilson, Joan, 6
Hoover, Herbert, 67

Indochina. *See* France; United States Foreign Policy; Vietnam
Intermediate-Range Nuclear Arms Reduction (INF) Treaty, 9, 133–35; and détente, 136, 148; and future of NATO, 135–38. *See also* Troops, U.S.: commitment of
Integration, European, 9, 42, 44, 48, 50, 73, 90, 159n. 43. *See also* European unity
Iran Hostage Crisis, 126–28
Isolationism, 2, 34, 52, 56, 67, 73, 77, 151
Italy, 21, 25, 100, 142

Jackson, Henry, 112–13
Jackson-Nunn Amendment, 107–8
Jackson-Vanik Amendment, 112
Japan, 41, 42, 44, 105, 137
Johnson, Louis, 19, 28, 31, 36, 41, 45, 58–60, 156n. 16
Johnson, Lyndon B., 6, 101, 145; and de Gaulle, 90, 93, 100
Joint Chiefs of Staff (JCS), 45, 52, 101; military plans of, 13–15, 27

Kaplan, Lawrence S., 19, 26, 27
Kennan, George F., 24, 37–39, 47, 149
Kennedy, John F.: and Berlin crisis, 87; and France, 6, 87, 89, 91; and U.S. troops in Europe, 141, 142, 144
Khrushchev, Nikita, 141, 148–49
Kissinger, Henry, 7, 99; and Mansfield Amendment, 104–7, 175n. 38; and Nixon, 95–115, 117; and nuclear weapons, 102, 104, 174n. 24. *See also* Détente; National Security Council; United States Foreign Policy
Korean War: and armament of West, 13; and NATO, 4–5, 12, 30, 33–51; and U.S. military commitment, 33, 36–38
Kosygin, Alexei, 101

LaFeber, Walter, 4, 5
LeMay, Curtis, 4, 13, 17, 19
Linkage, 6–8, 96, 105, 109, 175n. 31. *See also* Dual-Track Decision

Lippmann, Walter, 41
Lisbon force goals, 68–70, 75, 77. *See also* Truman, Harry S.
Lovett, Robert A., 23, 25, 70

McCloy, John J., 63–65, 71
McMullen, Clements, 18, 29
McNamara, Robert, 87, 100, 141, 144, 145
Mansfield Amendment, 101, 104–7, 175n. 38
Marshall, George C., 20, 22–26, 48, 66–68
Marshall Plan, 28, 59–60, 63; European recovery under, 12; and NATO, 5, 35, 38–40, 46, 47
May, Ernest R., 5
Military aid, 13, 27, 40–41, 47, 53, 60. *See also* Troops, U.S.: in Europe; Truman, Harry S.
Military Committee paper number 48 (MC-48), 48, 53–54, 75
Military service rivalry, 57–58, 67, 76–77, 164n. 18
Missiles: Air Launched Cruise Missile (ALCM), 121–22; cruise, 7–8, 116, 124–25, 127–29, 132, 133, 135; Ground Launched Cruise Missile (GLCM), 121, 124, 125; Intercontinental Ballistic Missile (ICBM), 102, 110, 143–44; Pershing II, 7, 116, 124–25, 127–29, 132, 133, 135; Submarine Launched Ballistic Missile (SLBM), 111, 114. *See also* Anti-Ballistic Missile; SS-20 Affair; Weapons, nuclear
Monnet, Jean, 65, 70–72, 77–78, 82, 90
Monroe Doctrine, 32, 151
Montgomery, Bernard, 14, 27, 37, 41
Multilateral Nuclear Force (MLF), 92, 93, 145, 146
Multiple Independently Targetable Reentry Vehicle (MIRV), 101, 103, 109–10. *See also* Missiles
Mutual Balanced and Force Reduction (MBFR), 7, 106–8, 114, 148

Mutual Defense Assistance Act, 40
Mutual Defense Assistance Program, 28, 30

National Security Council (NSC): and Nixon administration, 95–97, 103, 106, 108, 171–72n. 3; and NSC-30, 16; and NSC-68, 39–41, 44, 58–61, 165n. 22. *See also* Nitze, Paul
NATO (North Atlantic Treaty Organization): and burden sharing, 136, 140, 142, 146, 150; Defense Committee of, 29, 52–54, 56, 66, 147; and defense preparedness, 19, 53; and European unity, 2, 146, 150, 152; and France, 5–6, 30, 37–38, 42, 47–49, 81–83, 94, 148; and French withdrawal from NATO command, 84–93, 146–47; future of alliance, 9–10, 136–40, 150–53; and Germany, 3, 5, 9, 34, 37–38, 72, 142, 145, 146, 150; and Great Britain, 21, 29, 34–36, 146; headquarters of, 139–40; historical importance of, 1–3, 12–13, 32; impact of Korean War on, 4–5, 12, 30, 33–51; Nuclear Planning Group of, 6, 147; opposition to, 31–32, 136–37, 159n. 43; organization of, 29; origins of, 11–32; role in promoting stability, 2, 8–9, 11–12, 151–53; and Soviet Union, 2, 7, 8, 28, 35; and SS-20 Affair, 116–20, 123, 129, 133; Standing Group of, 29, 47, 83, 147; and United Nations, 26, 28, 31; and United States, 1–10, 30, 33–34, 43, 50–53. *See also* Détente; Intermediate-Range Nuclear Arms Reduction (INF) Treaty; Nixon, Richard M.; Germany: rearmament of; Troops, U.S.: in Europe
Neutralism, 6, 40. *See also* Soviet Union
Nitze, Paul, 38–41, 58–59, 64, 129, 164n. 18

INDEX

"Nixinger" foreign policy, 96–97, 108–9, 113
"Nixingerism" ("grand design"), 7, 96–97, 101, 104, 108, 114–15, 175n. 31
Nixon administration. *See* Kissinger, Henry; Nixon, Richard M.
Nixon Doctrine, 6, 7, 96, 103–4
Nixon, Richard M.: and arms control, 96, 100–104, 109–11; and China, 95, 104, 105, 108–9; and de Gaulle, 99; and détente, 96–115, 117, 173n. 14; and foreign policy, 95–115, 118; and Kissinger, 95–112, 114, 115; and NATO, 98–108, 172n. 5, 173n. 13; and nuclear weapons, 100, 104; and peace movement, 99, 106; resignation of, 108, 115; and Soviets, 96–115; and Third World, 103, 105, 175n. 31; and Watergate, 98, 105, 115
Norstad, Lauris, 85, 145–46
North Atlantic Council (NAC): and Harmel Report, 6; and Lisbon force-goal statement, 68–70; and military forces, 68–69
North Atlantic Treaty, 1, 11–12, 25–29; Senate ratification of, 3, 26; signing of, 19, 26. *See also* Bevin, Ernest; NATO; European unity
Norway, 21, 157–58n. 27
Nuclear war, 117, 129–30, 132, 134, 144–46
Nuclear weapons. *See* Weapons, nuclear

Panama Canal, 127
Peace Movement. *See* Antinuclear movement
Persian Gulf, 126, 129
Pleven Plan, 48, 65–66, 70. *See also* European Defense Community (EDC); France: and NATO

Reagan, Ronald: and arms control, 128, 129; and Carter, 126–27; and dual-track decision, 8, 128; and Soviets, 9, 130–31; and zero/zero option, 128–29, 134. *See also* Antinuclear movement; Nuclear war; SS-20 Affair
Rio Treaty, 23, 31
Robin, Gabriel, 86, 91
Roosevelt, Franklin D., 24

Schell, Jonathan: *The Face of the Earth*, 130. *See also* Weapons, nuclear
Schmidt, Helmut, 8, 120, 122–23, 125, 126–27
Schuman Plan, 44, 47
Schuman, Robert, 48, 49, 65, 69, 71–72
Senate, U.S.: and NATO, 3, 25–26
Smith, Gaddis, 7–8, 20
Southeast Asia Treaty Organization (SEATO), 2, 31, 47, 140
Soviet Union: and atomic bomb, 33, 34, 36–37, 39, 41, 45, 60; expansionism of, 4, 40–41; as military power, 4, 5, 7, 22, 53–54, 62, 76, 147–48, 157n. 19, 165n. 31; and NATO, 2, 7, 8, 26, 28, 35; and United States, 116–34. *See also* Détente; SS-20 Affair; United States Foreign Relations
Spain, 100
Sputnik, 84, 143. *See also* Soviet Union: as military power
SS-20 Affair, 7; and challenge to NATO, 116, 133; and non-conversion agreement, 119–20; and opportunity for West, 116–24, questions for future historians, 133–34; and Soviets, 116–17, 119–20, 123, 129, 133. *See also* Dual-Track Decision
Strategic Air Command (SAC), United States, 4, 67; and Korean War, 13; problems in, 16–17, 57–58; reforms in, 13, 17, 19, 29; weapons used by, 29, 75
Strategic Arms Limitation Talks (SALT): SALT I, 96, 99, 101, 104,

188 INDEX

108–10, 114, 176n. 46; SALT II, 8, 101, 108–10, 113–14, 117–21, 124, 126, 128, 133
Suez crisis, 3, 82
Supreme Allied Commander Atlantic (SACLANT), 9, 143, 147
Supreme Allied Commander Europe (SACEUR), 83, 85, 87, 145, 147; Eisenhower as, 30, 49, 62, 66, 69, 77
Supreme Headquarters Allied Powers Europe (SHAPE), 9, 83, 143
Sweden, 24–25, 157n. 27

Taft, Robert, 41–42, 67, 77
Tito, Marshal, 21, 27, 41
Trade Reform Bill, 112, 115
Trade sanctions, 126
Trevor-Roper, Hugh R., 12–13
Troops, U.S.: in Asia, 46; commitment of, 33, 62–67, 101, 103, 105, 136–48; in Europe, 8, 9, 11, 27, 44, 60, 62, 73, 107–8, 152–53; in Korea, 46, 60. *See also* Korean War; Mansfield Amendment; Vietnam War
Truman administration, 4, 42, 49, 58–59, 71–74, 140. *See also* Truman Doctrine; Truman, Harry S.
Truman Doctrine, 2, 3, 6, 39, 60, 78
Truman, Harry S., 20, 27, 37, 66; and European Defense Community, 71–74; and German rearmament, 45–49, 64, 66; and Indochina, 42; and Korean War, 33, 46, 48, 49, 60; and military aid to Europe, 36, 47–48, 56, 68; and military spending, 57–61, 69–70, 74–75; and Mutual Defense Assistance Program, 28, 39–41, 158n. 36; and NATO, 4, 11, 19, 26, 34–35, 49–51; and nuclear weapons, 28–29, 49; and Soviet Union, 21, 28, 37; and war planning, 15–16, 57. *See also* Brussels Pact; Cold War
Turkey, 21, 33

United Nations, 26, 28, 31
United States Foreign Policy, 11, 39, 49; and defense preparedness, 15–19, 21, 57; and détente, 95–115; and Far West, 137, 143; and German rearmament, 38–39, 44, 45, 63–66; in Indochina, 42, 44, 49, 50; and military power, 4, 13, 15, 40, 53–56, 155n. 2; and NATO, 30, 33–34, 43, 50–53; and nuclear weapons, 54–56, 74–75, 76–80. *See also* Antinuclear movement; Soviet Union; United States Foreign Relations
United States Foreign Relations: United States–British relations, 22, 43, 55, 67, 68, 77–79; United States–German relations, 37–40, 44, 45, 49, 63–64, 76–80; United States–Far West (Asian) relations, 137, 143, United States–French relations, 42, 47–49, 78, 81–83; United States–Soviet relations, 7, 15, 20, 116–24; and U.S. role in Europe, 40, 53, 135–53. *See also* Berlin: blockade of; Cold War
United States Mission to NATO, 3; 40th Anniversary Symposium, 3–4

Vance, Cyrus, 117, 119, 123, 126
Vandenberg, Arthur H., 3, 26, 28, 31, 41, 56, 158n. 31
Vandenberg Resolution, 26. *See also* Vandenberg, Arthur H.
Vietnam, 141, 143
Vietnamization, 103
Vietnam War, 6, 42, 89, 93, 97, 104, 117–18, 145–46

War planning, 15–16, 27
Warsaw Pact, 99, 101, 106–8, 125, 141, 144, 148, 150
Weapons, nuclear, 7, 53, 83, 156n. 12; atomic bombs, 15–20, 34; H-bomb (hydrogen bomb), 28, 74; neutron bomb, 8, 17; and Soviets, 9, 28, 33, 36–39, 41, 45, 60; and U.S., 16, 74–76, 146–47. *See*

also Antinuclear movement; Enhanced Radiation Warhead (ERW); Missiles; National Security Council (NSC)
Wells, Samuel F., Jr., 6
Western European Union (Western Union), 14, 27, 138, 145, 150

West Germany, 3–5, 9, 14, 89; and "middle power" concept, 41–43; and NATO, 33–34, 72, 142, 150; rearmament of, 14, 37–39, 44–49, 64–65, 78
Wilson, Woodrow, 24, 31
World War II, 4, 11, 54, 56, 145

Contributors

ROBERT H. FERRELL (Ph.D., Yale) is Distinguished Professor Emeritus at Indiana University, Bloomington, and the author or editor of books on American diplomatic history, including *Peace In Their Time, American Diplomacy: A History,* and *Harry S. Truman and the Modern American Presidency.*

JOAN HOFF-WILSON (Ph.D., Berkeley), professor of history at Indiana University, Bloomington, specializes in twentieth-century foreign policy and the modern presidency. She is the author of *American Business and Foreign Policy, 1920–1933* and *Ideology and Economics: U.S. Relations with the Soviet Union, 1918–1933.* Her study of the Nixon presidency will be published in 1991.

LAWRENCE S. KAPLAN (Ph.D., Yale) is University Professor of History and Director of the Lyman L. Lemnitzer Center for NATO Studies at Kent State University. He has written and edited many books on NATO's history, including *A Community of Interests: NATO and the Military Assistance Program, NATO and the United States: The Enduring Alliance* and *NATO after Forty Years.*

WALTER LaFEBER (Ph.D., Wisconsin) is Noll Professor of History at Cornell University. His recent books include *The American Age: U.S. Foreign Relations at Home and Abroad Since 1750; The Panama Canal: The Canal in Historical Perspective,* 2d edition; and *America, Russia, and the Cold War,* 6th edition.

ERNEST R. MAY (Ph.D., UCLA) has been a member of the Department of History at Harvard University since 1954 and is currently a Charles Warren Professor of History. He is the author of numerous books on nineteenth- and twentieth-century U.S. diplomatic history, including *Lessons of the Past: The Use and Misuse of History in American Foreign Policy* and *Thinking in Time: The Use of History for Decision-Makers* (with Richard E. Neustadt).

CONTRIBUTORS

GADDIS SMITH (Ph.D., Yale) is Larned Professor of History at Yale University where he has been a member of the Department of History since 1961. Among his publications are *Dean Acheson* and *Morality, Reason and Power: American Diplomacy in the Carter Years*, a study of Carter's foreign policy.

SAMUEL F. WELLS, JR. (Ph.D., Harvard) is Deputy Director of the Woodrow Wilson International Center for Scholars in Washington, D.C. He previously directed the European Institute (1985–1988) and the International Security Studies Program of The Wilson Center (1977–1985) and has taught International History and Defense Studies at the University of North Carolina at Chapel Hill. Among his publications are *The Ordeal of World Power*; co-author), *Security in the Middle East*; co-editor), and *Strategic Defenses and Soviet-American Relations*; co-editor). He has also written several articles for foreign affairs journals.

AMERICAN HISTORIANS AND THE ATLANTIC ALLIANCE
was composed in 10/12 New Baskerville
on a Xyvision system with Linotron 202 output
by BookMasters, Inc.;
printed by sheet-fed offset on 55-pound, acid free,
Glatfelter B-16 paper stock,
Smyth sewn and bound over .088" binders' boards
in Holliston Roxite B cloth;
also adhesive bound with paper covers printed in two colors
on 12-point stock and film laminated
by BookCrafters, Inc.;
text designed by Will Underwood;
cover designed by Diana Gordy;
and published by
THE KENT STATE UNIVERSITY PRESS
Kent, Ohio 44242